| exploring |

Illustrator CS3

| exploring |

Illustrator CS3

Annesa Hartman

Ken Sholar

DELMAR
CENGAGE Learning

Exploring Illustrator CS3
Annesa Hartman &
Ken Sholar

Vice President, Technology and
Trades ABU:
David Garza
Director of Learning Solutions:
Sandy Clark
Managing Editor:
Larry Main
Senior Acquisitions Editor:
James Gish
Product Manager:
Nicole Calisi
Editorial Assistant:
Sarah Timm
Marketing Director:
Deborah Yarnell
Marekting Manager:
Kevin Rivenburg
Marketing Specialist:
Victoria Ortiz
Director of Production:
Patty Stephan
Production Manager:
Andrew Crouth
Content Project Manager:
Andrea Majot
Technology Project Manager:
Kevin Smith
Cover Image:
Joshua On High
© David Arsenault,
oil on canvas

For product information and technology assistance, contact us at
Cengage Learning Customer & Sales Support, 1-800-354-9706

For permission to use material from this text or product,
submit all requests online at **cengage.com/permissions**
Further permissions questions can be emailed to

Library of Congress Control Number: 2007025333

ISBN-13: 978-1-4180-5257-7

ISBN-10: 1-4180-5257-4

Delmar Cengage Learning
5 Maxwell Drive
Clifton Park, NY 12065-2919
USA

Cengage Learning products are represented in Canada by Nelson
Education, Ltd.

For your lifelong learning solutions, visit
delmar.cengage.com

Visit our corporate website at **www.cengage.com**

Notice to the Reader
Publisher does not warrant or guarantee any of the products described herein or perform any independent
analysis in connection with any of the product information contained herein. Publisher does not assume, and
expressly disclaims, any obligation to obtain and include information other than that provided to it by the manufacturer. The reader is expressly warned to consider and adopt all safety precautions that might be indicated by
the activities described herein and to avoid all potential hazards. By following the instructions contained herein,
the reader willingly assumes all risks in connection with such instructions. The publisher makes no representations or warranties of any kind, including but not limited to, the warranties of fitness for particular purpose or
merchantability, nor are any such representations implied with respect to the material set forth herein, and the
publisher takes no responsibility with respect to such material. The publisher shall not be liable for any special,
consequential, or exemplary damages resulting, in whole or part, from the readers' use of, or reliance upon, this
material.

4 5 6 7 11 10 09 08

For my father, Terry Hartman—the most inspiring teacher I know.

For my parents, Johnnie and Chiyo.

contents

CONTENTS

contents

contents

CONTENTS

| *preface* |

INTENDED AUDIENCE

You are here. Destination, Adobe Illustrator. Your guide, this book. *Exploring Illustrator CS3*, like other books in the Delmar Cengage Learning Design Exploration series, takes an inventive approach to the introductory study and application of popular computer graphic software programs.

A new student to digital illustration, a computer graphics or arts educator, or a professional graphic artist looking for fresh ways to use Adobe Illustrator will find this book's content relevant, straightforward, and engagingly accessible. It speaks clearly to the artist in all of us, approaching what could be complex design concepts practically, visually, and in the context of the many tools, effects, and workflow features currently available for both print and Web artwork creation in Adobe Illustrator CS3.

BACKGROUND OF THIS TEXT

Pablo Picasso once exclaimed, "Computers are useless. They can only give you answers." True, perhaps. However, accompanied by the right questions, such answers can bring an enlightened perspective to mundane tasks, complicated procedures, and traditional methods of creative endeavor. Today's successful graphic artists realize the importance of not just having a foundation in design principles and knowing the tools, but the skills to communicate clearly and collaboratively with others in the innovation process. The artist's highlighted in this book were asked, "What suggestions for success would you give to the emerging graphic artist?" All emphasized the need for one to be adaptable to change and alterations, to be professional, organized, and prompt in all matters of his/her business, to be personable to others, and yet persistent in self-promotion. And finally, to keep learning, exploring, and engaging with all that this expansive world offers, such as this book!

This full-color book:

- explores the questions that face today's illustrator-artist and provides some educated answers through the use of Adobe Illustrator's digital tools and features;
- offers process-oriented lessons developed from actual implementation in classrooms and production firms;
- develops an understanding of core concepts related to digital artwork creation through fundamental design elements (line, shape, value, texture, and color) and methods;
- and, most importantly, opens the door for continued, self-guided discovery.

As you will learn in the first chapter, Illustrator is a powerful program for the reworking, repurposing, and reproduction of artwork, as well as for the development of completely new digital imagery. Its fundamental way of making illustrations, which is explained and demonstrated step-by-step in this book, is through the use of something called vectors, making lines and shapes point by point. Yes, having taken a few traditional drawing and design classes can more quickly move along your understanding of how Illustrator works, but they are not necessary. This book addresses not only the fundamentals of using Illustrator, but also the creation of digital artwork in general and within the context of established elements of art and design. All you really need to get started is some motivation to venture forth.

TEXTBOOK ORGANIZATION

Like all books in Delmar Cengage Learning's Design Exploration series, the instructional design of this book—its organization and features—is the result of the collaborative efforts of dedicated authors and production staff. The book began with two months of researching the content and layout of other Illustrator books and the writing styles of textbooks in general. We talked with many digital artists and computer graphics instructors and students about their training needs, both with general design concepts and practical application. Confirming our suspicions, we discovered that learning the best practices for integrating design concepts with tool-based software programs is becoming increasingly complicated (so many tools, so little time) and that clear instruction, practice, and practical application are essential. Just as essential is the need for learning experiences to be fun and exploratory, providing timely, innovative ways for artwork creation. The way in which the content of this book is organized and presented is the result of our findings from this interesting investigation.

Each chapter builds upon itself, and material is presented in a linear fashion, introducing design elements and Illustrator tools and features on a "need-to-know" basis. This streamlines the amount of information a reader must know to successfully render a task. However, we don't discourage jumping around to get certain facts when you need them, especially if you are already somewhat familiar with the program. As well, to accommodate those who appreciate alternative methods of learning information, we provide both textually and visually succinct explanations of the important concepts to grasp in each chapter. For those who prefer structured, hands-on experiences, step-by-step lessons are provided; for those who prefer to wander around a bit, final project files, samples, and suggestions for further exploration are available for deconstruction.

The following is a brief overview of the concepts and skills covered in each chapter. Since this book is all about a design program, notice that the content in most chapters corresponds to the fundamental design elements of line, shape, value, texture, and color, and then finally composition and space.

Chapter 1: **A Discovery Tour** Right away build a logo in Illustrator, and discover the purpose of the Illustrator program.

Chapter 2: **The Lay of the Land** Get comfortable with the Illustrator interface, and learn the important landmarks of the program to get around with ease.

FEATURES

The following list provides some of the salient features of the text:

▶ Learning goals are clearly stated at the beginning of each chapter.

▶ Instructional focus is on a visually oriented introduction to basic design elements and the function and tools of Illustrator, meeting the needs of design students and professionals alike.

▶ Client projects involve tools and techniques that a designer might encounter on the job.

▶ Provide an inside look at how artists' working in the field come up with their ideas and inspirations.

▶ "Exploring on Your Own" sections offer suggestions and sample lessons for further study of content covered in each chapter.

▶ "In Review" sections are provided at the end of each chapter to test reader understanding and retention of the material covered.

▶ A CD-ROM at the back of the book contains support files to complete the books' exercises.

E.RESOURCE

This guide was developed to assist instructors in planning and implementing their instructional pro-grams. It includes sample syllabi for using this book in either an 11- or 15-week semester. It also provides answers to the "In Review" questions, PowerPoint slides highlighting the main topics, and additional instructor resources.

ISBN: 1-4180-5258-2

FILE SETUP

Located in the back of this book is a CD-ROM containing all files for completing the lessons in this book. These lesson files are compatible with Illustrator CS3. For a trial version of Illustrator CS3, visit *http://www.adobe.com/downloads/*.

Before starting any of the lessons, create a folder on your local computer named My Lessons (or what-ever name you prefer). From the CD, drag a copy of the lesson files to the folder. As you work on the lessons, open the lessons, assets, and sample files from this location. You can then also save your work in the same place.

HOW TO USE THIS TEXT

The features discussed in the following sections are found in the book.

▶ Charting Your Course and Goals

The introduction and chapter objectives start off each chapter. They describe the competencies the reader should achieve upon understanding the chapter.

▶ Don't Go There

These boxes highlight common pitfalls and explain ways to avoid them.

▶ Explorer Pages

These sections showcase the imagery, insights, and work flow processes of successful graphic artists.

charting your course

If you are the adventurous type with an inclination to jump into new experiences feet first, this chapter is for you. If you prefer to proceed with caution because you are more of a "stand-on-the-edge-and-dip-your-toes-into-the-water" type, this chapter is also for you. We begin with a hands-on investigation of Adobe Illustrator, but depending on your learning style, you can choose to "do" the discovery tour or simply read it. Perhaps, you are a type A, such as ourselves, and will choose both options. In this chapter you will also discover the purpose and scope of this program, shedding some light on such impending questions as, "What's so great about Illustrator? What does it do? How can it help me?"

goals

In this chapter you will:

- Get excited about Illustrator
- Build a logo
- Explore the use of some of Illustrator's tools and features
- Discover the purpose of Illustrator, who uses it, and why

▶ **Don't Go There!**

In this particular lesson, you have been making shapes with a stroke (outline) color only, no inside fill color. (If you recall, you played with strokes and fills somewhat in Chapter 1, but it is covered more in Chapter 5.) The rule for successfully selecting and moving an object is: You must click on a part of the object that has color applied to it. If, for example, you click in the center of an object where no fill color is indicated, you end up deselecting the object—oops!

▶ In Review and Exploring on Your Own

Review questions are located at the end of each chapter and allow the reader to assess his or her understanding of the chapter. The section "Exploring on Your Own" contains exercises that reinforce chapter material through practical application.

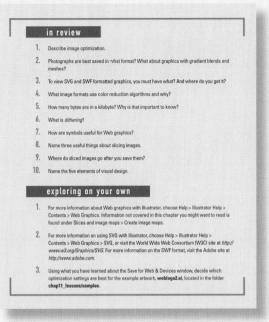

in review

1. Describe image optimization.

2. Photographs are best saved in what format? What about graphics with gradient blends and meshes?

3. To view SVG and SWF formatted graphics, you must have what? And where do you get it?

4. What image formats use color reduction algorithms and why?

5. How many bytes are in a kilobyte? Why is that important to know?

6. What is dithering?

7. How are symbols useful for Web graphics?

8. Name three useful things about slicing images.

9. Where do sliced images go after you save them?

10. Name the five elements of visual design.

exploring on your own

1. For more information about Web graphics with Illustrator, choose Help > Illustrator Help > Contents > Web Graphics. Information not covered in this chapter you might want to read is found under Slices and image maps > Create image maps.

2. For more information on using SVG with Illustrator, choose Help > Illustrator Help > Contents > Web Graphics > SVG, or visit the World Wide Web Consortium (W3C) site at *http://www.w3.org/Graphics/SVG*. For more information on the SWF format, visit the Adobe site at *http://www.adobe.com*.

3. Using what you have learned about the Save for Web & Devices window, decide which optimization settings are best for the example artwork, **weblogo2.ai**, located in the folder **chap11_lessons/samples**.

▶ Adventures in Design

These spreads contain client assignments showing readers how to approach a design project using the tools and design concepts taught in the book.

ABOUT THE AUTHORS

Annesa Hartman holds a Masters in Teaching with Internet Technologies, focusing her attention on instructional design for online technologies, and Web and graphic design concepts and programs. Currently, she is an Instructional Designer for Landmark College's Institute for Research and Training in Putney, Vermont, where she designs and develops online courses for educators. For over 10 years she also has taught computer graphic courses and is a freelance graphic designer with clients from around the world. She is the author of *Exploring Photoshop CS2*, *Exploring Illustrator CS2*, *Exploring Photoshop CS3*, and *Producing Interactive Television*. When she is not pushing pixels, she is performing in community theater and teaching yoga classes.

Ken Sholar holds a Bachelor of Arts degree in Art from CSU Stanislaus. Currently, he is a lab manager at the MAGIC Lab, a computer lab dedicated to the advancement of art and technology, at Modesto Junior College in California. He has created online courseware for the Computer Graphics department at MJC and is also the author of *Exploring Photoshop CS3*. When not in cyberspace, he enjoys reading and wandering aimlessly in the Sierra Nevada foothills.

ACKNOWLEDGMENTS

Annesa Hartman:

In writing a software book, the author faces many challenges. Chief among these is the short time frame in which to write the book and the creation and acquisition of the materials, lesson sources, and images for it. I find my material (and inspiration) through close friends, family, students, and professional colleagues. First, a special thanks goes to my co-author Ken Sholar for his endless energy and expertise. Another special thanks goes to my mother, Carolyn Murov, who is never without a camera around her neck. She is a graphic artist by profession, and provided many of the photographs I used throughout the book. A big thanks also to Andrea Linkin-Butler, Dave Garcez, Gregory Sinclair, Arthur Mount, Kevin Hulsey, Brooke Nuñez, Reggie Gilbert, Ann Paidrick, Janet McLeod, and Karen Claffey for providing real-world content that Ken and I have used in demonstrating Illustrator concepts and design techniques. Thanks also to Charmaine Wesley and my dear boyfriend, Dave Marx. As well, my experience with the staff of Delmar Cengage Learning, during the creation and marketing efforts of all editions of this book, has been utterly commendable—thanks for your patience and expertise. Finally, many kudos to the students and instructors in the Graphic Design department at Modesto Junior College, California, where I am an adjunct online instructor, alumni, and daughter of one of the college's dedicated fine arts and computer graphics faculty, Terry Hartman. Dad, I very much enjoy discussing with you the idiosyncrasies of current technology books and instructional methods, and putting into practice with our students interesting and innovative ways to learn about graphic design. Mostly I appreciate your love and support. This book is for you.

Ken Sholar:

I want to thank Annesa Hartman for giving me the opportunity to participate in this literary journey. I also would like to thank Delmar Cengage Learning for their support and countless hours in bringing this book to fruition. I wish to give special thanks to those teachers that have guided and brought me here to this point in my life: Jim Griffin, Paul Pronoitis, Joel Hagen, Terry Hartman, and Richard Savini. And most of all, I want to thank my family, friends and loved ones for all their emotional support: my parents, Denise E. Yu, the Hartman family, the Tip Tankard crew, and the students, staff and faculty of the Computer Graphics and Computer Science departments at Modesto Junior College.

Delmar Cengage Learning and the authors would also like to thank Toni Toland for ensuring the technical accuracy of this text.

QUESTIONS AND FEEDBACK

Delmar Cengage Learning and the authors welcome your questions and feedback. If you have suggestions you think others would benefit from, please let us know and we will try to include them in the next edition.

To send us your questions and/or feedback, you can contact the publisher at:

Delmar Cengage Learning
Executive Woods
5 Maxwell Drive
Clifton Park, NY 12065
Attn: Media Arts & Design Team
800-998-7498

Or Annesa Hartman at:

Landmark College
Instructional and Graphic Designer
P.O. Box 820
River Road South
Putney, VT 05346
ahartman@landmark.edu

Or Ken Sholar at:

Modesto Junior College
435 College Ave.
Modesto, CA 95350
sholark@mjc.edu

COME TO VERMONT & LIVE YOUR DREAM

↩ CONTACT
✉ EMAIL
⚹ LOGIN
✛ SITE MAP

| WELCOME | FIND HOMES | FOR BUYERS | VACATION RENTALS | LOCAL INFO | RESOURCES | ABOUT US |

ANDREA LINKIN-BUTLER

All Realtors are NOT alike! Find out why we are top real estate experts. Call us: 800-808-5917.

OUR SPECIAL OFFERS
Buyers Want Your Home for as Little as Possible.
Are you thinking of selling your home? You should know exactly what it's worth before making such an important decision.
Find Out More >
View All Offers >

Representing Buyers in Vermont

Stratton Buyer Brokerage

FEATURE PROPERTY

Intervale Townhouse #1
Two level, end unit townhouse in a gorgeous country setting.
Location: Private shuttle to the slopes!!
Price: $22,000 *Season*
VIEW THIS PROPERTY
VIEW ALL PROPERTIES

| a discovery tour |

charting your course

If you are the adventurous type with an inclination to jump into new experiences feet first, this chapter is for you. If you prefer to proceed with caution because you are more of a "stand-on-the-edge-and-dip-your-toes-into-the-water" type, this chapter is also for you. We begin with a hands-on investigation of Adobe Illustrator, but depending on your learning style, you can choose to "do" the discovery tour or simply read it. Perhaps, you are a type A, such as ourselves, and will choose both options. In this chapter you will also discover the purpose and scope of this program, shedding some light on such impending questions as, "What's so great about Illustrator? What does it do? How can it help me?"

goals

In this chapter you will:

- **Get excited about Illustrator**
- **Build a logo**
- **Explore the use of some of Illustrator's tools and features**
- **Discover the purpose of Illustrator, who uses it, and why**

JUMPING IN

You have a problem. It is your first day on the job and the creative director arrives at your desk with a logo design cursorily sketched on a somewhat used dinner napkin. See Figure 1–1. She needs the sketch recreated on the computer right away, so it can be printed on business cards by the end of the week. What do you do?

a. Pack up your belongings and move to the mountains.

b. Politely explain that it is "just not possible."

c. Learn Adobe Illustrator.

figure | 1–1 |

A logo sketched on paper.

figure | 1–2 |

Completed lesson: A logo redrawn using Illustrator.

The best answer is "c," of course! Without a doubt, learning Adobe Illustrator will solve your problem and your success as a graphic designer will be greatly advanced. Let us not waste another minute, and get started.

Lesson: Connect-the-Dots Logo Tour

This lesson is an initial foray into what Illustrator can do. It is not meant to get into any great detail—that is coming soon enough in later chapters. Rather it is an opportunity to experience how you might solve a common problem: recreating a traditional drawing (a logo design) into a digital format using Illustrator. See Figure 1–2. Assuming you have already scanned the dinner napkin sketch onto your computer, follow these steps using Illustrator.

Importing the Sketch

1. Open Illustrator.

2. From the menu bar at the top of the program, choose File. From the drop-down menu, choose Open. In the dialog box that pops up, find your local hard drive and browse for the Exploring Illustrator folder **chap01_lessons**. Open the file **chap1L1.ai**. Bypass the Welcome window by pressing the Close button.

> **Note:** As mentioned in the File Set-up, to save your work, you must make a copy of the chapter lessons to your local hard drive and select files from that location.

In the middle of the document, you will see a blank artwork area with a black border. This is your drawing space. To the left of the interface is your toolbox. See Figure 1–3. You will access the toolbox more than any other part of Illustrator.

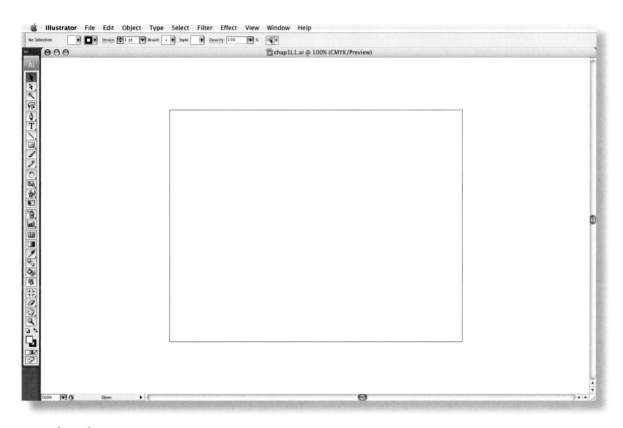

figure | 1–3 |

The Illustrator viewing area.

3. Press Shift-Tab to hide unnecessary window panels and docks.

4. Choose View > Actual Size. Your viewing area should look similar to Figure 1–3.

5. Choose Window > Layers to open the Layers panel. Layers are a way of organizing parts of an image. You can add, delete, rearrange, hide/unhide, lock/unlock, and duplicate layers. In this lesson, the layers have already been created for you.

> **Note:** Panels appear to the right of the interface, and they allow you to monitor and modify your work. By default, Illustrator panels are stacked in groups within docks. For example, the Color panel is stacked with the Color Guide panel in the default dock. If you prefer, select and drag the title tab of just the panel you want to use (in this example, the Layers tab) to another area of the screen to detach it. Panels are explained in Chapter 2, "Lesson 1: Interface Highlights."

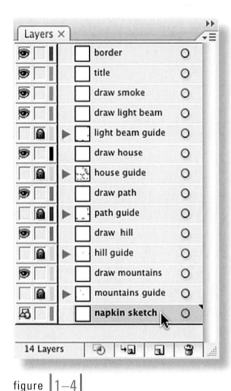

figure |1–4|

The Layers Panel with the napkin sketch layer selected.

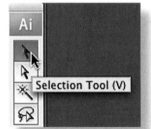

figure |1–5|

The Selection tool selects objects on the document.

6. Click once on the bottom layer—**napkin sketch**—to select it. See Figure 1–4. If you do not see all the layers, click on the lower-right corner of the Layers panel window—a double-headed arrow will appear on the border. Then, drag down the arrow to expand the window.

7. Choose File > Place and browse for **chap01_lessons/assets/ logo.jpg**. Click Place to import the image into Illustrator. This is the original scanned sketch, which will be used as a template to trace the new logo design. Select the Selection tool (black arrow) in the toolbox, if not already selected. See Figure 1–5.

8. Click and drag on the imported image and center it over the artwork area.

9. Click on the blank box to the left of the layer name—**napkin sketch**—to lock the layer. A little lock icon will appear. See Figure 1–6.

10. Choose File > Save As to save your file. Rename it **chap1L1_ yourname.ai**, and save it in your lessons folder.

Drawing the Background Mountains

1. Click on the blank box to the far left of the layer name— **mountains guide**—to unhide the layer. An icon appears that looks like a series of geometric shapes. See Figure 1–7.

> **Note:** This icon indicates that a template object on this layer is visible. Objects on template layers are usually used as guides you can trace over. Other layers are visible when you see an "eye" icon in the visibility column of the Layers panel.

figure |1–6|

Lock the napkin sketch layer, so it cannot be edited.

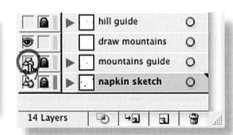

figure |1–7|

Reveal the dots hidden on the mountains guide layer.

A series of numbered dots appears on the document, strategically placed over the mountain drawn in the sketch. You will create the logo as if you were drawing an image in a connect-the-dot activity book.

2. Click the **draw mountains** layer to select it. See Figure 1–8. This layer will contain your final drawing of the mountains.

3. Prepare the color you will use for the mountains. Click the Fill color box on the toolbox to bring it forward. See Figure 1–9.

4. Choose Window > Swatches to open the Swatches panel.

> **Note:** Illustrator panels are stacked in groups within docks. For example, the Swatches panel is stacked with other panels related to quick item selection, such as Brushes and Symbols. To make things easier, select and drag the title tab of the panel you want to use (in this example, the Swatches panel) to another area of the screen to detach it.

5. In the Swatches panel, choose the 40% Black color swatch as the Fill color. See Figure 1–10.

6. Select the Pen tool in the toolbox. See Figure 1–11.

7. Place the Pen tool on point 1 on the document, and click once. Then click on point 2 to create a straight path. Continue clicking each point—3, 4, 5, 6, and 7.

> **Note:** If you make a mistake, choose Edit > Undo—Command-Z (Mac) or Ctrl-Z (Windows)—or hit Delete on your keyboard.

8. Click once on point 1 to close the path. You now have a completed mountain shape. See Figure 1–12.

9. Hide the **mountains guide** and **draw mountains** layers by clicking on the icons to the far left of each layer. (One icon looks like a series of shapes, the other like an eye.) See Figure 1–13.

10. Save your file (File > Save).

Drawing the Hill

1. Unhide the **hill guide** layer to see the dots that will guide your drawing. See Figure 1–14 on the next page .

figure | 1–8 |

Select the **draw mountains** layer.

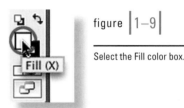

figure | 1–9 |

Select the Fill color box.

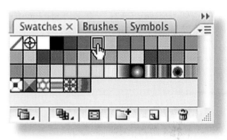

figure | 1–10 |

Select the 40% Black color swatch as the Fill color.

figure | 1–11 |

Select the Pen tool in the toolbox.

▶ Don't Go There!

If you are unable to draw on your chosen layer, even though the Pen tool is selected, this means the layer is either locked or hidden, or that you are on the wrong layer. In this case, an icon appears that looks like a pencil with a line through it.

figure |1-12|

Completed mountain shape.

figure |1-13|

Hide the contents on the **mountains guide** and **draw mountains** layers.

figure |1-14|

Unhide the **hill guide** layer.

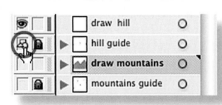

2. Click the **draw hill** layer to select it. This is the layer you will draw on.

3. Prepare the color you will use for the hill. Click the Fill color box on the toolbox to bring it forward.

4. In the Swatches panel, choose the color Black.

5. Select the Pen tool in the toolbox.

6. Place the Pen tool on point 1 on the document, and click.

7. This next step is a little tricky. At point 2, click, hold, and then drag the Pen tool to the right of the point to create a curved path. As you pull on the point, it creates a curve to form the rounded hill shape. See Figure 1–15. Remember, if you make a mistake, Edit > Undo is always there for you— Command-Z (Mac), Ctrl-Z (Windows).

8. Continue clicking each point 3, 4, and 5, creating straight paths.

9. Click once on point 1 to close the path. You now have a completed hill shape. See Figure 1–16. Do not worry if your lines are not perfect. You will get a lot more practice as you learn Illustrator.

10. Click on the icon to the far left of each layer—**hill guide** and **draw hill**—to hide them. (One icon looks like a series of shapes, the other an eye.)

11. Save your file.

Drawing the Path

1. Unhide the **path guide** layer to see the dots that will guide your drawing.

2. Select the **draw path** layer. This is the layer you will draw on.

3. Prepare the color you will use for the path. Click the Fill color box on the toolbox to bring it forward.

4. In the Swatches panel, select the 40% Black swatch (seventh swatch in the top row).

5. With the Pen tool, connect the dots starting and ending with point 1. The finished path should look something like Figure 1–17.

6. Click on the icon to the far left of each layer—**path guide** and **draw path**—to hide them.

7. Save your file.

Drawing the House

1. Unhide the **house guide** layer to see the dots that will guide your drawing. Hmmm, a bit more complicated, but you can do it! See Figure 1–18 on the next page.

2. Select the **draw house** layer. This is the layer you will draw on.

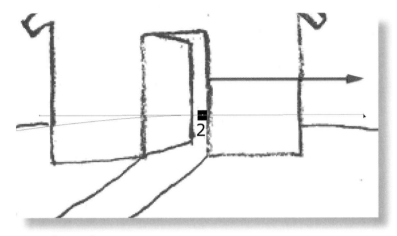

figure |1–15|

Click, hold, and drag to create a curved path.

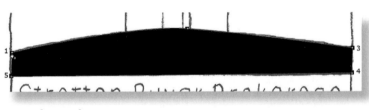

figure |1–16|

Completed hill shape.

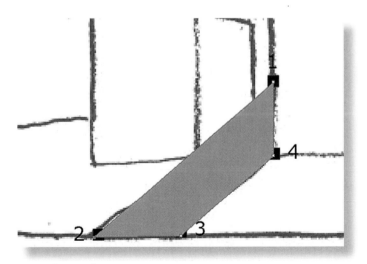

figure |1–17|

Completed path shape.

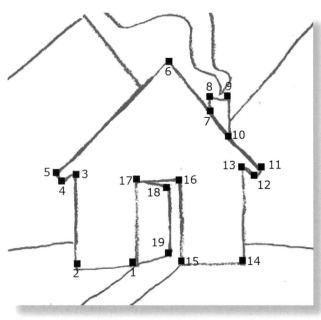

figure |1–18|

Reveal the guide dots to create the house shape.

figure |1–19|

Choose the "none"
option to have no
color fill.

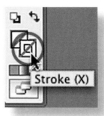

figure |1–20|

Set the stroke
(outline) color.

3. Set the color for the house. Click on the Fill box in the toolbox and choose the "none" option (white box with a red line through it). See Figure 1–19.

> **Note:** You will work with no fill to make it easier to draw the house.

4. Click on the Stroke box in the toolbox to bring it forward. See Figure 1–20.

5. Select the Black color swatch in the Swatches panel to set the stroke (outline) color to black.

6. Select the Pen tool.

7. Place the Pen tool on point 1, and click. Then, click once on each point—2, 3, 4, 5, 6, etc. When you have connected all the dots, close the path by clicking on point 1.

8. With the path you drew still selected, click the Fill box in the toolbox and choose the Black swatch. The house now should be black. See Figure 1–21.

figure |1–21|

Completed house drawing.

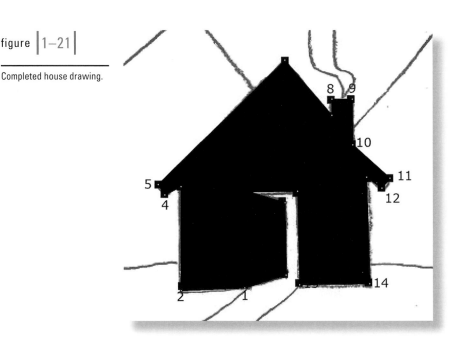

| CHAPTER 1 | **11**

9. Click on the icons to the far left of each layer—**house guide** and **draw house**—to hide them.

figure |1–22|

Set the stroke box to "none."

10. Save your file.

Drawing the Light Beam

1. Unhide the **light beam guide** layer to see the dots that will guide your drawing.

2. Select the **draw light beam** layer. This is the layer you will draw on.

3. Set the Stroke box in the toolbox to "none." See Figure 1–22.

4. Click the Fill box in the toolbox to bring it forward of the Stroke box.

5. For the fill color, select the 40% Black swatch in the Swatches panel.

6. With the Pen tool, connect the dots to create the light beam shape. See Figure 1–23.

7. Choose Window > Transparency and set the Opacity to 75%. See Figure 1–24. This makes the gray color slightly transparent.

8. Hide the **light beam guide** and **draw light beam** layers.

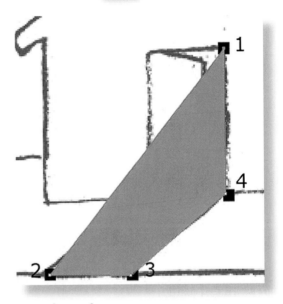

figure |1–23|

Completed light beam shape.

Making Smoke

1. Select the **draw smoke** layer.

2. Choose Window > Brushes.

3. From the brush list, select the Dry Ink brush. See Figure 1–25 on the next page. If the brush is not visible, click and drag the lower-right corner of the Brush panel to see more brushes.

4. From the toolbox, select the Paintbrush tool (the ninth tool in the toolbox). See Figure 1–26 on the next page.

5. From the toolbox, choose "none" for the fill color.

figure |1–24|

Set the color opacity.

> **Note:** When using a brush, the color comes from the color of the stroke and not from the color of the fill.

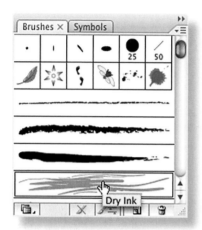

figure | 1–25 |

Select the Dry Ink brush.

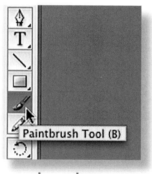

figure | 1–26 |

Select the Paintbrush tool.

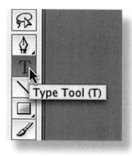

figure | 1–28 |

The Type tool in the toolbox.

6. Draw some smoke coming out of the chimney with the Paintbrush tool. Click and drag a wavy line. See Figure 1–27.

7. Save the file—you are almost there!

Creating the Title

1. Select the **title** layer.

2. Select the Type tool in the toolbox. See Figure 1–28.

3. Choose Type > Size > Other from the menu bar. The Character window pops up. For Font, choose Arial/Regular. For Size, enter **50** pt. See Figure 1–29.

4. Position the Type tool at the beginning of the word *Stratton* on the template.

5. Click down (you will see a blinking cursor). Then type **Stratton Buyer Brokerage**. See Figure 1–30.

figure | 1–27 |

Create smoke using the Paintbrush tool and Dry Ink brush.

figure | 1–29 |

The Character window for adjusting type.

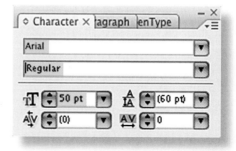

Stratton Buyer Brokerage

figure | 1–30 |

Completed text line.

6. With the Selection tool (black arrow), click and drag on the text block to position it in place. Click once away from the type to deselect it.

Making the Final Border

1. Now for the final touches. Select the **border** layer in the Layers panel.

2. Select the Rectangle tool in the toolbox. See Figure 1–31.

3. In the toolbox, select "none" for the fill color.

4. For the stroke, select a black swatch from the Swatches panel. Your final color selections should look like Figure 1–32.

5. Starting at the top-left edge of the logo's frame, click and drag to the opposite corner of the frame, creating a rectangular border around the image. See Figure 1–33.

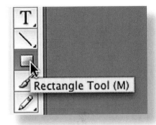

figure | 1–31 |

The Rectangle tool in the toolbox.

figure | 1–32 |

Fill and Stroke options for the logo border.

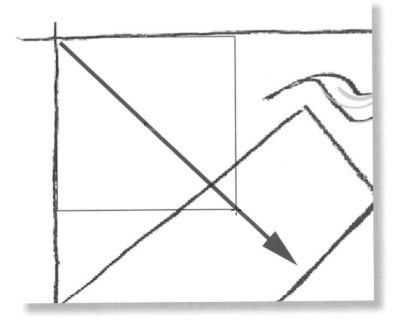

figure | 1–33 |

Draw a rectangle from corner to corner of the napkin sketch's frame.

figure | 1–34 |

Unhide the drawing layers.

Unveiling the Final Logo

1. Unhide the drawing layers by clicking to reveal the eye icon on each of them. The layers are **border**, **title**, **draw smoke**, **draw light beam**, **draw house**, **draw path**, **draw hill**, and **draw mountains**. See Figure 1–34.

2. Hide the **napkin sketch** layer. Your final image is revealed. See Figure 1–35.

3. Save your file—you have done it!

ABOUT ILLUSTRATOR

Adobe Illustrator is a great resource to reproduce, redo, revise, rework, and re-envision traditionally and digitally created artwork and imagery. Even if you are new to drawing or working digitally, Illustrator (along with this book) is a great place to start stirring up some creative energies. It also gets you out of many time-crunching, sticky, and unsuspected situations that await you as a graphic designer and offers a versatile new environment to draw, paint, and edit graphic images.

figure | 1–35 |

Completed Illustrator logo.

Lucky for you, each new version of Illustrator is significantly more sophisticated than the previous version. As the demand grows for more malleable and cross-product integration of digital content, new tools and effects are introduced and workflow techniques are added and improved, as is the product's ability to fuse into all types of graphic disciplines (i.e., interactive media, animation, print, and the Web). For all its capabilities it is no wonder Illustrator has been the most popular digital drawing program on the market since its inception—a necessary provision for print, Web and interactive designers, architects, animators, and traditional artists.

Fundamentally, however, Illustrator has not changed that much. Its underlying magic is the use of vectors, a way in which computer-generated objects are drawn using points and lines. You got a taste of this in the logo design lesson. Alternatively, digital images created by pixels—square-like elements gathered in a grid—are mainly handled using Illustrator's companion product, Adobe Photoshop. Chapter 3 goes into greater detail of the differences between these two ways of generating digital graphics, respectively known as vectors and bitmaps. For now, however, you should know Illustrator has the ability to:

- Create, color, edit, and add special effects to original or traced drawings.

- Effectively format and render type and enhance typographic layout and design.

- Produce objects and design layouts that can be resized and reformatted for print, Web, and multimedia publication without losing their quality (resolution).

- Export graphics to other vector-based formats, such as Macromedia's Flash (SWF) and the Web vector standard SVG (Scalable Vector Graphics). More on this in Chapter 11 of this text.

SUMMARY

As you have discovered, Illustrator is a powerful program for the reworking, repurposing, and reproduction of artwork, as well as the development of completely new digital imagery. Its fundamental way of making illustrations is through the use of vectors, making lines and shapes point by point. Without a doubt, Illustrator is a vital part of any graphic designer's repertoire.

in review

1. What is the purpose of a template image in Illustrator?

2. What are layers? How are they useful?

3. How do you know when a layer is hidden?

4. What is opacity?

5. Name at least two uses of Illustrator.

6. Who uses Illustrator?

exploring on your own

1. Visit the Illustrator area of the Adobe site: *http://www.adobe.com/cfusion/designcenter/ search.cfm?product=Illustrator&go=Go*. The official Adobe site has a wealth of information on Illustrator, including developer resources, third-party plug-ins, and inspirational customer stories and examples using Illustrator.

2. Do a search for Illustrator artists on the Web and explore what other artists are creating using Illustrator. Many artists' sites have tutorials for further learning. Also, see the "Explorer Pages" in this book for more inspiration from others. Some example sites and resources include:

   - *http://www.techvector.com*—Reggie Gilbert is TechVector, an avid Illustrator user, skateboarder, and snowboarder.

   - *http://www.arthurmount.com*—Arthur Mount, a non-stop illustrator with a hefty client list.

   - *http://www.ebypaidrick.com*—Ann Paidrick, of Eby-Paidrick Designs, creates beautiful, photo-realistic designs: a feast for the eyes.

- *http://www.janetmcleod.com*— Janet McLeod, a Toronto artist with a lyrical, hand-drawn sense to her work. Her client list includes editorial, advertising, and educational publishing companies.

- *http://www.lifeinvector.com*—Brook Nunez, illustrator, has an extensive gallery of her beautiful, diverse collection of work.

- *http://www.khulsey.com*—Kevin Hulsey, a master of cut-away technical illustrations, shares a site full of computer graphic illustration tutorials, tips and tricks for students.

- *Best Practice: The Pros On Adobe Illustrator*, by Toni Toland. Published by Thomson Delmar Learning, this book inspires readers to explore the creative process and technical skill behind the work of leading contemporary digital artists.

NY2007

©2007 Annesa Hartman

| the lay of the land |

2

charting your course

In Chapter 1, you were a sightseer on the Illustrator tour bus. You got to wander around, visit a few tourist attractions like the Layers panels and the Pen tool, and even build something you can slap into a scrapbook and say, "I did that!" Chapter 2 prepares you for the longer journey into Adobe Illustrator. Now you actually open up the atlas and take a good look at the program's landscape. In one lesson, you will visit the historical landmarks of the Illustrator interface—the most important parts of the program that you get from point A to B. Then you put on your binoculars (theoretically!) and take a closer look at the program's navigational features.

goals

In this chapter you will:

- **Feel comfortable with the Illustrator interface**
- **Set and delete Preferences**
- **Navigate around the workspace**

HISTORICAL LANDMARKS

I, Annesa, live at the end of a long, winding dirt road in the backwoods of Vermont. The UPS guy gets lost every time he comes to deliver a package. I usually get a phone call from the dispatcher inquiring about how to get to my house. Instead of giving street names already indicated on any map or sophisticated GPS (global positioning system), I point out a few notable landmarks: go across the covered bridge, stay to the left of the big pine tree, turn at the tilted mailbox, and go straight up the driveway to the end. In a matter of minutes, UPS is at my door. My point is: You can be handed a detailed map of an unknown—at least to you—area, but that does not necessarily mean you can find the way to where you want to go, at least not as directly. You can memorize the map, but you will soon realize—after having talked to some of the locals—that a few historical landmarks can help you find your destination much faster. You learn the shortcuts or discover there is more than one way to go, depending on which direction you are coming from. The Illustrator interface or work area is no exception. For example, in Illustrator there are at least two ways to get to every tool: click on it in the toolbox or use a keyboard shortcut (Edit > Keyboard Shortcuts). You will learn all the secret routes over time, but for now let us get familiar with some tried-and-true historical landmarks, including the artboard, toolbox, menu bar, panels, status bar, context menus, and preferences.

Lesson 1: Interface Highlights

In this lesson, you identify the main interface elements of Illustrator.

Identifying Landmarks

1. Open Illustrator. Bypass the Welcome window by pressing the Close button. See Figure 2–1.

figure | 2–1 |

Illustrator's Welcome window.

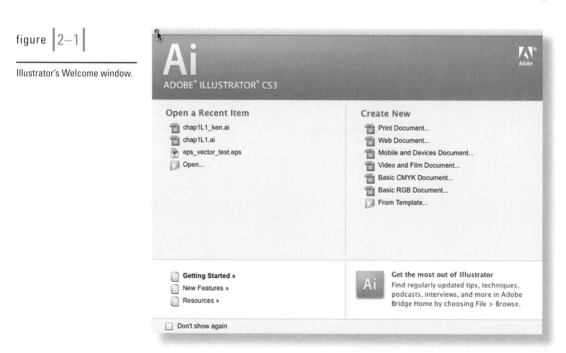

2. Choose File > New from the menu bar at the top.

3. Type **myfile** for the document name in the New Document dialog box. Choose Print for New Document Profile. Select OK. See Figure 2–2.

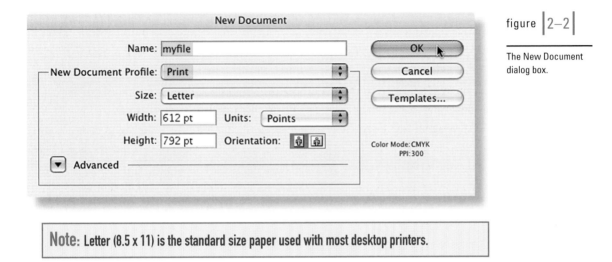

figure |2–2|

The New Document dialog box.

Note: Letter (8.5 x 11) is the standard size paper used with most desktop printers.

4. Depending on whether you are using a Macintosh (see Figure 2–3) or Windows (see Figure 2–4) computer, the nuances of the interface look slightly different. In general, however, the landmarks are the same. Compare your open Illustrator interface with Figure 2–3 or Figure 2–4, and note where the various parts of the program are located.

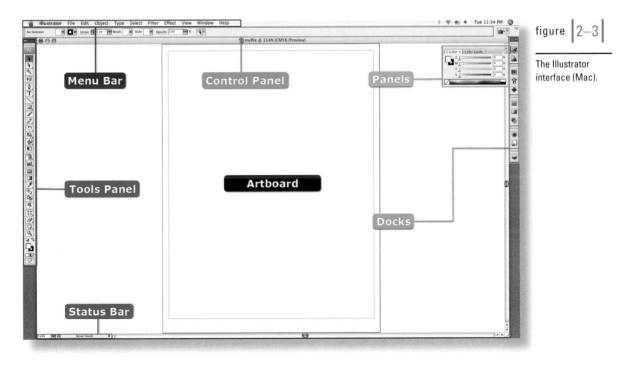

figure |2–3|

The Illustrator interface (Mac).

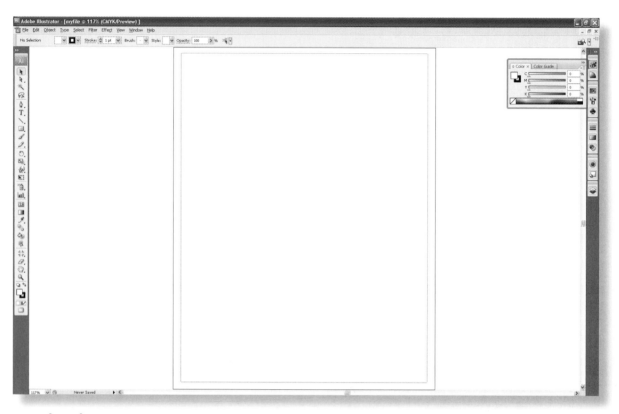

figure |2–4|

The Illustrator interface (Windows).

- *Artboard:* The artboard is the big white space in the middle of the screen. When you chose File > New in Step 2 above, you created a specified size for the artboard. The area bounded by the solid line is the region that contains your artwork. However, most printers cannot print right to the edge of this region. Therefore a printable "safe" area is defined within the dotted line. (If the dotted line is not visible, go to View > Show Page Tiling in the menu bar at the top of the screen.) The white space outside the artboard is called the "scratchboard" *(or "scratch area").* This is your doodling space, where you can create, edit, and store images that you might use on the final artboard area.

- *Tools Panel/Toolbox:* To the left of the screen is the Tools panel. It contains the tools necessary to select, create, edit, and manipulate illustrative objects. When you place your cursor (pointer) over a tool, the name of the tool appears—this is called a "tool tip," and it is incredibly helpful when you first learn which tool is which. There are several more tools than initially visible in the toolbox; some tools have tools hidden beneath them (sneaky). When you see a small triangle in the lower-right corner of a tool icon, click and hold on the icon and more tools are revealed. For a very useful visual of each tool and what it does, see Help > Illustrator Help > Work Area > Tools. At the top of the Tools panel, click on the double-arrow to toggle between the single-column (see Figure 2–5) and the classic two-column (see Figure 2–6) formats.

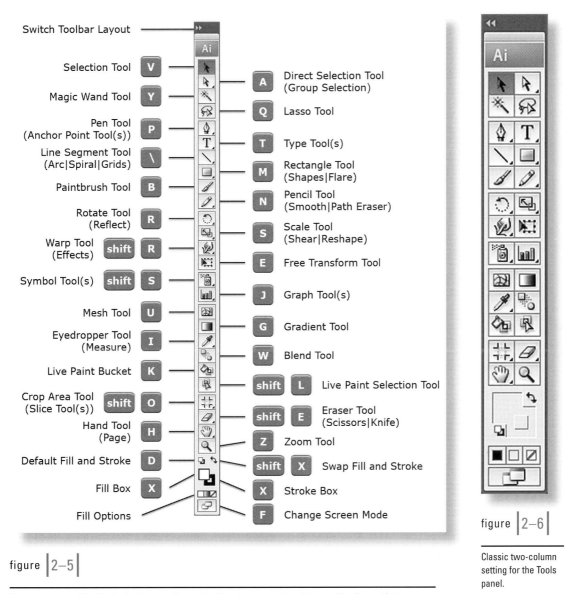

Switch Toolbar Layout

Selection Tool — V
Magic Wand Tool — Y
Pen Tool (Anchor Point Tool(s)) — P
Line Segment Tool (Arc|Spiral|Grids) — \
Paintbrush Tool — B
Rotate Tool (Reflect) — R
Warp Tool (Effects) — shift R
Symbol Tool(s) — shift S
Mesh Tool — U
Eyedropper Tool (Measure) — I
Live Paint Bucket — K
Crop Area Tool (Slice Tool(s)) — shift O
Hand Tool (Page) — H
Default Fill and Stroke — D
Fill Box — X
Fill Options

A — Direct Selection Tool (Group Selection)
Q — Lasso Tool
T — Type Tool(s)
M — Rectangle Tool (Shapes|Flare)
N — Pencil Tool (Smooth|Path Eraser)
S — Scale Tool (Shear|Reshape)
E — Free Transform Tool
J — Graph Tool(s)
G — Gradient Tool
W — Blend Tool
shift L — Live Paint Selection Tool
shift E — Eraser Tool (Scissors|Knife)
Z — Zoom Tool
shift X — Swap Fill and Stroke
X — Stroke Box
F — Change Screen Mode

figure | 2–5 |

Single-column setting for the Tools panel. Figure identifies the name of each tool and its shortcut key.

figure | 2–6 |

Classic two-column setting for the Tools panel.

- *Menu Bar:* On the top of the screen is the menu bar, which contains drop-down selections of various features, tools, and commands within Illustrator. Do not bother memorizing everything in the menu bar; it will come on a need-to-know basis.
- *Control Panel:* On the top of the screen, below the menu bar, is the Control panel. This is similar to the Options bar in Adobe's Photoshop. It offers quick access to options, commands, and other panels related to the current page item or objects you select. This type of panel is context sensitive, which means it displays different information depending on what artwork is selected. Try it out. Open the logo lesson (**chap1L1_final.ai)** from Chapter 1. Select objects on the artboard (paths or text) and watch the content for each selection change in the Control panel.

- *Panels:* Panels, usually located to the right of the interface, allow you to monitor and modify your work. You select panels from the menu bar under the Window heading. Panel windows come grouped together. To separate them, click on their title tabs and drag them to another area of the screen. See Figure 2–7. Of course, you can dock any panel back into a group or dock by dragging the separated panel's title bar over the desired panel's group or dock. To close unneeded panels, click on the Close button in the upper-right corner of any panel. To bring a closed panel back, go to Window on the menu bar and select the panel name. Or, to temporarily hide all the visible panels, press Shift-Tab. To bring them back, press Shift-Tab again. (If you press just Tab, you hide or unhide all panels including the toolbox.)

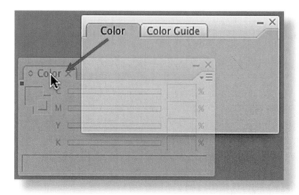

figure | 2–7 |

Separate or group panel windows.

- *Docks:* Docks are well-organized vertical bars composed of panels/groups displayed in either an iconic or full-size format. By default, a dock is located on the right side of the screen in a single column. Docks, however, can occupy either the left or right side of the screen in any number of columns. While a dock is collapsed (icons), clicking on any icon will expand the icon's panel/group. To view all panels in full-size, click on the double-arrow at the top of the dock to expand the dock. If you want to conserve valuable workspace, click on the double-arrow at the top of the panel/group or dock to collapse it to icons.

- *Status Bar:* The status bar is located at the lower-left edge of the document window. It contains the Zoom pop-up and Status pop-up menu items. The Zoom pop-up allows you to change the magnification of the document window. The Status pop-up contains specific information, such as under the Show menu the Version Cue status for your open file, current tool in use, date and time, number of undos and redos, and the document's color profile.

> Note: The Status pop-up also offers access to the Adobe Bridge application (Reveal in Bridge . . .), a stand–alone program that serves as the central location for increased productivity and file management with Adobe Creative Suite applications.

- *Context Menus:* When you Ctrl-click (Mac) or right-click your mouse (Windows), you will discover what are called context menus. These are drop-down menus that give you quick access to various features of a tool you might be using. See Figure 2–8.

Marking the Territory

1. Place the cursor (do not click!) over the Rectangle tool in the toolbox. Notice that a text equivalent (a tool tip) of the tool name appears. Next to the tool name a short-cut key is indicated. See Figure 2–9.

2. Click and hold on the Rectangle tool to open more Shape tool options. See Figure 2–10.

3. Select the Star tool.

4. Click and drag on your artboard to create a star shape. Make two or three.

5. Place the cursor over one of your stars, and hold down Command (⌘) (Mac) or Ctrl (Windows) to change the cursor to the Selection tool.

6. Keeping Command/Ctrl selected, click and move the star to a different location on the artboard. By selecting or releasing Command/Ctrl, you can toggle between the highlighted tool and the Selection tool. This is a nifty trick to quickly make, select, and move objects.

7. Hold down Option-Command (Mac) or Alt-Ctrl (Windows) while you click and move one of the stars. Release the mouse button first, and if your coordination is good, you will make a duplicate of the star. The Option/Alt key makes duplicates of currently selected objects. (Or, you can take the longer route and choose Edit > Copy, then Edit > Paste.) See Figure 2–11.

> **Note:** If you make a mistake, choose Edit > Undo, or Command-Z (Mac) or Ctrl-Z (Windows).

Here are a few things you should know about Undo.

- Repeatedly choose Edit > Undo to undo, in reverse order, the last operations you performed. To redo, choose Edit > Redo, or Command-Shift-Z (Mac), or Ctrl-Shift-Z (Windows).

- Depending on the amount of memory available on your computer, you can undo an unlimited number of the last operations you performed.

figure | 2–8 |

Ctrl-click (Mac) or right-click (Windows) to get to the context menus.

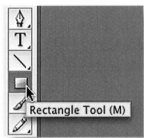

figure | 2–9 |

The tool tip for the Rectangle tool is revealed.

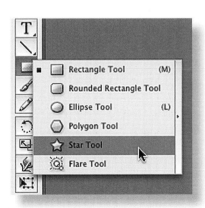

figure | 2–10 |

Click and hold on the Rectangle tool to reveal more Shape tool options.

figure |2–11|

Make stars.

- You can use Undo even after you have chosen the Save command, as long as you have not closed and reopened the file.
- If an operation cannot be undone, the Undo option is dimmed.

8. We are done with this file and identifying interface landmarks, so choose File > Save. For Format, make sure Adobe Illustrator Document is selected. Save **myfile.ai** in your lessons folder; you will use it again in the next lesson. Click OK to accept the default Illustrator Options.

> Note: The ".ai" at the end of your filename is the native file extension for all Illustrator files. Any file with this extension on the end was created in Adobe Illustrator.

Lesson 2: Getting Personal

Every time you open Illustrator and begin to open windows, set import options, determine ruler units, and grid and guide colors (basically customize things to your liking), Illustrator creates a file on your hard drive that defines these preferences. This is really great when you want to reopen the program and have everything preset your way. Let us set some preferences and see how this works.

Setting Preferences

1. Open Illustrator.

2. Choose File > Open and look for **myfile.ai**.

> Note: If you do not have a **myfile.ai**, choose **chap2L2.ai** in the **chap2_ lessons** folder.

3. Close any open panel windows (except for the toolbox) by clicking on the Close icon in the upper-right corner of each panel window. See Figure 2–12.

4. Select the Paintbrush tool in the toolbox. Notice that the cursor is changed to look like the tool selected. See Figure 2–13.

5. Choose Window > Brush Libraries and select the Artistic > Artistic_ChalkCharcoalPencil option. See Figure 2–14. Pick one of the artistic brushes in the library panel and proceed to paint some strokes on the artboard.

6. Let us change some preferences. Choose Illustrator > Preferences > General (Mac) or Edit > Preferences > General (Windows). Any change you make in this box will be recorded in a Preferences file for the next time you open the program. There are a lot of Preference options; we will only tinker with a few, but it is a good idea to look through all of them.

7. Under the General option, select the Use Precise Cursors and deselect Show Tool Tips. See Figure 2–15 on the next page. Tool tips come up by default when you place your cursor over a tool in the toolbox, and the name for the tool is revealed along with the keystroke shortcut for selecting it.

8. Go to the drop-down menu at the top of the Preferences window and change General to Guides and Grids. Change the Grid Color to Magenta.

9. Select OK to close the Preferences window.

10. Test your preference choices. First, roll your cursor over a tool in the toolbox and notice that the text equivalent Tool Tip is no longer available.

11. Choose the Paintbrush tool and notice that the cursor icon has changed. It is no longer in the shape of the brush icon; rather, it is a cross mark. This cross mark indicates a precise cursor—the center of the cursor is the exact spot where you will draw—which is much more accurate than the traditional icon cursor.

12. Choose View > Show Grid to see the magenta-colored grid.

13. Save your file. Name it **myfile2.ai**.

14. Choose Illustrator > Quit Illustrator (Mac) or File > Exit (Windows) to shut down the program.

15. Reopen the program and **myfile2.ai**.

16. Notice your Preferences have not changed.

Deleting Preferences

1. If you want to go back to Illustrator's default preference settings, first close Illustrator—Illustrator > Illustrator Quit (Mac) or File > Exit (Windows).

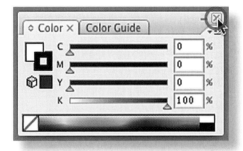

figure |2–12|

Close unneeded panel windows.

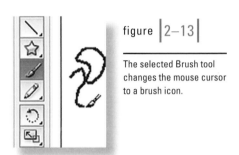

figure |2–13|

The selected Brush tool changes the mouse cursor to a brush icon.

figure |2–14|

Choose an artistic brush to paint on the art.

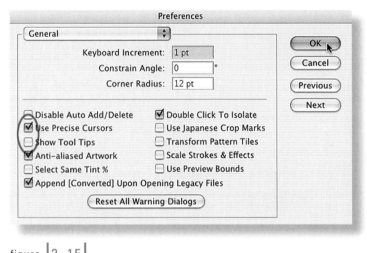

figure |2–15|

Select the General Preferences.

2. Depending whether you use a Mac or a Windows computer, do one of the following:

- In Windows, go to the **Documents and Settings\user name\ApplicationData\Adobe\ Adobe Illustrator CS3 Settings** folder. Delete the **AIPrefs** file.

Note: Before deleting the **AIPrefs** file, rename it and move it to the desktop as a safety copy.

- In Mac OS, go to the **Preferences** folder in the **System** Folder (Mac OS 9.x) or **Username/Library/Preferences** folder (Mac OS X). Open the **Adobe Illustrator CS3 Settings** folder and place the **Adobe Illustrator Prefs** file in the trash.

Note: Before deleting the **Prefs** file, rename it and move it to the desktop as a safety copy.

3. Once you have deleted the Preferences file, reopen Illustrator to view the default setup. It will look something like Figure 2–16.

figure |2–16|

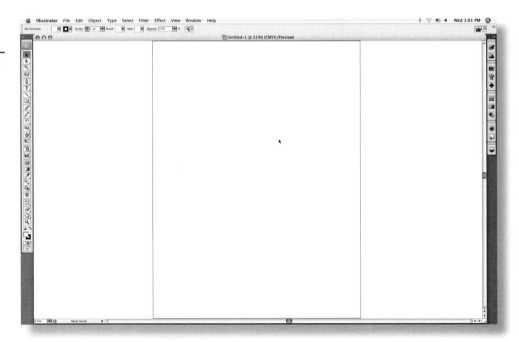

The Illustrator interface with its default preferences.

A CLOSER LOOK

You now have a bird's-eye view of the Illustrator landscape. Next, you will take a closer look at some of the navigational features of the program, such as the Hand and Zoom tools, the Navigator panels, Screen and View modes, and the status bar.

Lesson 3: Navigational Features

Magnification Tools

1. In Illustrator, open the file **chap2L3.ai** in the folder **chap2_lessons**.

> **Note:** If you get a convert color mode warning window, choose CMYK.

2. Choose View > Fit in Window to magnify the file to fit in the window area.

3. Notice the document title bar indicates the current magnification of the artwork. See Figure 2–17. Depending on the size of your document window, this number will vary. Try

figure |2–17|

The document title bar indicates the current magnification of the artwork.

this: Scale-down the lower-right corner of your document window and choose View > Fit in Window. The artwork is repositioned in the window area, indicating a new magnification level in the document title bar.

4. Choose View > Actual Size to set the document to 100% scaling. This shows you the actual size of the artwork if it were to be printed on paper.

5. Select the Zoom tool in the toolbox. Refer to Figure 2–5. Click once on the artwork to zoom in. Click again to zoom even closer.

6. Hold down Option (Mac) or Alt (Windows) to reverse the Zoom tool (notice the minus sign in the Zoom tool cursor). Continue to hold down Option/Alt, as you click once on the artwork to zoom out. Click again to zoom even farther away.

7. Let us zoom into a particular area of the artwork. With the Zoom tool selected, click and drag from upper-left to lower-right a rectangular shape over the copyright notice in the lower-left corner of the document. With this area marqueed, let go and notice how the area selected zooms in close. Cool! See Figure 2–18.

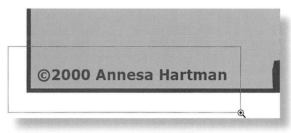

8. Select the Type tool (the "T") in the toolbox and change the text from 2000 to **2007**. To do this, click and drag on the last zero to highlight it, and then press the "**7**" key. See Figure 2–19.

figure |2–18|

9. Select the Hand tool in the toolbox (the tool above the Zoom tool). Click and drag with the Hand tool

Select an area to zoom in close.

figure | 2–19 |

Change the text with the Type tool.

©2007 Annesa Hartman

figure | 2–20 |

The completed artwork.

figure | 2–21 |

The nifty Navigator panel.

over the document, pushing it down until you see the NY2000 text on the left edge of the artwork.

10. Select the Type tool and change NY2000 to **NY2007**. To exit the Type tool, choose the Selection tool and click anywhere in the scratch area on the artboard.

11. Select View > Actual Size to see the completed artwork. Alternatively, double-click on the Zoom tool in the toolbox. See Figure 2–20.

The Navigator Panel

1. Another way to get a proper view of your artwork is to use the nifty Navigator panel. Choose Window > Navigator to open it. A small view of your artwork with a red border around it is shown in the Navigator window. See Figure 2–21.

2. In the Navigator panel, slide the small arrow in the lower-part of the window to the right, to magnify the document, or to the left, to reduce it. Notice the red border adjusts in the viewing window to indicate what area is viewable in the document.

> Note: Instead of moving the slider to zoom in and out, you can click on the mountain–like icons on each side of the slider. Also, you can type in a zoom percentage in the lower–left corner of the Navigator window.

3. Magnify the graphic by sliding the arrow in the Navigator window to the right. The red border area should grow smaller in the window.

4. Locate a specific area of the graphic by placing the cursor over the red border area in the Navigator window (notice the cursor changes to the Hand tool). Click and drag the red-border area, until you locate the copyright (©) symbol in the lower-left corner of the document.

Other Viewing Modes

1. Choose View > Actual Size to see the completed artwork.

2. Select the Selection tool in the toolbox. Marquee a selection of the Brooklyn Bridge by dragging from upper-left to lower-right. See Figure 2–22. Notice the edges (paths) of the artwork are visible for editing.

3. Turn these edges (paths) off by choosing View > Hide Edges. (We do not like to hide the edges of our artwork because then we cannot see the selected paths when editing, and sometimes we accidentally select View > Hide Edges when we do not mean to. This feature might come in handy someday, so it is good to know it is there.)

4. Choose View > Show Edges.

5. Choose View > Show Artboard to view the outline of the document. Remember that the artboard is the visible region that contains your artwork.

6. To view the artwork in outlines, choose View > Outline. This option views only the paths of the artwork, not the paint attributes. Viewing artwork without paint attributes speeds up the time it takes to redraw the screen when working with complex artwork. It also makes it easier to select things in a detailed illustration.

7. Choose View > Preview to see all the artwork attributes again.

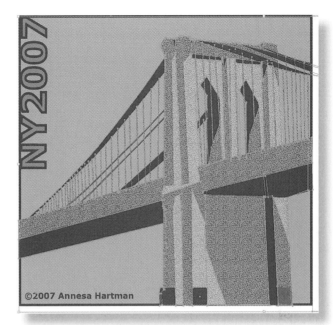

figure |2–22|

Edges, colored green in this figure, are visible for editing the artwork.

Screen Modes and Status Bar

1. You can also view artwork at different screen sizes. In the toolbox, you can choose Maximized Screen Mode, Standard Screen Mode, Full Screen Mode with Menu Bar, or Full Screen Mode (without Menu Bar). See Figure 2–23, and try out all four options.

2. In the toolbox, choose Standard Screen Mode. Notice the status bar in the lower-left corner of the document window. It contains pop-up information for Zoom options and Document status options. See Figure 2–24.

3. From the pop-up menu near the magnification number, choose a new magnification for the artwork.

4. From the pop-up menu near the document status indicator, explore each of the following options: Version Cue Status, Current Tool use, Date and Time, Number of Undos and redos available, and Document Color Profile. (More on that option later.)

5. Close the file. You are done with this lesson.

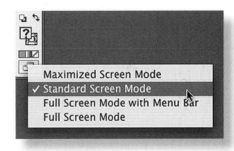

figure |2–23|

Select screen modes in the toolbox.

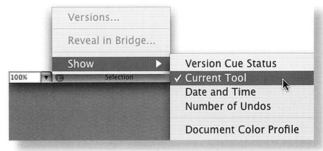

figure |2–24|

The status bar.

SUMMARY

After exploring this chapter you have a better command of the interface elements and navigational features of Illustrator. No more wandering around dark alleys trying to find your way. With a little practice, you will be zooming in and out, selecting tools, and opening and closing panel windows with ease. Who needs a sophisticated GPS when you have historical landmarks and shortcut keys to aid you on your Illustrator journey?

in review

1. Explain the difference between the scratchboard and the artboard.

2. The nonprintable area of a document is indicated by what visual on the Illustrator artboard?

3. What does .ai at the end of a filename indicate?

4. What are tool tips? How can you turn them off?

5. What is a precise cursor?

6. Identify the shortcut key to undo a mistake.

7. What steps are necessary to go back to Illustrator's default preferences?

8. What is the difference between View > Actual Size and View > Fit in Window?

exploring on your own

1. Create a new file and explore the different shape options available in the toolbox—rectangle, rounded rectangle, ellipse, polygon, stars, and flares. Use the Navigator panel to practice zooming in and out of the document window. Reset your Preferences.

2. There are many ways to customize your experience in Illustrator. Explore the various options for how your workspace could be set up by choosing Window > Workspace. See Figure 2–25. Keep in mind that you do not want to customize too much while you are doing the lessons in this book or things might get confusing; all lessons in this book are based on the default (Panel) arrangement of the workspace and keyboard shortcuts. Options for workspace setup include:

   - *Basic Workspace:* Minimizes the workspace area into the most basic, docked versions of the panels.

   - *Panel:* Resets workspace to the default Illustrator setup.

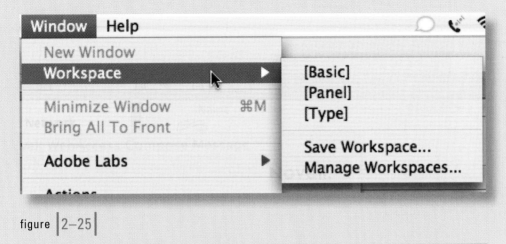

figure |2–25|

Customize your workspace.

- *Type:* Sets workspace with open panels used mostly for typographic creation and editing.

- *Save Workspace:* Saves your favorite workspace setup (panels, menus and keyboard shortcuts) for quick access every time you use the program.

- *Manage Workspace:* View and delete your saved workspaces.

Also, in Illustrator, read the section "Work area" under Help > Illustrator Help.

3. Once you get the hang of the general features of Illustrator, you can set personalized keyboard shortcuts under Edit > Keyboard Shortcuts.

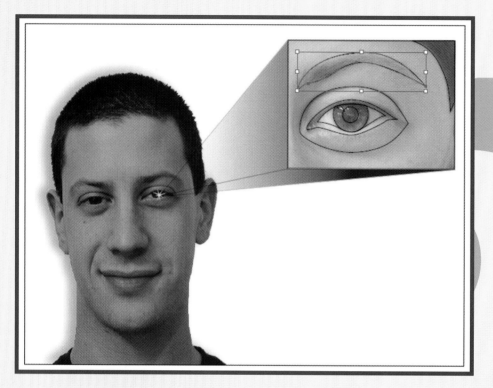

| survival techniques |

3

charting your course

Now that you have gotten your feet wet with Illustrator, you are ready go in a little deeper. Chapter 3 is essential for aspiring graphic artists. If you can grasp this chapter, you will be well equipped for creative expeditions not only in Illustrator, but also in any computer graphics program.

In this chapter you find out that Illustrator—because it uses vector technology—opens up a world of possibilities for you, the artist. We will start with a brief explanation of what it takes to be an Illustrator artist, and then venture into the differences between vector and bitmap images, as well as image formats. In conclusion, we will guide you through a hands-on deconstruction of an Illustrator file with design elements in mind.

goals

In this chapter you will:

- **Find out that being an Illustrator artist is more than just knowing the tools**
- **Develop a basic understanding of the two types of digital images: bitmap (raster) and vector**
- **Learn about image formats and get an overview of common image format types**
- **Find out how Illustrator, through the understanding of fundamental design elements, can be used as an effective art medium**
- **Explore the use of Illustrator's tools and features with design elements in mind**

IT'S MORE THAN COOL TOOLS

We are going to tell it to you straight: Being a graphic artist is not about knowing how to use the millions of tools in the hundreds of computer graphics software programs available. That is like saying you are going to master all the tools at Home Depot before you build a house. Why learn how to use a miter saw before you need something cut?

Obviously, it helps to know what tools do exist. And having some versatility with a few common tools—such as a hammer if you are building a house, or the Pen tool if you are working in Illustrator (see Chapter 4)—does make things easier. Such knowledge allows you to better conceptualize how a project might come together. Truly mastering all the tools and features of a program, however, comes when you have a real-life project—with schedules and deadlines and picky clients. And that kind of experience comes with time.

More important to comprehend is not the tools, but rather the principles behind how the tools are used. Understanding how digital images are created is key to your survival as a successful graphic artist. This includes knowing an image's distinguishing characteristics, its format type, and—in particular to Illustrator—how it is created in relation to fundamental design elements. Most books on Illustrator do not get into any of this until much later (if it all), and we believe it is a crime against the designer intellect. That would be like sending you out on an African safari with a shotgun and no training on when and how to use it. We do not want to be responsible for your being swallowed by a lion, so please read on.

CHARACTERISTICS OF BITMAPS AND VECTORS

There are two types of digital graphics: bitmap (or raster) and vector. The designer's understanding of bitmaps and vectors is as important as the mechanic's knowledge about what is under the hood of a car. If you want the creative engine to work, you need to know how the parts fit together. Having a clear picture of the differences between bitmaps and vectors enables you to more effectively create, format, edit, and alter digital artwork—as we mentioned before, not just in Illustrator, but in every computer graphics program you might encounter. That being said, if it seems too technical at first, do not worry—the differences will become obvious once you start working with digital graphics. The key point is to be aware that these differences exist, as shown in Figure 3–1.

About Bitmap Images

When describing bitmaps, we like to think of beautiful mosaics composed of individual tiles. Each tile has its own color and location, and when combined with other tiles it produces a complete image, pattern, or design. To equate this with computer graphics, each complete image, pattern, or design is what would be defined as a bitmap, and each tile—individual piece of the bitmap—is a pixel, a square element containing specific information (bits), such as color and location data. Figure 3–2 demonstrates this makeup.

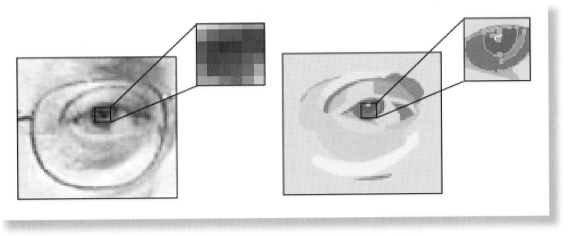

figure | 3-1 |

On the left is an example photograph composed of pixels (small elements of data in a bitmap grid) that describe the image's color and size. On the right is an illustration composed of vectors, specific points that define the object's outline using a mathematical coordinate system.

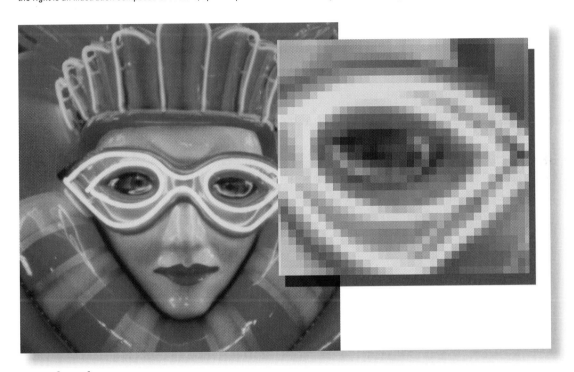

figure | 3-2 |

Zooming in close to a bitmap image can reveal its individual pixels.

A bitmap image contains a fixed number of pixels (information), measured by pixels per inch (ppi). This measurement is called the image's resolution. An image with a high resolution contains more pixels than an image of the same dimensions with a low resolution. For example, the

1-by-1-inch black-and-white photo in Figure 3–3 was designed to go to print and the printer requested the image to be delivered with a 150 ppi resolution. (Note: For information about resolution related to printing, see Chapter 10.) The total number of pixels in this image would be 22,500 (150 ppi × 150 ppi = 22,500). If it were to be viewed on a screen, such as a Web browser, 72 ppi is a recommended resolution, making a total image resolution of 5,184 pixels. Setting the proper resolution of an image is key to effectively saving it for its intended use. Also keep in mind that the higher the resolution of an image, the bigger the file size and usually the better its visual quality. We will come back to the topic of resolution in Chapter 10 and Chapter 11, when we get into specifics about preparing images for print and Web output.

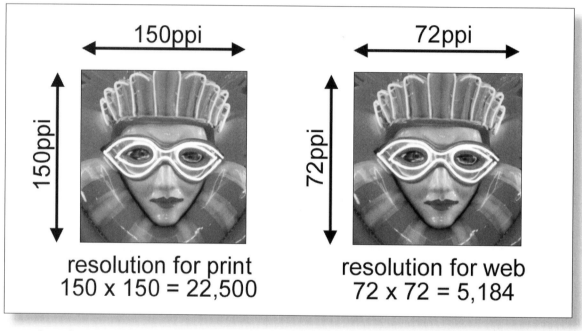

figure |3–3|

A bitmap image of the same dimensions (for example, 1-by-1-inch) can have a different resolution (number of ppi) depending on its intended use.

To sum up the discussion of bitmap images, remember this: They are unique because they are composed of a grid of pixels, and their visual quality, file size, and intended use are dependent on resolution; they are most common for continuous tone images, such as photographs; and they are really good at representing subtle gradations of color and shading.

About Vector Graphics

To visualize vectors just think of those coloring books where you connect a series of dots and a complete image appears. You explored this in Chapter 1, when you made a logo. Each dot defines a particular point in space with lines in between. Each line, in turn, connects to create the shapes that comprise an object or illustration. Unlike the static pages of a coloring book, however, the cool thing about connecting dots in Illustrator is that you can add, delete, and edit those dots and lines over and over until you get your vision just right. Its flexibility is its asset, and this is what makes drawing digitally truly fun.

If you recall, bitmap images are dependent on their resolution, which makes them tricky to work with; however, with vectors this is not the case. In Illustrator, instead of trying to push around square pixels, you actually construct an image with straight and curved paths, point by point. Additionally, a vector image can be scaled big or small and its quality always looks good. Therefore, graphics made with vectors are usually bold and illustrative, with qualities that retain crisp lines and solid colors when scaled to various sizes and used for different purposes, like text and logo treatments, for example.

In short, it's good to know that vector graphics are made up of points and lines that describe an object's outline or shape. See Figure 3–4. In contrast to bitmap images, vector images are resolution independent—they do not depend on pixels to determine their visual quality. They can be scaled any size and printed to any output device without loss of detail or clarity. Vectors are what Illustrator is all about.

figure |3–4|

On the left is an illustrative vector image. On the right are the editable lines that comprise it.

Convergence of Image Types and Image Formats

Before moving on, we should mention a couple more vital points about vectors and bitmaps. Programs such as Adobe Photoshop and Fireworks, and GIMP are designed to work specifically with bitmap-constructed images. Adobe Illustrator and Flash, and CorelDRAW are designed to work with vector-based graphics. However, most programs—to some extent—have the ability to import and translate both vector and bitmap graphics. Illustrator in particular has the option to convert vector objects into bitmap objects. This process is called rasterization. For example, by selecting Object > Rasterize in Illustrator, a basic shape can be converted from vector outlines to bitmapped pixels. You might do this if you want to apply a certain effect or filter that works only on bitmapped objects. You can also convert bitmaps into vectors with Illustrator's Live Trace feature. See "Adventures in Design: Going Live," at the end of Chapter 6.

There also are different image formats for different types of images. A format is described by an extension at the end of the filename, like image.jpg, mywork.tiff or paper1.doc. An image's format helps you identify whether it is composed of bitmaps or vectors. A file format also indicates the file size, visual quality, and compression settings (if any) of the image. A highly compressed image is lower in file size and visual quality than an uncompressed or minimally compressed image. There are many kinds of image file formats depending on where you are going to use the image (i.e., print, Web, or exporting into another program). Most graphic programs support the use of the following:

Bitmap-based formats:

- *BMP:* A limited bitmap file format not suitable for Web or print.

- *GIF:* A highly compressed format mainly used for Internet graphics with solid colors and crisp lines.

- *JPEG:* A compressed format used for Internet graphics, particularly photographs.

- *PNG:* A versatile bitmap compressed format used mainly for Internet graphics.

- *TIFF:* Saves bitmap images in an uncompressed format, most popular for print and compatible for virtually all image editing and page layout applications.

> Note: To maintain the highest quality, images are usually saved uncompressed in TIFF format. However, in Illustrator you can apply certain types of compression, such as LZW, on a TIFF, which compresses the file without discarding detail from the image.

Vector- and bitmap-based formats:

- *EPS:* Flexible file format that can contain both bitmap and vector information. Most vector images are saved in this format.

- *PICT:* Used on Mac computers and can contain both vector and bitmap data.

- *SWF:* The Flash™ file format. A common vector-based graphics file format for the creation of scalable, compact graphics for the Web and handheld devices.

- *SVG:* An emerging XML-based, vector format for the creation of scalable, compact graphics for the Web and handheld devices.

Importing and Exporting

In Illustrator, you can import (place into the program) images and files saved in many types of formats. To import files into an existing document and view a list of all readable documents Illustrator supports, choose File > Place. See Figure 3–5. When placing an image or file into a document, you have an option to "link." See Figure 3–6. When the link button is checked, the placed file uses the source image as an external reference to the document reducing the overall document file size. When linking files, remember to keep the linked files at hand; without them, the document will not show your work properly. If the link button is unchecked, the placed file is embedded into the document. These embedded files become part of the document and, as a result, they may increase the document's file size significantly. To import files as a new document, choose File > Open.

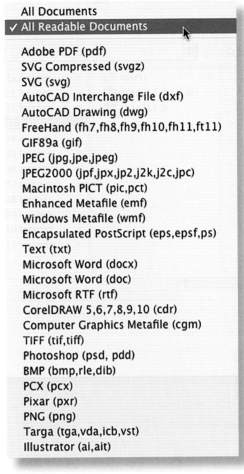

figure | 3–5 |

Choose File > Place to import files into Illustrator.

> **Note:** If you decide to link images or files to your document you always have the option to embed them later. Choose Window > Links for options to embed and/or re-link misplaced images.

You can also export (save) your Illustrator work into different formats depending on where it will go next in the design process—print, the Web, or imported into another program. To export a file and view a list of file formats, choose File > Export. See Figure 3–7.

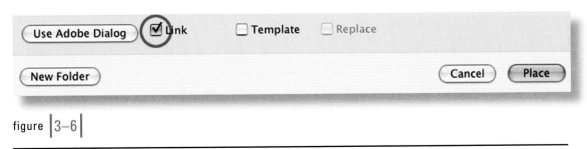

figure | 3–6 |

The option to link rather than embed a file or image is available when you place the file or image into the program.

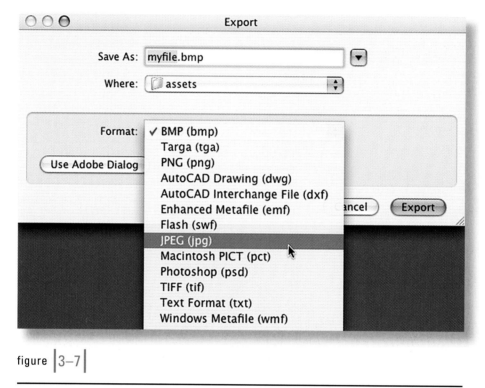

figure |3–7|

Choose File > Export to save Illustrator artwork in a different format.

DESIGN ELEMENTS WITH ILLUSTRATOR

The approach to creating an illustration in Illustrator is not unlike traditional drawing and painting. Whether sketching by hand or computer mouse, the elements of design are essentially the same. With this in mind, you are ready to learn the tools and techniques of Illustrator as they apply to the fundamental building blocks of visual art.

"The corresponding structural elements of art are line, shape, value, texture, and color," according to the authors of *Art Fundamentals, Theory and Practice.* "In art the artist is not only the contractor but also the architect; he or she has the vision, which is given shape by the way the elements are brought together."

Each chapter of this book builds on the elements of art as they pertain to your growing understanding of Illustrator. With the elements of line, shape, value, texture, and color, a direct correlation can be made with how a vector illustration is constructed to the structural elements of art and design. As you will learn in Chapter 4, a digital illustration is composed of vector objects, each having one or more paths (shapes) made of line segments having anchor points at each end. Each object's lines and shapes become unique, unified, and/or spatially whole by application of value, texture, and color. On a cursory level, you will explore this relationship in the next lesson, "Adam's Eye." Additionally, a visual diagram of this correlation might help. See Figure 3–8.

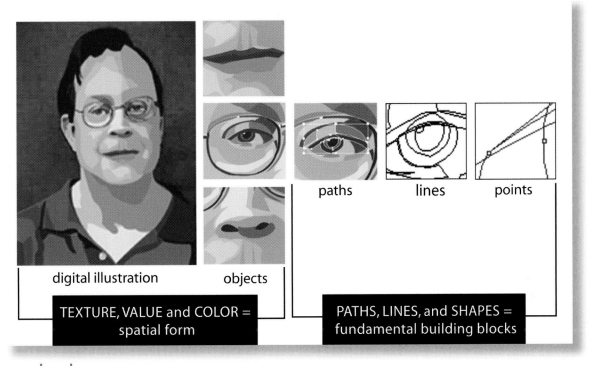

digital illustration   objects   paths   lines   points

TEXTURE, VALUE and COLOR = spatial form

PATHS, LINES, and SHAPES = fundamental building blocks

figure | 3–8 |

Anatomy of an illustration with the elements of art and design in mind.

As an artist uses watercolors, charcoal sticks, or clay to bring a vision to form, the graphic designer uses Illustrator as a medium toward a creative end. See Figure 3–9. Its numerous tools and features are designed to support the elements inherent in visual artwork and beyond.

Lesson: Adam's Eye

In this lesson, you take a guided tour of a previously created Illustrator file. Step-by-step, you import and place a bitmap image, add a warp effect, unlock layers, and explore the different stages of vector object construction—all the while keeping design elements in mind. See Figure 3–10 of the completed lesson.

figure | 3–9 |

Notice how line, shape, value, and texture make up the illustration of René Descartes, shown here. Value is indicated by the light and dark shapes in the drawing. Textural line effects bring out the subtle softness and depth of his hair and robe. Note: René Descartes can be considered one of the foremost fathers of vector illustration. A seventeenth-century mathematician and philosopher, he developed analytic geometry, in particular coordinate systems, which provide a foundation for describing the location and shape of objects in space.

figure |3–10|

Completed lesson: Adam's Eye.

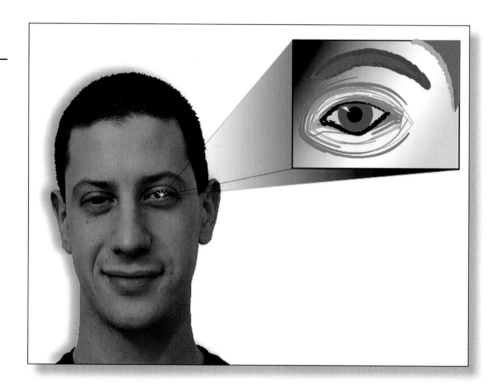

figure |3–11|

The Layers panel.

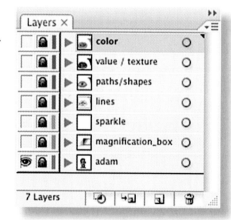

Setting Up the File

1. Open Illustrator. If a Welcome screen appears, click the close button on the screen's title bar.

2. Choose File > Open and, on your local hard drive, browse for the Exploring Illustrator folder **chap3_lessons**. Open the file **chap3L1.ai**.

> **Note:** As mentioned in the File Set-up, to save your work, you must make a copy of the chapter lessons to your local hard drive, and select files from that location.

figure |3–12|

The Layers visibility option is indicated by an eye icon on the left of the Layers panel.

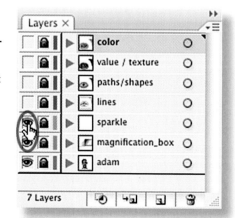

3. Choose Window > Layers to open the Layers panel. See Figure 3–11. Layers organize the various elements of an Illustrator document. There are already several layers created for this document.

4. Unhide the layers **magnification_box** and **sparkle** by turning on the visibility option for each layer in the Layers panel. See Figure 3–12 and Figure 3–13.

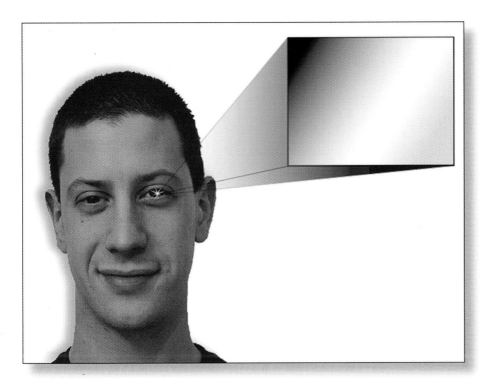

figure |3–13|

Unhiding Layers reveals more parts of the illustration.

Importing a Bitmap

1. Select the layer **sparkle**. See Figure 3–14.

2. Click Create New Layer at the bottom of the Layers panel (next to the trash can icon) to make a new layer above the **sparkle** layer. See Figure 3–15.

3. Double-click on the new layer (**Layer 8**) to open the Layer Options. Alternatively, click on the arrow with three horizontal lines in the upper-right corner of the Layers panel and select Options for "Layer 8." See Figure 3–16.

4. For the layer name enter **eye_bitmap**, and click OK. See Figure 3–17.

5. With the **eye_bitmap** layer highlighted, choose File > Place from the menu bar.

6. Browse for **chap3_lessons/assets** and place the **adam_eye.jpg**.

7. Choose Window > Transform. In the Transform panel window (or, using the Control panel of the selected .jpg) enter W: **240 pt**, and H: **180 pt** to reduce the bitmap's size. See Figure 3–18.

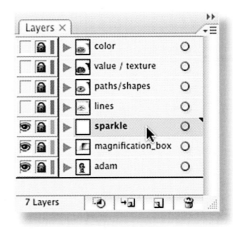

figure |3–14|

Sparkle layer is selected (highlighted in blue).

figure |3–15|

The Create New Layer option.

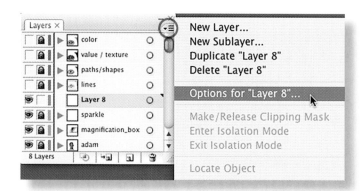

figure |3–16|

Open the Layer options.

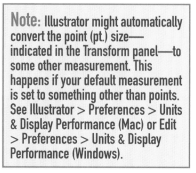

Note: Illustrator might automatically convert the point (pt.) size—indicated in the Transform panel—to some other measurement. This happens if your default measurement is set to something other than points. See Illustrator > Preferences > Units & Display Performance (Mac) or Edit > Preferences > Units & Display Performance (Windows).

8. Click and drag the bitmap image to fit into the magnification box. For precise positioning, press the up/down and right/left arrow keys on the keyboard to move the image in 1-pt. increments. See Figure 3–19.

9. In the Control panel at the top of the screen, click on the Embed button if it is available. See Figure 3–20. If you have inadvertently deselected the bitmap, select it again to show the Embed option. By embedding the image, you ensure the placed image will be saved with the document, and filters and effects can be applied to it.

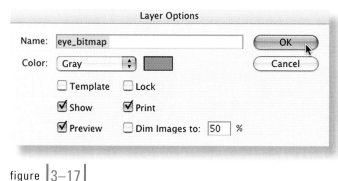

figure |3–17|

Name the Layer.

Note: Another way to embed an object: uncheck the "link" button in File > Place, as discussed earlier in the chapter.

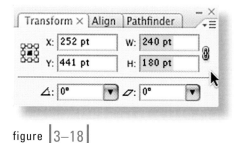

figure |3–18|

Size the bitmap exactly using the Transform panel window.

10. For fun, choose Effect > Warp > Fisheye (be sure the bitmap is selected). In the Warp Options window, adjust the Bend option by moving the slider to 72%. Preview the effect on the bitmap by selecting the Preview option. See Figure 3–21. (Note: You might need to move the Warp Options window aside to see the eye bit-map effect on the document below.) Click OK to close the Warp Options window.

11. Double-click the **eye_bitmap** layer to open the Layer Options. Select the Dim Images to option and set it at **75%**. This option dims the bitmap located on this layer, which will be useful when you trace over the image in the next section. Click OK.

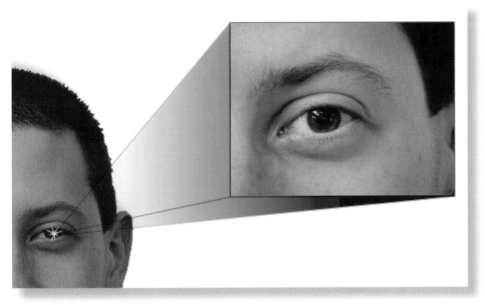

figure |3-19|

Position the eye bitmap.

figure |3-20|

Select the Embed button on the Control panel.

12. Lock the **eye_bitmap** layer by selecting the lock option on the left of the Layers panel. See Figure 3–22 on the next page . You should lock a layer—making it safe from editing—when you are working on other layers.

13. Choose File > Save As to save your file. Rename it **chap3L1_yourname.ai**, and save it in your lessons folder.

Exploring Lines

1. Unhide and unlock the **lines** layer in the Layers panel. Some lines, traced around the image of the eye, have already been created. Constructing lines and paths are the first step in the illustrative process.

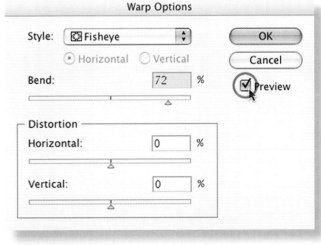

figure |3 –21|

Preview the Fisheye Warp settings.

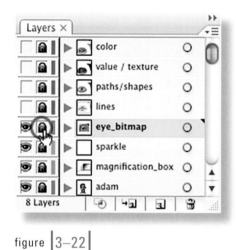

figure |3–22|

Lock a layer to make it safe from editing.

figure |3–23|

The Selection tool is the black arrow that allows you to select objects in your document.

2. Choose the Selection tool in the Toolbox. See Figure 3–23.

> **Note:** By default your toolbox should be open. If not, choose Window > Tools to open the panel.

3. Explore selecting the different paths on the eye image. Notice how each line segment is composed of connecting anchor points. See Figure 3–24.

4. Each line created is indicated in the **lines** layer. To see the sub list of lines (labeled <Path>), click the gray arrow next to the **lines** layer icon. To quickly select the various lines/paths in the document, click on the circle to the right of any of the layers. See Figure 3–25. To hide the layer's sublayers, click on the triangle again.

5. Let us make a new line object by outlining the eyebrow of the eye bitmap image. First, select the Zoom tool in the toolbox (the magnifying glass icon toward the bottom of the panel), and then click once on the **eye_bitmap** to magnify it.

> **Note:** If you make a mistake, double-click on the Zoom tool icon in the toolbox to zoom out to full view, and then try again.

6. Select the Pencil tool in the toolbox. See Figure 3–26.

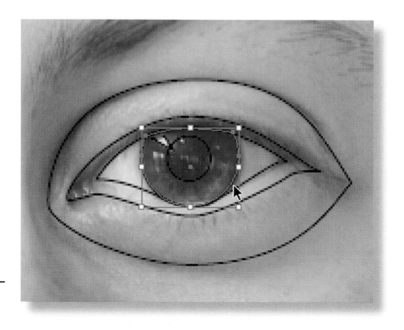

figure |3–24|

Select lines and paths.

7. With steady hand, click and drag a continuous line around the eyebrow, ending in the same place you started. See Figure 3–27. If you make a mistake, choose Edit > Undo Pencil, and try again.

> **Note:** There are numerous ways to edit and reshape the line you created, which will be covered in later chapters. For now, just get a feel for what it is like to trace over an image.

8. Save your file.

Filling a Shape

1. Unhide the **paths/shapes** layer. Notice the lines created filled with flat shading, resulting in distinct shapes.

2. Select your eyebrow. From the Control panel click on the down arrow of the Fill option (first drop-down arrow). Select the 80% Black (dark gray) swatch to fill the eyebrow. See Figure 3–28.

3. From the Control panel, click on the down arrow of the Stroke option (second drop-down arrow). Select the 80% Black swatch for the eyebrow's stroke. See Figure 3–29 and Figure 3–30.

Adding Value and Texture

1. In the Layers panel, unhide the **value/texture** layer. Notice the variations of line—width, intensity and quality—that add value and texture to the illustration.

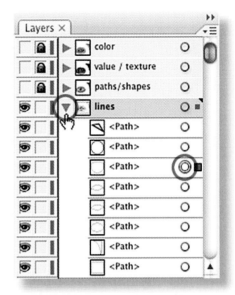

figure | 3–25 |

To organize all the elements of an illustration, layers are further subdivided into sublayers—each sublayer contains one element or object.

figure | 3–26 |

The Pencil tool is just one of the tools to create lines and paths.

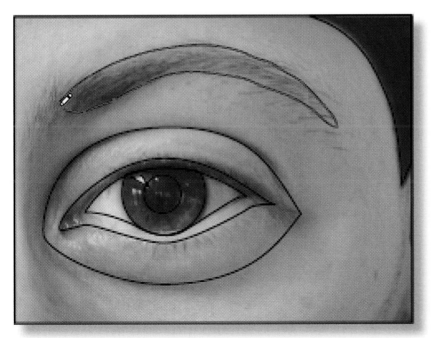

figure | 3–27 |

Drawing an eyebrow with the Pencil tool and your mouse takes a steady hand.

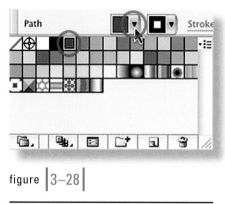

figure | 3–28 |

The Swatches panel; available through the
Control panel.

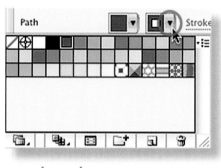

figure | 3–29 |

Select a color for the stroke (outline) of the shape.

2. Select your eyebrow. From the Control panel click on the down arrow for the Brush panel (or choose Window > Brushes). See Figure 3–31.

3. In the Brush panel, choose the Charcoal art brush.

See Figure 3–31 and Figure 3–32. A charcoal-like style is added to the stroke (outline) of the eyebrow. Explore the other available brushes by selecting them in the Brush panel as they automatically update on the selected path.

figure | 3–30 |

The filled eyebrow shape.

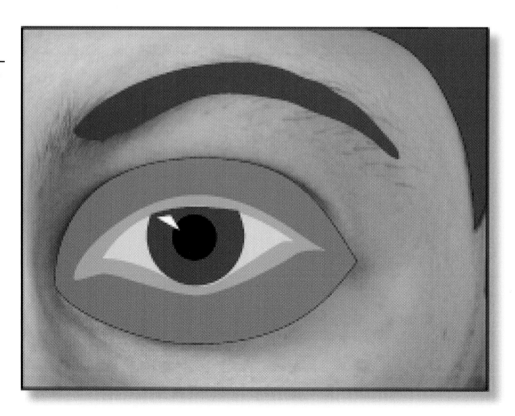

Adding Color

1. Unhide the **color** layer. As crazy as they are, colors have been added to the eye image, creating an illusionary effect and mood.

2. Select your eyebrow. Click on the Fill box in the toolbox to open the Color panel. See Figure 3–33.

3. In the Color panel, click on the color spectrum bar in the lower-part of the window to select a fill color. See Figure 3–34.

> **Note:** If your color panel does not look like Figure 3–34, you might need to expand it. Click repeatedly on the double-headed arrow located on the Color panel's title tab to cycle through options.

4. Change the stroke (outline) color of the eyebrow. First, click on the Stroke icon in the toolbox to bring the stroke option forward so you can edit it. See Figure 3–35.

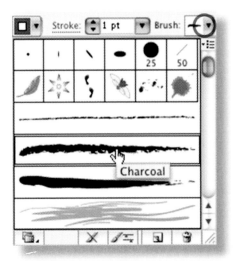

figure | 3–31 |

Select the Charcoal brush in the Brushes panel.

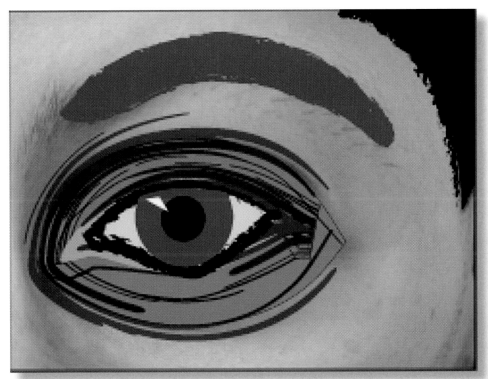

figure | 3–32 |

The eyebrow outline has texture and value.

figure |3–33|

The Fill box in the
toolbox.

5. In the Color panel, click on the color spectrum bar in the lower-part of the window to select a color for the eyebrow's stroke.

6. Hide the **eye_bitmap** layer by toggling its visibility off in the Layers panel. If the Layers panel has disappeared, choose Window > Layers.

7. Choose View > Fit In Window.

8. Save your file.

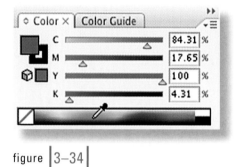

figure |3–34|

Choose a color in the Color panel.

figure |3–35|

Bring the Stroke option forward in the Tool panel.

SUMMARY

Vital survival techniques for gung-ho graphic artists were revealed in this chapter. You learned tools are cool, but knowing about digital image construction and design elements is what really keeps you alive in the Illustrator jungle. Briefly described were characteristics of bitmap and vector graphics, image formats, and resolution, all which help prepare you for the idiosyncrasies of drawing digitally. Lastly, you progressed through the creation of an illustration by building on the elements of design, including line, shape, value, texture, and color.

in review

1. Briefly describe the differences between bitmap and vector graphic types.

2. Illustrator's underlying magic is its ability to work with what type of images?

3. Bitmap images are most common for what type of images? Why?

4. Text and logo treatments are created best as what type of graphic? Why?

5. What is image resolution? Why is it important to know?

6. What is an image file format?

7. What are the five elements of art that can be explored in Illustrator?

exploring on your own

1. Access the Help > Illustrator Help menu bar option. Under Contents, read the section "About vector graphics" under Drawing > Drawing basics. In the section "Importing, exporting and saving," read the following topics: Importing Bitmap images, Importing files, and Exporting artwork.

2. Do an online search for "design elements" and/or "design principles" and read up on traditional design concepts and current trends.

Explorer pages

ARTHUR MOUNT

Asbury Park for *Dwell Magazine*. Compliments of Arthur Mount.

About Arthur Mount

Arthur Mount is from Berkeley and the San Francisco Bay area, where he received his Bachelor of Fine Arts in drawing from the California College of the Arts in 1995. He and his wife left in 2001, fleeing high house prices, lived in Pasadena for a couple years, where their son was born, and then moved to beautiful Portland, Oregon.

Arthur has been working as an illustrator since 1996, but he did not get serious about it until around 2000. His work has appeared in a number of magazines and periodicals, including *Dwell*, *Wallpaper*, *Fortune*, *Sunset*, *GQ*, *ESPN*, and the *New York Times*. His commercial clients have run the gamut, including L'Oreal, Apple, Boeing, AT&T, Google, Sprint, Red Bull, Volkswagen, W Hotels, and many others. He has been published around the world, and has won a few awards along the way.

"I enjoy what I do, and appreciate the flexible schedule it gives me to spend time with my family and other interests," he said.

To view more of Arthur's work, visit *http://www.arthurmount.com*.

Illustration for Google.
Compliments of Arthur Mount.

About the Work of Arthur Mount

"For the *Dwell Magazine* illustrations of Asbury Park, I worked closely with the designers at *Dwell* as well as an architecture firm in New York that was developing blocks of downtown Asbury Park," Arthur said. "Working from photos of the existing site and architectural elevations and sketches, I was to render the finished development in place, as well as adding a street scene with people, cars, etc. Pulling everything together under a tight deadline was quite a task, particularly since at that time the building designs were not completed and only existed as flat, unfinished 2D drawings. In addition to the scene seen here, I also drew a scene from the other side of the development from across a small body of water, as well as a cutaway, showing aspects of the development's interior. This was my first of many assignments with *Dwell*, and it's still one of my favorites. After completing the project, my wife and I took a trip to Asbury Park and its vicinity to see where the development was to be realized."

Illustration that accompanied an article about NASCAR in America Airlines' in-flight magazine, *American Way*. Courtesy of Arthur Mount.

Fire and Ice

"Being a successful illustrator is a business," Arthur said. *"Do what you enjoy and be as creative as possible, but if you want to do it for any length of time and not have to find another job somewhere else, you must find a way to make it work for you."*

 Learn more about this artist via podcast at *http://www.designexploration.com/podcasts.*

Illustration for Celebrity Cruises by Arthur Mount.

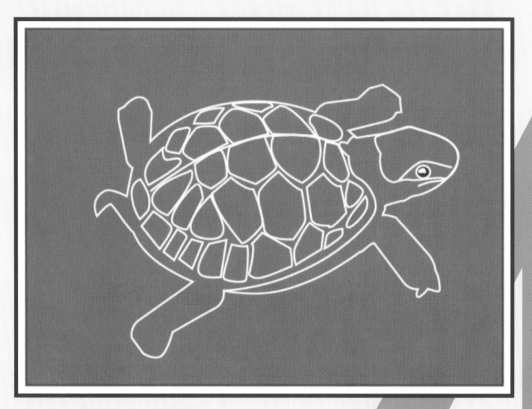

| drawing lines and shapes |

4

charting your course

Chapter 3 introduced you to the essential elements of visual imagery—line, shape, value, texture, and color. By focusing on the first two elements—line and shape—Chapter 4 further solidifies your understanding of how to draw in Illustrator. Illustrator has numerous tools to produce lines and shapes. Some of them create geometric shapes, others more freeform styles, and one in particular—the Pen tool—offers a more precise drawing experience. As you practice the methods for drawing lines and shapes, you will also encounter useful terminology for describing various shapes and the vector points, line segments, and paths from which they are made.

goals

In this chapter you will:

- **Review the process of creating illustrations in Illustrator**

- **Learn the difference between open lines and closed lines/shapes**

- **Draw and transform basic shapes and describe shape types in design**

- **Explore the freeform drawing tools**

- **Discover the characteristics of Bezier lines and curves using the Pen tool**

- **Create, move, and edit straight and curved paths**

- **Combine straight and curved paths into object shapes**

- **Select and edit individual anchor points**

THE SIMPLICITY OF LINES AND SHAPES

Look closely at Figure 4–1. It is a candlestick, right? Look at it again. This time, squint your eyes and focus on its form—the outline and shapes that distinguish the object. It has a cylindrical shape at the top, some various shaped circles along the stem, each connected by smaller cylinders, and a cone-like base. What initially looks like an intricate candlestick is essentially a series of geometric shapes. See Figure 4–2. It is the eye of the artist that has the ability to visually break down objects into simple and familiar lines and shapes, to look at common objects as objective forms.

figure | 4–1 |

An intricate candlestick.

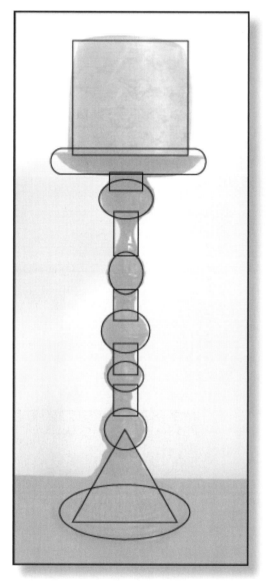

figure | 4–2 |

On closer inspection, the candlestick is composed of basic geometric shapes.

When looking, and thus drawing objects in this way certain questions might arise: What is a line and what is a shape? A line, in drawing, is simply an edge or a boundary. Within Illustrator, and most other graphic drawing programs, a line can have several different names. Generally speaking, a line can be referred to as a stroke, an outline, or a path. Lines can be either opened or closed. A closed line is usually referred to as a shape. See Figure 4–3 through Figure 4–7 for clarification. Lines can also have different values (thicknesses) and colors, which we discuss in Chapters 5 and 6.

With an artist's eye, you will practice your line and shape design abilities in the next series of lessons using basic shapes, freeform, and precision drawing tools and techniques.

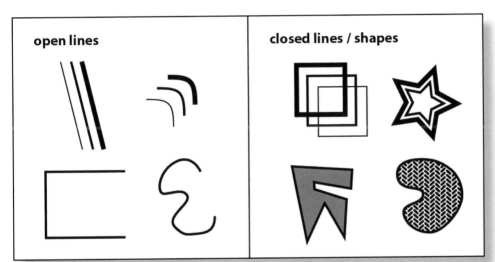

open lines

closed lines / shapes

figure | 4–3 |

A *shape* is defined as a line enclosing an area. In the study of design, shapes actually have specific definitions depending on what they look like, such as geometric, rectilinear, biomorphic, and irregular.

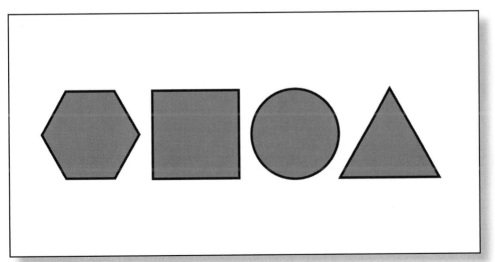

figure | 4–4 |

Geometric: shapes are constructed mathematically.

figure |4–5|

Rectilinear: shapes are bound by straight lines, which are not related to each other mathematically.

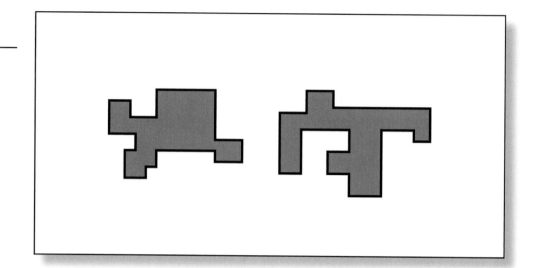

figure |4–6|

Biomorphic (organic): shapes are bound by free-flowing curves, suggesting fluidity and growth.

figure |4–7|

Irregular: shapes are bound by straight and curved lines, which are not related to each other mathematically.

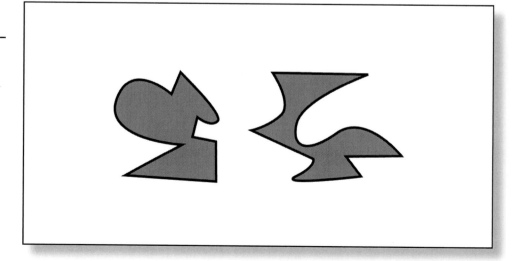

GEOMETRIC, FREEFORM, AND PRECISION DRAWING

To match the visual image you might have in your mind's eye with what actually materializes on the Illustrator artboard depends on three things: the tools you use, the methods you use, and the process by which you go about the endeavor. Take for example, our idea to draw a turtle. Should we make the turtle look cartoon-like or more like the real thing? To make a cartoon-like turtle, we opted to trace over a photograph using the basic shape tools and then combine them. See Figure 4–8. To make it more like the real thing, we traced over a photograph, this time using the Pen tool, which gave us the flexibility to draw a more complex reptile. See Figure 4–9. Both methods produced an illustration of a turtle, each with a different visual result depending on the tools we used.

figure |4–8|

A simple drawing of a turtle using geometric shapes, then adding color and texture.

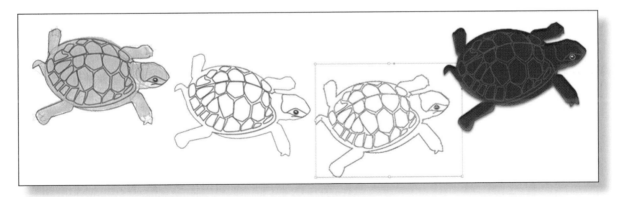

figure |4–9|

A more complex drawing of a turtle constructed using the Pen tool.

Now it is your turn to make lines and shapes using various tools and methods. You have had opportunity to play with some of these shape creation tools in Illustrator. In Chapter 1, you tackled the connect-the-dots logo design using the Pen tool, and in Chapter 3 you cursorily sketched an eyebrow in the lesson "Adam's Eye" using the more freeform Pencil tool. As promised, we will now be more specific about these tools, starting with Illustrator's options for creating geometric and freeform shapes, and then working with the more accurate Pen tool.

Lesson 1: Basic Lines and Shapes

In this lesson you practice creating geometric and freeform shapes. To do this, you draw on a template that defines the different shape types in art and design.

Setting Up the Stroke and Fill Attributes

1. In Illustrator, choose File > Open and open the file **chap4L1.ai** in the **chap4_lessons** folder.

2. Choose Shift-Tab to temporarily hide any panels and give yourself more room to work.

3. Before you begin to draw, you should set up the fill and stroke (outline) color attributes. First, select the default color option in the toolbox, making the fill area white and the stroke black. See Figure 4–10.

4. Click on the fill box (the white one) to activate. See Figure 4–11.

5. Choose the "None" option to indicate no color for the fill. See Figure 4–12.

figure | 4–10 |

Set the Stroke and Fill to the default.

figure | 4–11 |

Click the Fill box to activate it.

figure | 4–12 |

Choose the "None" option to indicate no color for the fill.

Making Geometric Shapes

1. Select the Zoom tool and zoom in close to the first quadrant of the file labeled **Geometric Shapes**. In the blank area below the row of geometric shapes, you will practice drawing the shapes. Let us call this the "drawing area."

2. Select the Rectangle tool in the toolbox.

3. Starting in the upper-left corner of the first quadrant drawing area, click and drag to create a rectangular shape. See Figure 4–13.

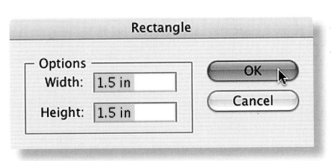

Geometric Shapes

figure | 4–13 |

Create a rectangle in the Geometric Shapes drawing area.

4. Practice moving the rectangle in different directions by pressing incrementally on the up/down or right/left arrow keys on the keyboard. You can also use the Selection tool to translate the shape.

5. Delete the rectangle by selecting it and pressing Delete.

6. Choose Illustrator > Preferences > Units & Display Performance (Mac) or Edit > Preferences > Units & Display Performance (Windows). Under Units, check that General is set to Inches.

7. Select the Rectangle tool. Place your cursor anywhere over the drawing area and click down once to open the Rectangles options box. Here, you can add in an exact width and height for the rectangle. To make a perfect square, enter **1.5 in** by **1.5 in** in the dialog box. Click OK to create the shape. See Figure 4–14.

Rectangle

Options
Width: 1.5 in   OK
Height: 1.5 in   Cancel

figure | 4–14 |

Set a specific, numeric size for shapes.

8. Practice making a few more rectangles or squares, either by clicking and dragging, or by clicking on the drawing area and indicating exact dimensions in the dialog box.

9. Select the Selection tool in the toolbox. Select one of the rectangle shapes you made, then hold down Shift and click on an edge of each of the other shapes to add them to the selection. See Figure 4–15.

figure | 4–15 |

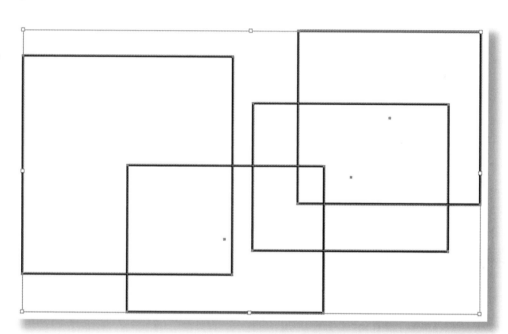

Select multiple shapes to delete them all at once.

10. Press Delete to delete the selected shapes and clear the drawing area.

11. Click and hold on the Rectangle tool in the toolbox to open the other shape options. See Figure 4–16. Choose the Rounded Rectangle tool.

12. Click once on the drawing area to open the Rounded Rectangle options. Enter **1.2 in** for Width, **1.2 in** for Height, and **0.2 in** for Corner Radius. See Figure 4–17. Click OK to see the result.

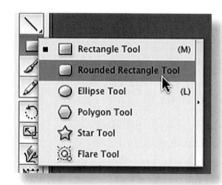

figure | 4–16 |

Select the Rounded Rectangle tool option.

figure | 4–17 |

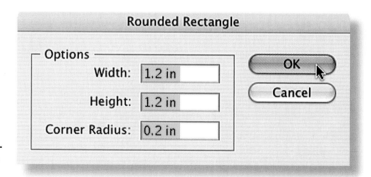

Enter options for the Rounded Rectangle tool.

13. If you do not find it intuitive to put in a number for the corner radius you can do it interactively. First select the Rounded Rectangle tool.

14. While you click and drag to create the shape keep pressing the mouse button and then press the up arrow key on the keyboard. The corner radius of the shape changes before your eyes!

15. With the mouse button pressed try holding the down arrow key. The corner radius goes in the opposite direction. What happens if you choose the right and left arrow keys?

16. Select all your rounded rectangles and delete them.

17. Click on and hold the Rounded Rectangle tool in the toolbox to open the Shape options. Choose the Ellipse tool.

18. Click and drag to create an ellipse shape on the drawing area. As you draw the shape, notice how it draws from the edge out.

19. To draw the shape from the center out first select the Ellipse tool.

20. Place your cursor over the drawing area and press Option (Mac) or Alt (Windows). Notice how the cursor changes to a circle with a cross mark in the middle.

21. Keeping Option/Alt pressed, click and drag to make the circle. Notice how your circle is now being constructed from the center out. This option is very helpful to create more accurately placed circular shapes.

22. Delete all your ellipse and circle shapes.

23. Click and hold the Ellipse tool in the toolbox to open the Shape options. This time choose the Polygon tool.

24. Now that you have an idea of how shapes are drawn, create some polygonal shapes. Try clicking and dragging to create the shapes. Try clicking and dragging and then, keeping your mouse button pressed, hold the up or down arrow keys to interactively add or subtract sides to the shape. We know this takes some coordination, but it is definitely a handy little trick. Using this method, see if you can make a triangle from the polygon shape. How about a circle?

25. Choose the Star tool in the Shape tool options list and practice the same method learned in the last step to draw and adjust the star shape. Use the up arrow key to make more points on the star, or the down arrow key to make fewer.

Transforming Lines and Shapes

1. Select and delete (Edit > Clear or hit Delete) all the geometric shapes you created in the first quadrant of the lesson file.

2. Make a new star shape in the first quadrant drawing area.

3. Choose the Selection tool (black arrow) in the toolbox and select the star shape. A Free Transform bounding box appears around the object, a box with positioning nodes (squares) on each corner and side. This bounding box is really a time saver—it is a Move, Scale, and Rotate tool in one. You will use it in the next steps and in later lessons.

> **Note:** If you do not see the bounding box around the object, go to View > Show Bounding Box to unhide this option.

4. To move the star, click on its edge (the black outline) and drag it to a new position on the drawing area. See Figure 4–18.

figure | 4–18 |

Move the star shape.

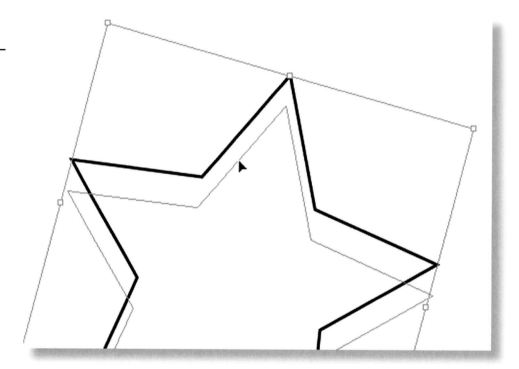

5. To scale the star, click on a corner of the bounding area and drag the shape to a new size. See Figure 4–19.

> **Note:** To uniformly scale, hold down Shift as you scale the object.

▶ Don't Go There!

In this particular lesson, you have been making shapes with a stroke (outline) color only, no inside fill color. (If you recall, you played with strokes and fills somewhat in Chapter 1, but it is covered more in Chapter 5.) The rule for successfully selecting and moving an object is: You must click on a part of the object that has color applied to it. If, for example, you click in the center of an object where no fill color is indicated, you end up deselecting the object—oops!

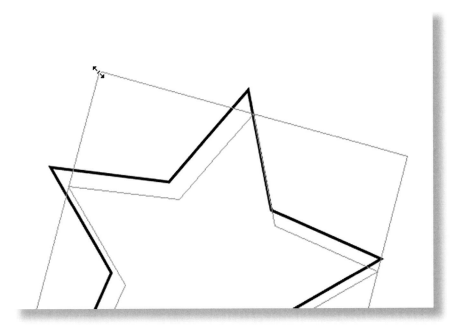

figure |4–19|

Scale the star shape.

6. To rotate the object, first place the cursor slightly outside one corner of the bounding box. The cursor shifts to an icon of a bent line with an arrow at each end. See Figure 4–20. Click and drag to rotate the object.

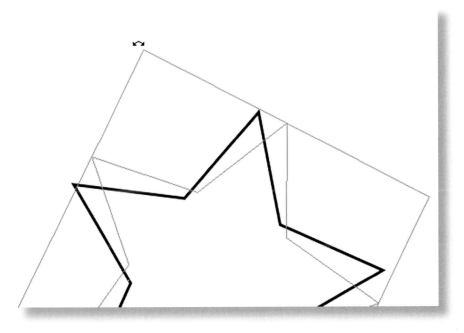

figure |4–20|

Rotate the star shape.

Making Rectilinear Shapes

1. Still working on the file **chap4L1.ai**, set your viewing area to the second quadrant labeled **Rectilinear Shapes**. Two rectilinear shapes have already been created. You will trace over these shapes.

2. Select the Line Segment tool in the toolbox. The Line Segment tool allows you to create individual straight lines called line segments—how convenient! See Figure 4–21.

figure | 4–21 |
_____
Select the Line Segment tool.

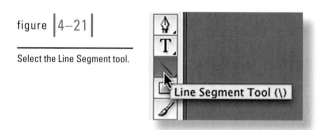

3. Place the cursor in the upper-left corner of the first rectilinear shape. Click and drag to the right, creating a line segment that defines the top of the shape. See Figure 4–22.

4. Continue making line segments to construct the shape. To make a line limited to 45 degree angles, constrain the line as you draw it by holding down Shift.

figure | 4–22 |
_____
Draw a line segment.

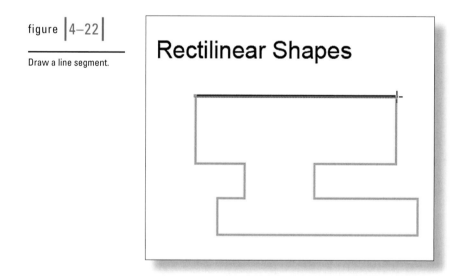

Note: To move or transform a line, hold down Command (Mac) or Ctrl (Windows). The Line Segment tool will temporarily switch to the Selection tool.

5. Go ahead and practice using the Line Segment tool to trace over the other rectilinear shape. Then make your own rectilinear shapes in the drawing area below the templates.

Making Biomorphic Shapes

1. Free yourself from the rigidity of the Line Segment tool and let us go organic. Set your viewing area to the third quadrant—**Biomorphic Shapes**.

2. Select the Pencil tool in the toolbox. See Figure 4–23.

3. With a steady hand, draw a continuous line around the first biomorphic shape. Yeah, we know it is not easy—this is why you learn the Pen tool later when you will have more control. Nevertheless, try it again. Delete the shape or select Edit > Undo Pencil and then redraw it. See how close you can get.

4. Try tracing the other biomorphic shape.

5. Make your own organic shapes in the drawing area below the templates.

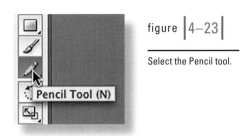

figure |4–23|

Select the Pencil tool.

Making Irregular Shapes and Grouping Them

1. Set your viewing area to the last quadrant—**Irregular Shapes**. These types of shapes have a combination of linear (straight) and biomorphic (curved) lines. You will use a different tool for each type of line.

2. Select the Line Segment tool in the toolbox. Trace the straight lines of the first shape. (Hint: There are three of them.) See Figure 4–24.

3. Click on and hold the Line Segment tool in the toolbox to open the other Segment options. Choose the Arc tool. See Figure 4–25.

4. Click where you want the arc to begin—in this case, the upper-left point of the first irregular shape—and drag to create the arc. See Figure 4–26.

> **Note:** When drawing lines with the Line Segment and Arc tools, each line created is separate from the next. Test this out. Choose the Selection tool in the toolbox and individually select each line created.

5. Let us group the individual lines of this irregular shape. Select one of the lines in the object, then hold down Shift and select each of the other three line segments of the shape.

> **Note:** Using the Shift key while selecting objects subsequently adds the objects to the selection.

6. Choose Object > Group from the menu bar to group the selected line segments.

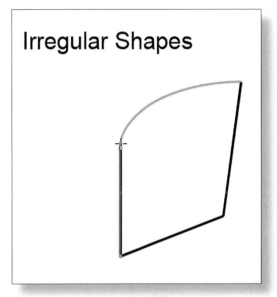

figure |4–24|

Trace lines with the Line Segment tool.

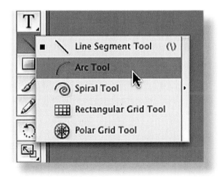

figure |4–25|

Select the Arc tool.

figure |4–26|

Create the arc shape.

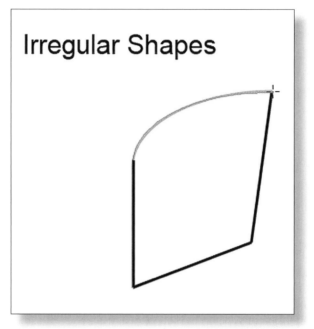

7. Using the Selection tool move the irregular shape to see its grouped state. By grouping line segments and shapes, they become easier to move around, scale, and rotate.

> **Note:** To undo a group, select the grouped object and choose Object > Ungroup.

8. Use the Line Segment and Arc tools to trace the other irregular shape.

> **Note:** To change the direction and degree of an arc, hold down the up or down arrow keys as you click and drag to draw the shape.

9. Create your own irregular shapes in the drawing area below the templates. Select the individual lines and arcs and group them together.

10. Save your file in your lessons folder if you wish.

Mastering the Precise Pen Tool

Annesa's first attempt with the Pen tool was mediocre at best. She felt as if she were drawing with an Etch-A-Sketch®. Remember that toy? Moving her computer mouse with any sort of grace reminded her of turning those awkward little white knobs. Luckily however, she never gave up learning how to use this tool. Now it is her weapon of choice—as it is for most other professional Illustrator artists—when drawing just about anything in the program. Think of the Pen tool as King Arthur's sword Excalibur (the one stuck in solid rock); it was unwieldy at first, but once mastered, mighty and faithful.

Exactly like Illustrator's other drawing tools you have encountered, the Pen tool creates vector-based lines and shapes. However, to be successful using the Pen tool, it helps to take a detailed look at a vector illustration's anatomy. See Figure 4–27. A vector illustration is composed of vector objects, such as the head, mouth, and eye of the turtle in Figure 4–27. Each object contains one or more paths (lines), which are composed of line segments. A line segment has an anchor point at each end. Anchor points are the most fundamental component of a vector illustration—they are the dots that connect paths. Through direction lines and direction points (together called direction handles), anchor points define the position and curve attributes of each line segment. Here is a little trivia for you: The name for the resulting curve attributes of a line segment are called Bezier (pronounced bay-zee-ay) curves. Pierre Bezier, a French mathematician, was the very smart fellow who developed the method for defining these curves mathematically. You will get to define your own curves—the Illustrator way—in the next lessons.

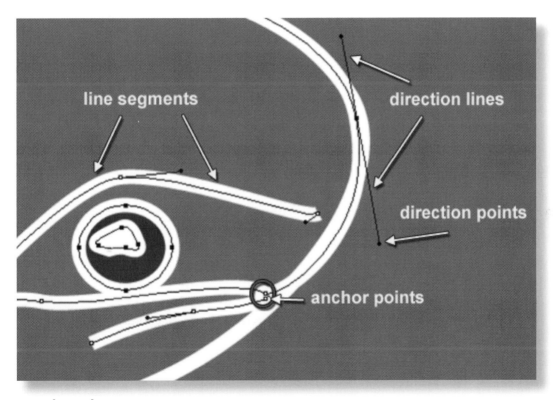

figure | 4–27 |

The turtle's head illustrates the various parts of a vector's anatomy.

Lesson 2: Drawing Precise Straight and Curved Paths

In this lesson, you practice drawing with the Pen tool to create, move, and adjust straight and curved paths.

figure |4–28|

────────────

Select the Pen tool.

Setting Up the Stroke and Fill Attributes

1. In Illustrator, choose File > Open and open the file **chap4L2.ai** in the folder **chap4_ lessons**.

2. Choose Shift-Tab to temporarily hide any panels. You will need lots of space to work.

3. Select the default color option in the toolbox, making the fill area white and the stroke black. See Figure 4–10.

4. Click on the fill box (the white one) to activate it. See Figure 4–11.

5. Choose the "None" option to indicate no color for the fill. See Figure 4–12.

Starting with Straight Lines

1. Zoom in close to the first quadrant of the lesson template labeled **Straight Paths**.

2. Select the Pen tool in the toolbox. See Figure 4–28.

3. Click on—but do not drag—the red dot on the top straight line. This defines the first point.

4. Click—do not drag—at the end of the line to create the straight segment. See Figure 4–29.

figure |4–29|

────────────

Click to make another anchor point at the end of the line segment.

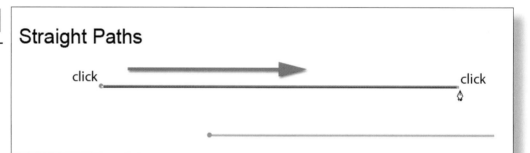

Don't Go There!

There is a big difference between a "click" and a "click and drag" to define an anchor point of a line segment. To create straight lines, you click once to make each point. If direction lines appear, you have accidentally dragged with the Pen tool. To fix this, choose Edit > Undo and click again. The click and drag action is used to make curves. Also, the first point you draw will not be visible until you click a second anchor point. It takes two anchor points to create a complete line segment.

5. Prepare to start another line segment by doing one of the following:

    -   Command-click (Mac) or Ctrl-click (Windows) anywhere away from all objects.
    -   Choose Select > Deselect.
    -   Click on the Pen tool icon in the toolbox.

    > **Note:** When the cursor for the Pen tool has a little cross mark next to it that is a sign you are ready to make a new path. See Figure 4–30.

figure |4–30|

A cross mark next to the Pen tool cursor sets the Pen tool to make a new path.

6. Using the guide, practice making another straight line segment under the first one you created. To do this, click on one end and then the other.

7. Press and hold Command (Mac) or Ctrl (Windows) to toggle to the Selection tool. Click on the line and practice moving it. Remember you can use the Free Transform bounding box to move, rotate, or scale any object.

    > **Note:** If you do not see the bounding box around the line, go to View > Show Bounding Box to unhide this option.

8. Choose Select > Deselect to deselect all objects.

9. Select the Pen tool and click on the red dot of the zigzag line.

10. Continue clicking points at each corner of the line until completed. See Figure 4–31.

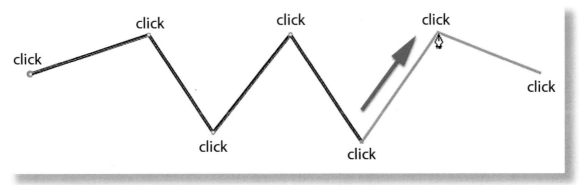

figure |4–31|

Anchor points to make a zigzag line.

11. Select (with the Selection tool) the zigzag path and practice moving, scaling, and rotating the line.

12. In the first quadrant area of the lesson, practice creating your own straight and zigzag paths.

Making Closed Straight Paths/Shapes

1. Still working in **chap4L2.ai**, choose View > Actual Size.

2. Zoom in on the second quadrant area labeled **Closed Straight Paths/Shapes**.

3. Select the Pen tool.

4. Click to place a point at the red dot of the triangle shape, then click at the next corner, and then the next.

5. To close the path, place the cursor over the starting point. Notice that the cursor has an open circle next to it. See Figure 4–32. This indicates you are ready to close this path. Click on the starting point to close the path.

> **Note:** Closing a path ends a path. In contrast to what you learned earlier, to end an open path you have to click the Pen tool in the toolbox or choose Command (Mac) or Ctrl (Windows) and click away from the path.

6. On your own, practice drawing closed shapes using the snowflake shape on the template as a guide.

Drawing Curved Paths

1. Still working in **chap4L2.ai**, choose View > Actual Size.

2. Zoom in on the third quadrant area labeled **Curved Paths**. To make things easier, guides indicating the direction lines and/or placement points for the path are provided.

> **Note:** In case you are wondering, direction lines and points do not print.

3. Select the Pen tool.

4. Click and hold on the red dot of the first curve. Begin to drag up to release the direction handles. Extend the handles to the length indicated on the guide. See Figure 4–33 and Figure 4–34. If you make a mistake, Edit > Undo Pen and try again.

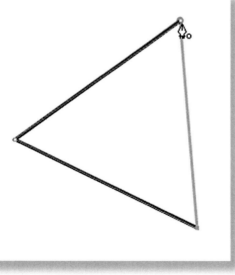

figure | 4–32 |

Close a path.

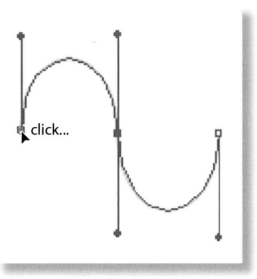

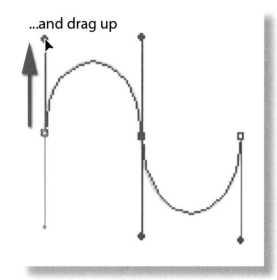

...and drag up

click...

figure |4–33| and figure |4–34|

Start off the curve.

5. To continue the curved path, click on the center anchor point and drag down the handle to match the guide. Your first curve is formed. See Figure 4–35 and Figure 4–36.

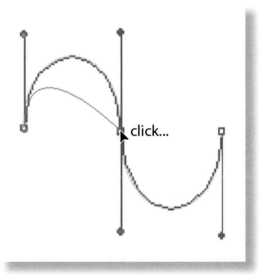

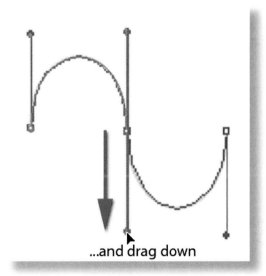

click...

...and drag down

figure |4–35| and figure |4–36|

Complete the first curved segment.

6. To complete the curved path, click and drag up on the last anchor point. See Figure 4–37 and Figure 4–38.

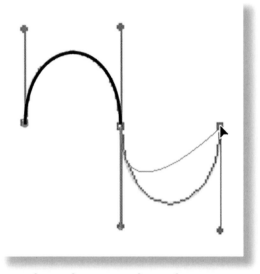 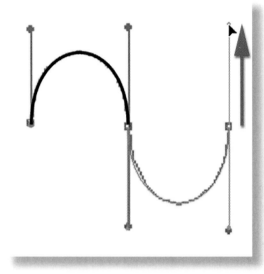

figure |4–37| and figure |4–38|

Finish the curved path.

▶ Don't Go There!

When first learning how to make curves, it is common to get what we call "click happy." The tendency is to click down many points while drawing, thinking to get a more accurate shape. However, in this case, more is not necessarily better. Keep it simple! The trick is in the placement and adjustment of the anchor points and direction handles; if you place them right, you can create simpler, cleaner lines. For example, to achieve a more symmetrical line, place points at the ends of a curve, rather than at the high point of a curve. See Figure 4–39 and Figure 4–40.

figure |4–39|

Place a point at the high point of the curve—not very efficient when creating symmetrical lines.

figure |4–40|

Place points at the ends of a curve and adjust the handles—more efficient.

7. Practice your anchor point placement on the second curve in the **Curved Paths** quadrant. In this example, the direction handles are not provided for you, but the point placements are. Position each point and drag the handles out sideways until you create each desired curve. (Hint: Drag your handles toward the next curve, rather than the one you just created.) See Figure 4–41.

8. Make some of your own curves in the drawing area of the **Curved Paths** quadrant.

Drawing Closed-Curved Paths/Shapes

1. Still in **chap4L2.ai**, choose View > Actual Size.

2. Zoom in on the last quadrant area, labeled **Closed Curved Paths/ Shapes**.

3. Select the Pen tool.

4. Let us create a circle with only two points. Click on the red dot of the circle and drag up to match the handle in the guide. See Figure 4–42 and Figure 4–43.

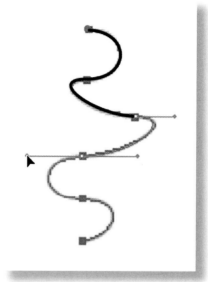

figure | 4–41 |

Practice curves.

> **Note:** If you hold down Shift as you drag, you can constrain the angle of the handles.

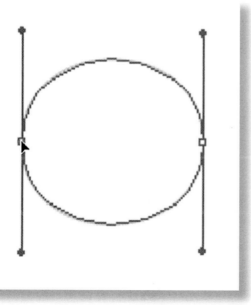

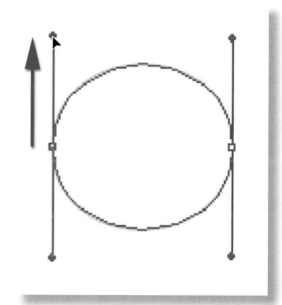

figure | 4–42 | figure | 4–43 |

5. Click on the point opposite the red dot and drag the handles down to form the top curve. See Figure 4–44 and Figure 4–45.

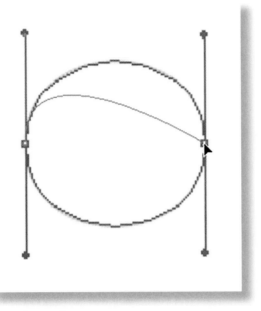

figure |4–44|

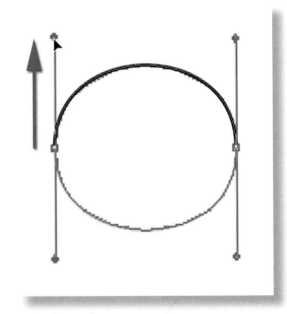

figure |4–45|

6. Click on the first point and drag the handles up to create the bottom curve and close the shape. See Figure 4–46 and Figure 4–47.

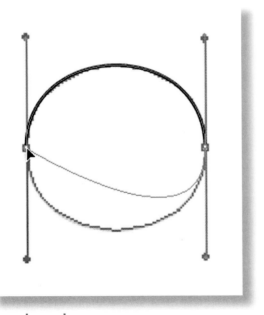

figure |4–46|

figure |4–47|

7. Practice your curved paths on the guide that looks like a flower. Because each petal of the flower is not a symmetrical curve, add points at the ends and the top of each petal curve to more easily get the correct shape. Check out Figure 4–48 to get the idea.

8. On your own, practice making more closed-curve shapes. Can you make a butterfly shape? Some tree leaves?

9. Save this file **chap4L2_yourname.ai**, if you wish. We are done with this lesson.

Lesson 3: Combining and Editing Straight and Curved Paths

So far you have got the almighty Pen tool drawing straight and curved paths. Next you use it to skillfully make and edit paths composed of both straight and curved segments.

Setting Up the Stroke and Fill Attributes

1. In Illustrator, open the file **chap4L3.ai** in the folder **chap4_lessons**.

2. Choose View > Actual Size.

3. Choose Shift-Tab to temporarily hide any panels.

4. Select the default color option in the toolbox, making the fill area white and the stroke black.

5. Click on the Fill box (the white one) to activate it.

6. Choose the "None" option to indicate no color for the fill. Now you are ready to start drawing.

Putting Straight and Curved Lines Together

1. Zoom in on the gear-like object in the upper-left of the file.

2. Select the Pen tool.

3. Click once on the red dot to define an anchor point.

4. Moving clockwise, click on the other end of the first curve and drag to make the curve segment. See Figure 4–49.

5. Click on the top point of the next curve in the shape. See Figure 4–50. Oops—the curve is going in the wrong direction. This is because you are attempting to draw around a sharp corner in the shape. To change the direction of the curve, you must "break" the direction handle. See Figure 4–51 and Figure 4–52.

figure | 4–48 |

Make a flower shape.

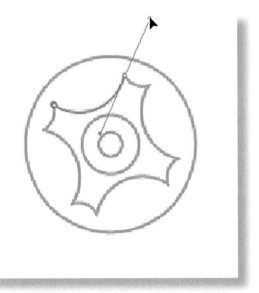

figure |4–49|

Click and drag to make a curve.

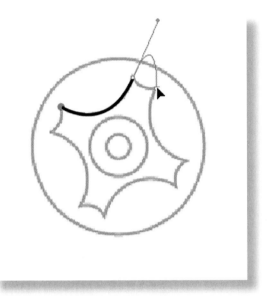

figure |4–50|

The curve goes in the wrong direction.

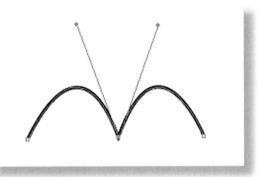

figure |4–52|

A broken direction handle creates a corner point, which changes the direction of the curve.

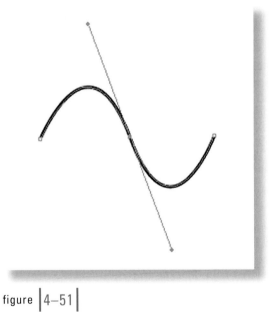

figure |4–51|

An unbroken direction handle produces a continuous curve.

6. To break the handle and delete the faulty anchor point, choose Edit > Undo Pen, or, use the short cut: Command-Z (Mac) or Ctrl-Z (Windows).

7. Place your cursor over the last anchor point. Notice the Pen tool has a little upside-down V shape next to it. See Figure 4–53. This indicates that the tool is prepared to delete the leading direction handle, converting the point to a corner point. Click on the point to delete and convert.

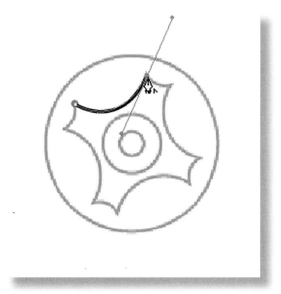

figure |4–53|

Convert the direction of the curve by breaking the direction handle.

figure |4–54|

Create the new curve.

8. Click and drag on the next top arch of the curve to produce the correct line. See Figure 4–54.

9. Place your cursor over the point you just placed until you see the upside-down V-shaped icon. Click on the point to break the direction handles.

10. Go to the next top arch of the curve and click and drag to make the line.

11. Continue drawing around the shape, breaking the direction handles as you draw each curve segment.

12. Two other templates have been provided to practice combining curved and straight line segments: a photograph of a pumpkin and the silly salamander. Hone your pen coordination skills and trace over these objects. Try to be efficient with your point placement—less is better, in this case. Also, practice drawing these outlines as one continuous line (i.e. close the shapes). Once again, if you make a mistake, our motto is always "delete and do over . . . and over . . . and over." It does get easier, we promise.

▶ Don't Go There!

If at this point you are ready to give up using the Pen tool, please hang in there! Like any new skill, it takes practice. Once you get it, however, we guarantee it will open up your Illustrator world. One thing we like to do if we find ourselves getting stuck is to delete the whole lesson or the part we are working on and try doing it again (and again) from step 1.

Converting and Editing Straight and Curved Paths

1. Still working in **chap4L3.ai**, choose View > Actual Size.

2. Zoom in on the lower section of the file labeled **Converting Straight and Curved Paths/Shapes**.

3. Choose the Direct Selection tool. See Figure 4–55.

> **Note:** The Direct Selection tool lets you select individual anchor points or path segments by clicking on them. Any direction lines and direction points then appear on the selected part of the path for adjusting. Cool!

4. Select the flower shape on the lesson file. Notice that all the points that comprise the shape are visible. Points that are hollow (white inside) are not selected. Points that are a solid color (in this case, red) are selected.

figure |4–55|

Choose the Direct Selection tool.

5. Select one of the points on the rounded part of one of the petals and move it up. See Figure 4–56. Notice how the unselected points stay anchored in position; hence the name anchor point.

6. Select one of the direction points (the end of a direction handle) and drag it out to make the petal wider. See Figure 4–57. Extend the other direction point.

7. Lengthen and expand each petal on the flower.

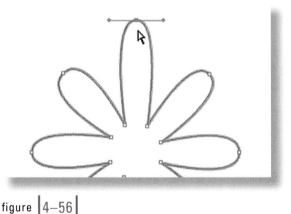

figure |4–56|

Edit a petal with the Direct Selection tool.

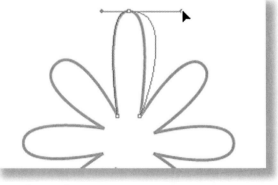

figure |4–57|

Adjust the petal by clicking and pulling on the direction lines.

8. Let us convert the flower into a star. Place your cursor over the Pen tool and click to open the other pen options (yep, there are options!) and select the Convert Anchor Point tool. See Figure 4–58.

9. Place the Convert Anchor Point tool over one of the petal points and click to convert the curved line to a straight line. See Figure 4–59. Continue clicking on each point to make the star.

> **Note:** If you get a warning that says something like, "Please use the Convert Anchor Point tool on an anchor point of a path" (see Figure 4–60), do not panic. It usually pops up when you missed the anchor point you were attempting to click on with the Convert Anchor Point tool. Click on the anchor point again. If the points are difficult to see, zoom in on the area on which you are working.

10. Change the star back to a flower. Click and drag out on each petal point to convert the straight lines to curved lines. See Figure 4–61 on the next page.

11. Let us change the flower into a circle. Place your cursor over the Convert Anchor Point tool in the toolbox and choose the Delete Anchor Point tool. See Figure 4–62. Notice, for future reference, the Add Anchor Point tool as well.

figure |4–58|

Select the Convert Anchor Point tool.

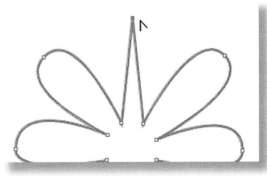

figure |4–59|

Convert an anchor point.

> **Ai** Please use the convert anchor point tool on an anchor point of a path.
>
> ☐ Don't Show Again
>
> OK

figure |4–60|

Warning for Convert Anchor Point tool usage.

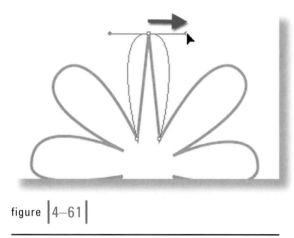

figure |4—61|

Convert to curves.

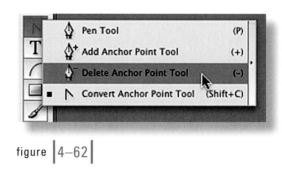

figure |4—62|

The often-needed Delete Anchor Point tool. Right next to it is the Add Anchor Point tool to click and add points to a shape.

12. Click on each of the innermost points of the flower shape to delete them and produce a circular shape.

13. Select the Direct Selection tool in the toolbox. For fun, select the angular shape (outlined in black) to the right of your mutated flower.

14. Select the Convert Anchor Point tool in the toolbox.

15. Click on and drag each point of the selected angular shape to match the gray template behind it. Remember, you can adjust the handles on a point at any time with the Direct Selection tool. What materializes? See Figure 4—63.

16. You have completed this lesson.

figure |4—63|

Create a profile of a face.

SUMMARY

This chapter covered a lot of important stuff about lines and shapes: what they are, how they are constructed, and what tools and techniques are used to create, edit, and adjust them. You practiced making various types of shapes, developed your hand–eye coordination with the powerful Pen tool, and mastered some foundation skills for a more flexible and precise drawing experience.

in review

1. What are some of the different names for a line in digital illustration?

2. Name the four types of shapes in design.

3. What keyboard command do you use to add objects to a selection?

4. What keyboard command do you use to draw an ellipse from the center out?

5. What part of an object must you click on to select it?

6. What is the purpose of a direction handle?

7. What is a Bezier?

8. What is the difference between a "click" and a "click and drag" when defining anchor points with the Pen tool?

9. What tool do you use to select individual anchor points?

10. How do you convert the direction of a curve?

exploring on your own

1. Access the Help > Illustrator Help menu option. Under Contents, read the topic on Drawing.

2. Practice your pen drawing skills by tracing over the sample images provided in the folder **chap04_lessons/samples**.

Explorer pages

KEVIN HULSEY

"The first step in a freelance illustration career is to create a portfolio of 10 or more samples of your best work," Husley said. *"Your abilities will be judged on your worst sample, not your best sample, so make sure that they are all equally high-quality."*

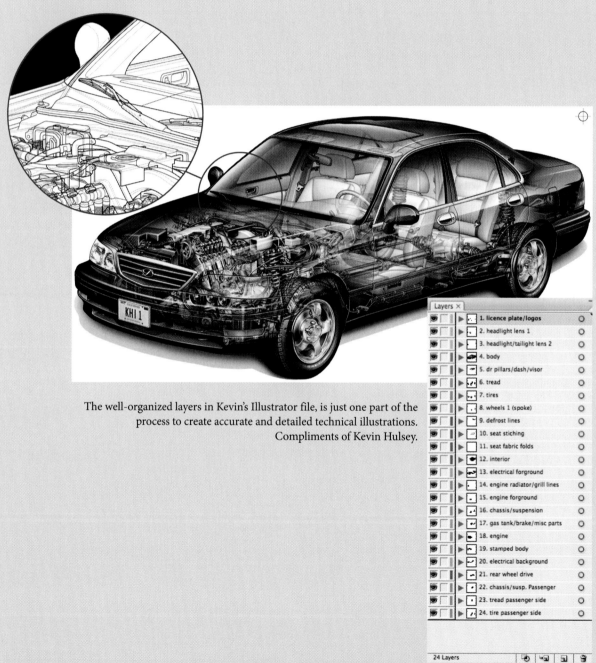

The well-organized layers in Kevin's Illustrator file, is just one part of the process to create accurate and detailed technical illustrations. Compliments of Kevin Hulsey.

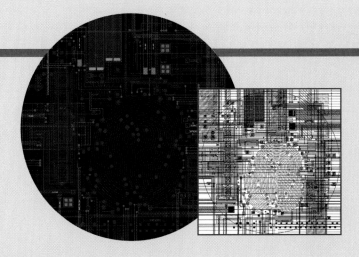

Rendition of an Intel fingerprint.
Compliments of Kevin Hulsey.

About Kevin Hulsey

Kevin Hulsey was born in Los Angeles, California, in 1955. His exposure to both commercial and fine art contributed to his development as an artist and illustrator.

Kevin's early work was heavily influenced by the Pop and Photo-Realist fine art movement of the 1960s. Artists Don Eddy and Richard Estes exerted the greatest influence with their sense of light, shadow, reflection, and realism. By the late 1970s Kevin was drawn to the commercial art world through his admiration for the work of David Kimble, Richard Leech, Tony Matthews, and Japanese technical illustrators Makoto Ouchi and Yoshihiro Inomoto.

Specializing in automotive and industrial cutaway illustration, Kevin has earned a reputation as one of the world's premiere technical illustrators. Since 1980, his talent has been recognized by the advertising industry; he has received numerous awards from Belding, Best in the West, *Communication Arts Magazine*, and the ADLA. Over the years, Kevin has worked for many of the top fortune 500 companies.

Although largely self-taught, Kevin has a strong background in architecture, drafting and design. He works in various mediums, including oils, acrylics, airbrush, and computer graphics in both fine and commercial art. His studio is located in Carmel, Calif.

Visit Kevin's informative Web site at *http://www.khulsey.com/*. The site includes detailed student tutorials and lessons on his technical illustration techniques and processes using Illustrator and Photoshop.

Digital camera design.
Compliments of Kevin Hulsey.

| using color |

charting your course

Color is an important aspect of illustrative work. We can easily spend 100 pages of this book discussing all the wonderful aspects of color in design. For now, however, let's start simple. This chapter covers some fundamental concepts of color, such as how color is reproduced, what color modes are, and an overview of some color theory you can't do without. You then get the chance to explore color in Illustrator, where a whole new aspect of your drawing can emerge.

goals

In this chapter you will:

- **Explore the concept of a color gamut**
- **Get acquainted with color models**
- **Learn what color mode to use**
- **Apply color to strokes and fills**
- **Explore the color features and tools in Illustrator**
- **Make gradients**
- **Learn how to pick colors using color chords**

SEEING IS NOT NECESSARILY BELIEVING

Have you ever heard the saying "What you see is what you get"? Well, that is not always the case when working with color on a computer screen. Monitors can view millions of colors, but even so, those are not all the colors available in our universe. Every device that has the capability to reproduce color has its own color range (or limits), which defines its color space or gamut (pronounced GAM-uht). The human color device—our eyes—can see many more colors than a computer or printer device. Take a good look at Figure 5–1. The chart indicates the visual (human), computer screen (RGB), and printer (CMYK) gamuts. (You will learn more about RGB and CMYK in the next section, "Choosing a Color Model.") Notice the marked areas indicating the gamuts. All the gamuts overlap, each able to view like colors; however, the CMYK gamut has the least amount of color possibilities.

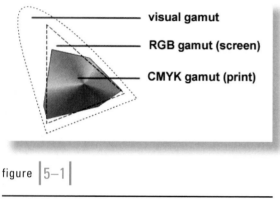

visual gamut

RGB gamut (screen)

CMYK gamut (print)

figure |5–1|

The visual, screen, and print color gamut areas.

So, if you pick a color for your digital image in Illustrator—which, by default uses the RGB gamut to display your artwork, even if you have specified a CMYK document—you might find the color to be completely different when you print it. Most likely the color you picked in Illustrator is not available in the printer's gamut. Admittedly this predicament is very frustrating, but there are ways to achieve the result you want. We can't cover all the solutions in this chapter, but we will get you started with some explanation of color models and modes and provide you with additional reading in the section, "Exploring On Your Own."

CHOOSING A COLOR MODEL

A color model is a system for describing color. You use color models when choosing and creating colors for your artwork. There are many different color models, but in computer graphics, and specifically in Illustrator, we will look at the following: Grayscale, RGB, Web Safe RGB, HSB, and CMYK.

Grayscale

The Grayscale color model is used to select tints of black ranging in brightness from 0% (white) to 100% (black). In Illustrator, when you convert color artwork into grayscale, the luminosity (tonal level) of each color in the artwork becomes a representation of a shade of gray. To work in grayscale, select an object you are working on and choose Grayscale in the Color panel options. See Figure 5–2.

> Note: Converting an image to grayscale is a great way to visualize contrast in your image. Select your image and choose Edit > Edit Colors > Convert to Grayscale. Choose Edit > Undo to convert your image back to full color.

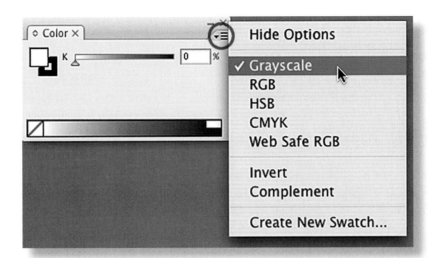

figure |5–2|

The Grayscale color model selected in the Color panel.

RGB and Web Safe RGB

The RGB model represents the primary colors of light—red, green, and blue (RGB). The mixing of red, green, and blue light in various proportions and intensities produces a wide range of colors in our visual spectrum. RGB color is also referred to as *additive* color. When R, G, and B light are mixed they create white—what occurs when all light is reflected back to the eye. (By the way, the absence of colored light is black—what you get when you turn out the lights at night.) When R, G, or B overlap each other, they create the colors cyan, magenta, or yellow (CMY). See Figure 5–3. Devices that reproduce color with light are using the RGB color model, such as your TV or computer monitor.

Each component—red, green, and blue—in the RGB color model is labeled with a value ranging from 0 to 255. This means you can have a total of 256 shades of red, 256 shades of green, and 256 shades of blue, and any combination thereof (about 16.7 million colors!). For example the most

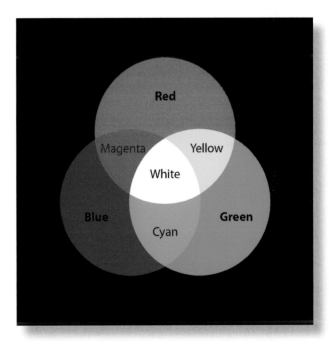

figure |5–3|

The RGB color model.

intense red color is represented as 255 (R), 0 (G), 0 (B), and a shade of deep purple is represented as 40 (R), 0 (G), 100 (B). See Figure 5–4.

Illustrator also includes the Web Safe RGB, a modified RGB model that indicates a spectrum of colors most appropriate for use on the Web. The color components in the Web Safe RGB

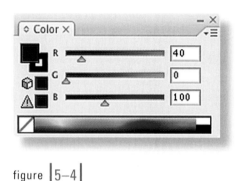

figure | 5–4 |

The RGB model selected in the Color panel.

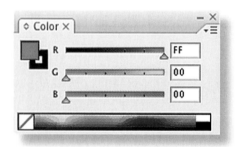

figure | 5–5 |

The Web Safe RGB model selected in the Color panel.

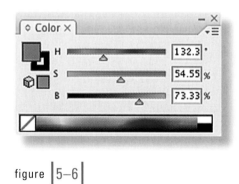

figure | 5–6 |

The HSB color model selected in the Color panel.

space are measured using hexadecimal, a combination of numbers and letters to represent a color. For example, a color of red in hexadecimal is indicated as #FF0000. See Figure 5–5.

HSB

Color can also be defined as levels of HSB—hue, saturation, and brightness. Hue identifies a main color property or name, such as "blue" or "orange." It is measured by a percentage from 0 to 360 degrees, as if picking colors from a standard color wheel. Saturation is the strength or purity of color. It is measured as an amount of gray in proportion to the hue, ranging from 0% (gray) to 100% (fully saturated). Brightness is the relative lightness or darkness of a hue, measured as a percentage from 0% (black) to 100% (white). See Figure 5–6.

As designers, we enjoy picking colors using the HSB color model because it offers a more natural way to identify and modify related colors. Take a look at the section, "Adventures in Design: The Moods of Color" at the end of this chapter.

CMYK

You learned that the RGB model reproduces color based on light. In contrast, the CMYK model reproduces color based on pigment or ink. The colors of CMYK are cyan (C), magenta (M), yellow (Y), and black (K, or Key). The colors in this model are *subtractive* because when you add these pigments to a white page or canvas they subtract or absorb some of the light, leaving what is left over to reflect back to your eye. When the colors overlap, interestingly, they produce red, green, and blue (RGB). See Figure 5–7.

The "black" part of the CMYK color model is a bit illusive. To print a true black color on white, a higher percentage of cyan is mixed with magenta and yellow; it is not an equal amount of each color as Figure 5–7 might lead you to believe. An equal mixing of just cyan, magenta, and yellow would actually result in muddy brown, not black, because of the absorption that occurs when ink hits paper. This is why black ink is used—in addition to the subtractive primaries cyan, magenta, and yellow—in four-color printing.

Each color component of the CMYK model is represented by a percentage ranging from 0% to 100%. To produce purple, for example, you mix 70% cyan, 100% magenta, 0% yellow, and 0% black. See Figure 5–8. In the print industry, this combining of the CMYK colors is appropriately called four-color processing. And the individual colors produced by the mixing of any of these four colors are identified as process colors. To help identify process colors as they would look when printed, you can purchase color swatch books. Swatch books contain samples of colors printed on various types of paper. The colors are coded with specific names, such as Pantone®107C or TRUMATCH 23-a7. You can match the color names with equivalent Swatch Libraries available in Illustrator. To see what we mean, go to Window > Swatch Libraries > Color Books > TRUMATCH or Window > Swatch Libraries > Color Books > PANTONE solid coated. Keep in mind, however, the issue of color viewed on screen versus print. Pantone 107C (a yellow color) will look slightly different on your monitor, which contains varying brightness and contrast levels, than on the printed swatch. If you know your artwork will go to print, trust the color you see on the printed swatch rather than the one on the screen.

> **Note:** To get the color visually equivalent (or as close as you can) while working in Illustrator, read up on "Keeping colors consistent" under Contents > Color Management in the Illustrator Help files (Help > Illustrator Help).

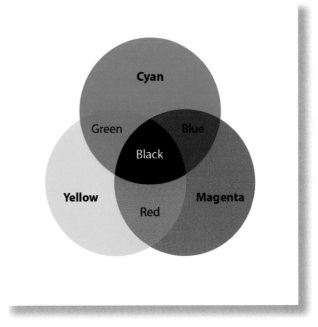

figure | 5–7 |

The CMYK color model.

In addition to process colors, another color type used in printing is spot colors. These are special colors composed of premixed inks that require their own printing plate rather than the four used for four-color processing. You will run into the process and spot color types as you work with colors in Illustrator, but do not worry about them right now. Preparing an image for a professional print job can easily become an advanced topic beyond the scope of this book. However, we will talk more about it in Chapter 10, "Print Publishing." For now, just remember, if your Illustrator artwork is going to print, choose colors within the CMYK model, or from spot color swatches.

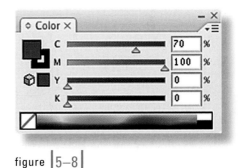

figure | 5–8 |

The CMYK color model selected in the Color panel.

GETTING IN THE MODE

Although you can select colors from various color models, ultimately you should set up your Illustrator artwork (document) to a specific color mode depending on the artwork's intended purpose. A color mode determines how your artwork is output, either for display on screen (RGB) or for print (CMYK). When you create a new document in Illustrator, you can specify the

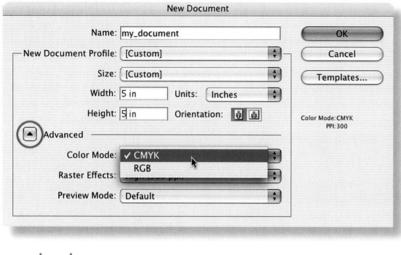

figure | 5-9 |

Identify a color mode under the Advanced tab in the New Document window.

color mode under the Advanced tab. See Figure 5–9. However, you can change the color mode at any time and without losing any information. To do so, choose File > Document Color Mode on the menu bar.

Why all this color mode business, you might be wondering. Well, remember, when it comes to color reproduction, what you see is not necessarily what you are going to get from print to screen and screen to print, but it does not hurt to try every means possible to get it close. Setting the proper color mode is one of those means.

APPLYING COLOR

When coloring vector-based illustrations, you have two possible parts of the drawing in which you can apply color: the stroke and the fill. The stroke is the path of an object or its shape, and the fill is the area enclosed by the path. You have applied color to both parts in previous lessons. You can change the color of a selected stroke or fill in many areas of the program—the

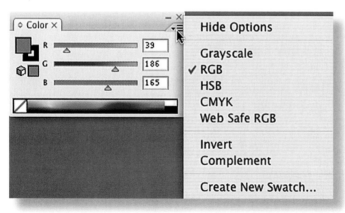

figure | 5-10 |

Select a color model to pick colors from in the Color panel.

Color panel, the Color Picker (double-click the Stroke or Fill box in the toolbox), the Swatches panel, the Control panel, or by using the Eyedropper or Live Paint Bucket tools. Also, for fills, you can create graduated color blends using the Gradient tool and Gradient panel. Each color selection option is described and put to practice in this chapter's lessons.

The Color Panel

The Color panel (see Figure 5–10) allows you to choose various color models and to switch between choosing and adjusting colors on the stroke and/or fill of a selected object.

The Color Picker

The Color Picker (double-click the Fill or Stroke box in the toolbox) is a somewhat sophisticated version of the Color panel, offering the option to view, select, and adjust colors of all the available color models in one window. You can also access your available swatches by clicking on the Color Swatches option. It can be overwhelming at first, so let's break it down for you. See Figure 5–11 through Figure 5–14.

In the area of the Color Picker indicated in Figure 5–12, you choose your colors. The spectrum bar on the right is where you pick the hue, such as red, blue, green. The large box to the left allows you to adjust the hue's saturation (moving horizontally) and brightness (moving vertically).

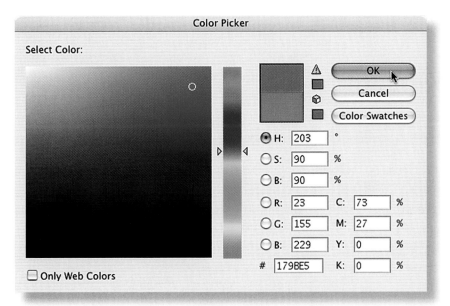

figure |5–11|

A full view of the Color Picker.

figure |5–12|

Choose your color in this area of the Color Picker.

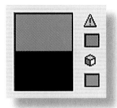

figure | 5–13 |

This area of the Color Picker indicates the current color selection and the original color selection for an object.

In Figure 5–13, you see the colors you are selecting in the Color Picker. Your current color selections are updated automatically in the top area of the box. The lower part indicates the original selected color of the object. Next to the color indicator are gamut warnings. They pop up when you have chosen a color that is outside either the Web Safe (the 3D box icon) or the CMYK (alert triangle icon) gamuts. When you click on the 3D box icon, the color shifts to the closest Web Safe color. Similarly, when you click on the alert triangle, the color shifts to the closest CMYK color. This is a really handy feature!

The last area of the Color Picker (see Figure 5–14) allows you to see and adjust colors in all four of the color models—HSB, RGB, CMYK, and Web Safe RGB.

The Swatches Panel

After spending hours picking your favorite colors, you should save them in the Swatches panel. See Figure 5–15. You can apply your saved colors to selected objects by simply clicking on your saved swatches in the panel window. You can also make swatch libraries to reuse in other documents or use one of the many already provided for you. The Swatches panel saves solid color selections, gradients, and patterns.

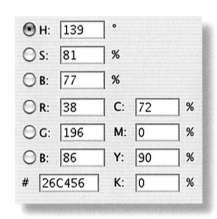

figure | 5–14 |

In the Color Picker, adjust colors in any of the four color models.

The Control Panel

To quickly change fill or stroke colors on a selected object, you can also access available swatches through the Control panel. This panel is usually located below the main menu bar. If its closed, choose Window > Control. See Figure 5–16.

The Eyedropper

The Eyedropper—located in the toolbox—is a tool common-to-many graphics programs. See Figure 5–28. With a click of the tool, the Eyedropper can take a sample of a color already used in a document (illustration or photograph) and copy it to another selected vector object or shape. This is very useful when you are trying to consistently match colors within your artwork.

The Live Paint Bucket Tool

The Live Paint Bucket tool (see Figure 5–17) is an improved variation of Illustrator's traditional paint bucket tool. And it is part of a more intuitive approach (feature) to painting in the program called "Live Paint." For information and to explore the new Live Paint and Live Trace features, see the section "Adventures in Design: Going Live." The Live Paint Bucket offers quick application of current paint attributes, such as fill, stroke, and brush colors and patterns. See Figure 5–18. To execute, you create a selection (one

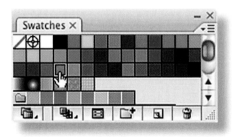

figure | 5–15 |

The Swatches panel.

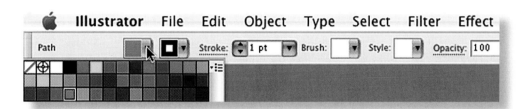

figure |5–16|

Change fill and stroke colors in the Control panel.

or more objects) with the Selection tool. Select the Live Paint Bucket tool, and click on the selection to make it a Live Paint Group. Then place your cursor over a face (filled surface) or edge of the selection to highlight an area, and click to apply the defined attribute. Groups of faces and edges can be selected and updated with the Live Paint Selection tool (right next to the Live Paint Bucket tool in the toolbox).

The Gradient Panel and Gradient Tool

figure |5–17|

The Live Paint Bucket tool.

Gradients are graduated color blends. They are useful to create smooth transitions of color in an object or across multiple objects to give them a more dimensional look. Gradients come in two types—linear and radial—both of which are explored in "Lesson 2: Vegas Lady, Part 2." See Figure 5–19. Gradients are created using the Gradient panel and their starting and endpoints are modified using the Gradient tool. See Figure 5–20 and Figure 5–21. You can also save your favorite gradients in the Swatches panel.

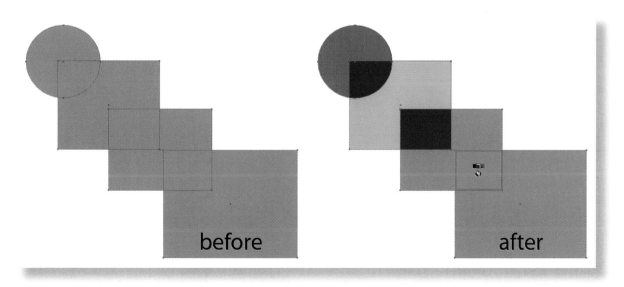

figure |5–18|

Fill overlapping paths with color using the Live Paint Bucket tool.

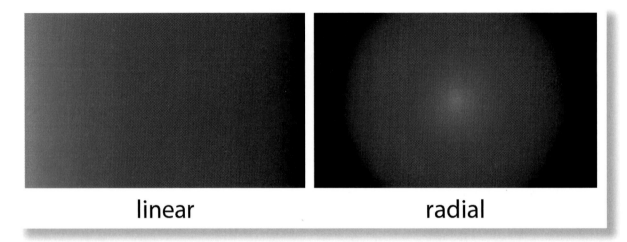

figure 5-19

Examples of linear and radial gradients.

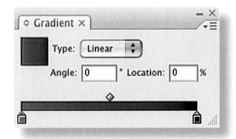

figure 5-20

The Gradient panel is used to create gradient color blends.

figure 5-21

Modify gradients with the Gradient tool.

Lesson 1: Vegas Lady, Part I

In this lesson you will apply solid colors to the strokes and fills of a pre-drawn image. You will choose colors from the Color Picker and Swatches panel, and create and save your own colors.

Setting Up the File

1. In Illustrator, open **chap5L1.ai** in the folder **chap5_lessons**.

2. Choose Window > Workspace > [Basic] in the menu bar to ensure you are starting with the default panel layout. This will reset the panels.

3. Choose Shift-Tab to hide any open panels/docks.

4. Select View > Fit In Window to see the original photo used as the drawing template.

5. Choose Window > Layers.

6. In the Layers panel, unhide the **coloring layer** to view the drawing in grayscale. See Figure 5–22.

7. Choose View > Outline to see how the image is constructed with numerous paths and shapes.

8. Choose View > Overprint Preview to view the fills and strokes.

9. Save this file in your lessons folder. Name it **chap5L1_ yourname.ai**.

Applying Color to Fills

1. In the Layers panel, expand the **coloring layer**, if not already expanded. To do this, click on the arrow to the left of the layer name, so the arrow points down. The paths and shapes that comprise the image are organized in separate sublayers. See Figure 5–23. To collapse the **coloring layer**, you can click on the arrow to reduce the clutter in the Layers panel. For now however, leave the **coloring layer** expanded.

> **Note:** You may not see all of the layers, paths, and shapes in the Layers panel. To see more, either use the scroll bar on the right side of the panel or resize the panel. To resize the panel, place your cursor over its bottom-edge or its lower-right corner (a double-headed arrow will appear), and then click and drag down. See Figure 5–24.

> **Note:** If the Layers panel is docked with other panels, click the title tab of the Layers panel and drag it away from the docked group to release it. Close the other, unneeded panels.

2. Expand the **head_dress** layer to see the individual paths, or sublayers.

3. Click the circle in the selection column of the **head_top** sublayer to select that object in the document. See Figure 5–25. (If you can't see the full names of the objects, resize the panel: place your cursor over its left edge and click and drag to the left.) The selection column of the Layers panel is located along its side with the scroll bar; when an object is selected, a colored selection box appears in this column.

4. Using the Color Picker, let's choose a new color for the top part of the headdress. Double-click on the Fill box in the toolbox to open the Color Picker.

> **Note:** The Color panel window also opens up. You can use the Color panel to select colors, too.

5. Select a deep red color by choosing a red hue from the spectrum and then adjusting the saturation and brightness levels of the color in the color box to the left. Alternatively, you can type the following in the RGB fields: R: **152**, G: **15**, B: **8**. Press Tab after each numeric entry. See Figure 5–26. Click OK.

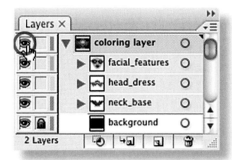

figure |5–22|

Unhide the coloring layer.

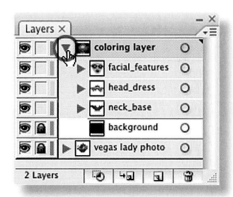

figure |5–23|

The expanded layer.

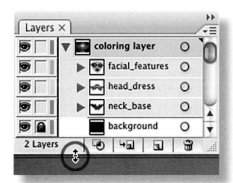

figure |5–24|

Expand the Layers panel.

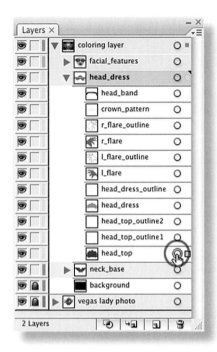

figure |5–25|

Select an object from the selection column in the Layers panel.

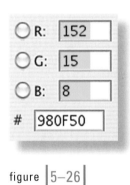

R:	152	
G:	15	
B:	8	
#	980F50	

figure |5–26|

Enter the RGB color.

6. Let's select the same color for the base of the Vegas lady drawing. With the Selection tool, click on the curved base object to select it. See Figure 5–27.

7. Choose the Eyedropper tool in the toolbox. See Figure 5–28.

8. Place the Eyedropper tool over the red headdress and click to take a sample of the color. The selected base will update with the sampled color. See Figure 5–29.

Note: You must first select the object you want to change, otherwise using the Eyedropper tool will just change the fill color, but not apply it.

9. Choose a color using the Swatches panel. Choose Window > Swatches to open the Swatches panel.

Note: If the Swatches panel is docked with other panels, click the title tab of the Swatches panel and drag it away from the docked group to release it. Close the other, unneeded panels.

figure |5–27|

Select the curved base.

figure |5–28|

Choose the Eyedropper tool.

figure |5–29|

Take a sample of color with the Eyedropper tool.

10. With the Selection tool, select one of the flares (feathers) of the Vegas lady drawing. See Figure 5–30. Click on the ocean blue colored swatch in the Swatches panel to apply the color. See Figure 5–31.

11. Apply the same blue color to the flare (feather) on the other side.

12. Save your file.

Applying Color to Strokes

1. In the Layers panel, select the sublayer **r_flare_outline** in the layer **head_dress**. To do this, click in the selection column of the sublayer located along the scroll bar side of the Layers panel. See Figure 5–32. In the toolbox, make sure the Stroke box is activated (in front of the Fill box) by clicking on it and the Fill box is indicated as "None." It is ready for you to add a new color to the stroke. See Figure 5–33.

2. In the Swatches panel, choose the magenta colored swatch for the stroke color.

3. Select the object **l_flare_outline** and apply the same magenta color.

4. Practice applying color to other strokes and fills on the document. Apply color to all the gray areas.

5. Save your file.

Saving Colors

1. Once you have picked colors for the image, you can save them to use over and over. Open the Swatches panel (Window > Swatches).

figure |5–30|

Select a flare on the lady.

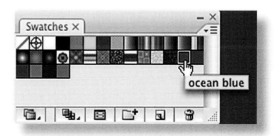

figure |5–31|

Select a swatch color.

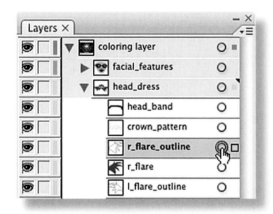

figure |5–32|

Select an object from the Layers panel.

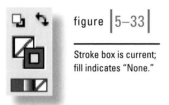

figure |5–33|

Stroke box is current; fill indicates "None."

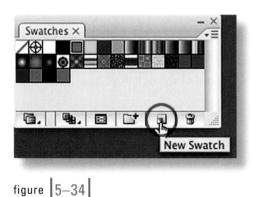

figure |5–34|

Add a new swatch.

2. Select the object **head_dress**. Notice that the color of the headdress is indicated in the Fill box in the toolbox. Click on the Fill box (to place it in front of the Stroke box) to activate it as the current color.

3. In the Swatches panel, click on the New Swatch icon in the lower-right of the panel window (next to the trash can) to add the current color. See Figure 5–34.

4. In the dialog box that pops up, enter a new, descriptive name for your new swatch. See Figure 5–35. Notice you can also change the color mode and color of the saved swatch. Click OK. If you need to get back to the Swatch Options for your new swatch, double-click on it in the Swatches panel.

5. You can also create a new swatch from the Swatches drop-down menu. Select one of the flares (feathers) on the Vegas lady. Click on the arrow with three horizontal lines in the upper-right corner of the Swatches panel. From the drop-down menu, select New Swatch. See Figure 5–36. Enter a name for the swatch and click OK.

Note: To delete a swatch, select it and click on the trash can icon in the Swatches panel.

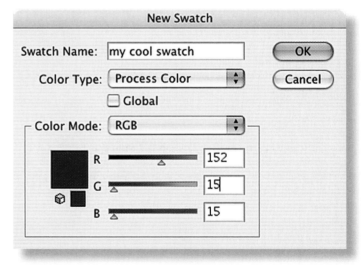

figure |5–35|

Name the swatch in the Swatch Options.

figure |5–36|

Create a new swatch from the Swatches drop-down menu.

6. Select each colored area in your image and save the colors in the Swatches panel.

7. Save your collected swatches into a library to use in another document. Click on the arrow with three horizontal lines in the upper-right corner of the Swatches panel. From the drop-down menu, choose Save Swatch Library as AI. Name your library **vegas_colors.ai** and save it in your lessons folder.

8. To open your swatches library, click on the arrow with three horizontal lines in the upper-right corner of the Swatches panel to open the Swatch Options. Choose Open Swatch Library > Other Library (at the bottom of the list).

9. Find your saved swatches library—**vegas_colors.ai**—in your lessons folder. Click Open, and the library will appear as a panel in the program.

10. Save your file—you are done with this version of the Vegas lady.

Lesson 2: Vegas Lady, Part 2

Using the pre-drawn image from Lesson 1, you will create gradients of color for the fill areas of the image.

Setting Up the File

1. In Illustrator, open the file **chap5L2.ai** in the folder **chap5_lessons**.

2. Choose Window > Workspace > [Basic] in the menu bar.

3. Choose Shift-Tab to hide unneeded panels/docks.

4. Choose View > Fit in Window.

5. Choose Window > Gradient.

> **Note:** If the Gradient panel is docked with other panels, select the title tab of the Gradient panel and drag it away from the docked group to release it. Close the other, unneeded panels.

6. Open the options for the Gradient panel. There are two ways to do this: 1) Click on the arrow with three horizontal lines in the upper-right corner of the panel and choose Show Options; or, 2) click twice on the up/down arrow in front of the Gradient's title tab. See Figure 5–37.

figure |5–37|

Open the Gradient panel options.

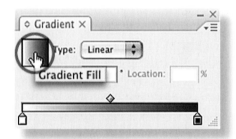

figure |5–38|

Click on the gradient fill box to create a default gradient on a selected object.

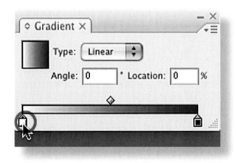

figure |5–39|

Select a color stop.

7. Save this file in your lessons folder. Name it **chap5L2_ yourname.ai**.

Applying a Linear Gradient

1. Select the red top headdress of the Vegas lady.

2. In the Gradient panel, click on the gradient fill box in the upper-left corner. This places a default gradient on the selected object. See Figure 5–38.

3. Let's change the colors of this default gradient. Choose Window > Color. Undock the panel if it is docked with others and choose Show Options from the Color panel drop-down menu. Keep things clean: close all panels except for the Color and Gradient panels.

4. In the Gradient panel, select Type: Linear.

5. Notice the color ramp at the bottom of the Gradient panel. It has two colors, one on each side, that blend. The markers under the ramp are called color stops. Click on the leftmost color stop to highlight it. See Figure 5–39.

> Note: The little triangle directly above the color stop will turn black when activated.

6. Notice that the Color panel changes to reflect the current selection. From the Color panel drop-down menu, choose the RGB model for color selection. See Figure 5–40.

7. Drag the Eyedropper tool along the RGB spectrum ramp at the bottom of the Color panel to select a new color for the gradient color stop. Pick any color. See Figure 5–41.

> **Note:** As you move the Eyedropper tool along the spectrum ramp, notice the gamut warning signs popping up. As discussed previously, you can click on either the Web or print gamut warnings to snap to an equivalent color within the gamut.

8. In the Gradient panel, click to select the rightmost color stop.

9. In the Color panel, choose the RGB color model, and assign this color stop a new color.

figure |5–40|

Choose RGB from the drop-down menu.

10. Type **90** in the angle box of the Gradient panel and press Enter to rotate the angle of the gradient.

11. Move the gradient slider (the diamond shape above the gradient ramp) to the right or left to adjust the midpoint of the gradient.

12. For fun, let's add another color to the ramp. Click under the ramp to create another color stop. See Figure 5–42.

13. Create a new color for the color stop in the Color panel.

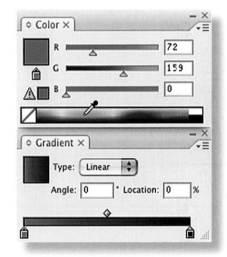

> **Note:** To delete a color stop, select it and drag it down and away from the Gradient panel.

14. Save your gradient by choosing Window > Swatches. From the Swatches drop-down menu, select New Swatch. Enter a name for your new swatch and click OK.

15. The new gradient appears in the Swatches panel.

figure |5–41|

Select a color in the Color panel. Notice how the color updates on the color stop of the color ramp in the Gradient panel.

> **Note:** If you do not see it, make sure Show All Swatches is selected from the Show Swatch Kinds menu in the lower part of the Swatches panel. See Figure 5–43.

16. Save your file.

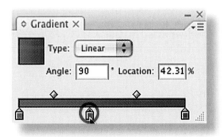

figure |5–42|

Click under the color ramp to add another color stop.

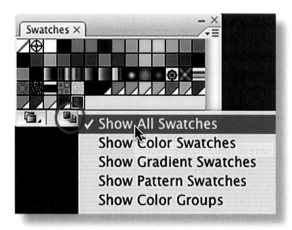

figure |5-43|

Select the Show All Swatches option.

Applying a Radial Gradient

1. Select the Zoom tool and magnify the Vegas lady's lips.

2. Let's apply a radial gradient to the upper and lower lips. Shift-click with the Selection tool to select both parts.

3. Click on the Gradient fill box in the Gradient panel to apply the last created gradient on the lips.

4. In the gradient box, choose Type: Radial.

5. Click the rightmost color stop. In the Color panel, select a red color to apply to the gradient.

> **Note:** As an alternative to selecting colors in the Color panel, you can drag a color swatch from the Swatches panel over the selected color stop.

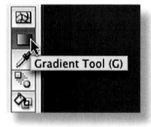

figure |5-44|

Select the Gradient tool.

6. Apply a lighter red color or white to the leftmost color stop.

7. Modify where the radial center starts on the gradient. To do this, click on the Gradient tool in the toolbox. See Figure 5-44.

8. Click and drag the tool vertically from the lower lip to the upper lip and notice how the gradient direction changes. See Figure 5-45. To readjust the gradient direction to your liking, drag the tool shorter or longer distances over the lips.

9. Save this gradient in the Swatches panel.

10. Using the methods you just learned, create other gradient combinations on the various shapes of the image. For example, use a radial gradient on the lady's eyeballs to make them more three-dimensional.

11. Save your final file.

figure |5-45|

Use the Gradient tool to adjust the radial gradient.

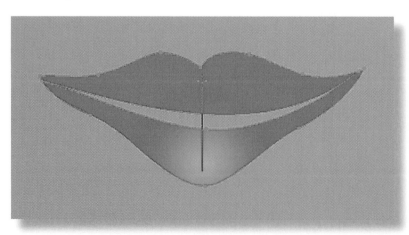

COLOR IN DESIGN

So many colors, so little time. This becomes apparent when you find yourself hours later still trying to decide what colors to use for your favorite masterpiece. To speed things up, you need to know how colors work together. In Illustrator you have several ways and color models in which to pick color, but how do you know what colors look good together? There is actually a whole art and science to creating a visually appealing palette of hues and, of course, numerous theories to back up the information. In general, these theories are based on an understanding of the color spectrum and usually in the form of a color wheel. See Figure 5–46.

As a starting point for picking colors, think in terms of color chords—combinations of colors that work well together. Six basic color chords are described as follows (there are others). For colorful examples of these color chords, open the **chords1.jpg** and **chords2.jpg** in the folder **chap5_lessons/samples**, and see Figure 5–48 and Figure 5–49.

- *Monochromatic:* Uses one hue (color) plus the addition of black, white, and/or grays.

- *Analogous:* Uses two to three hues, which are adjacent to each other on a standard color wheel (i.e., red, red orange, orange), plus the addition of black, white, and/or grays.

- *Achromatic:* Uses a combination of black, white, and/or grays. No hues.

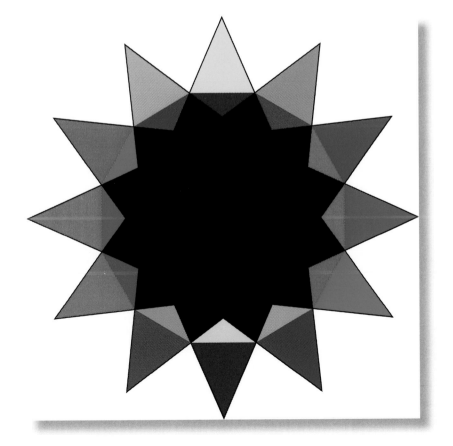

figure | 5–46 |

Example color wheel.

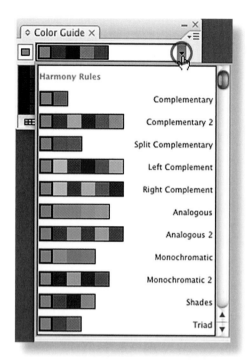

figure | 5–47 |

Use the Color Guide to pick colors that look good together.

- *Dyad (complement or opposite):* Uses hues that are opposite each other on the color wheel or color spectrum (i.e., orange and blue), plus the addition of black, white, and/or grays.

> **Note:** There is a quick way to find dyad colors in Illustrator. In the program, create an object and fill it with color. Select the object. Open the Color panel. From its Options drop-down menu, choose Complement.

- *Warm Hues:* Color hues that give the viewer a sense of warmth, such as reds, yellows, and oranges.

- *Cool Hues:* Color hues that give the viewer a sense of coolness, such as blues and greens.

Another great tool to use in the context of color harmonies is the Color Guide. Located under Window > Color Guide, this is a quick and easy way to find a list of different color harmony rules for your current forward color. By clicking on the arrow, the guide takes your selected color (fill or stroke) and provides you with a number of harmony rules, including analogous and complementary. See Figure 5–47. This is a great tool to keep in mind during your color journey.

To practice making your own color chord combinations, see the section, "Exploring On Your Own."

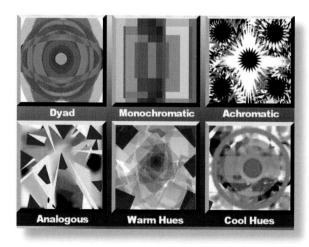

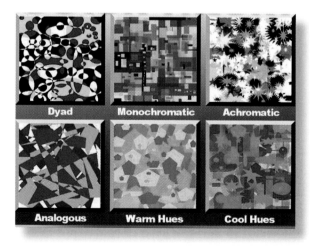

figure | 5–48 | and figure | 5–49 |

Example color combinations using color chords.

SUMMARY

This chapter introduced you to important concepts about color, including color models, modes, and gamuts. You applied color to strokes and fills using Illustrator's Color Picker, Color and Swatches panels, and the Eyedropper tool. Using color effectively in your artwork is more than just applying it to strokes and fills, however. It is also about picking colors that are visually enticing and preparing the colors correctly for the artwork's final, anticipated purpose.

in review

1. Define the term color gamut.

2. How do different color gamuts affect what colors look like in Illustrator?

3. What is a color model? How is it different than a color mode?

4. What color model represents the primary colors of light?

5. What is hexadecimal?

6. Briefly describe hue, saturation, and brightness.

7. Four-color processing uses what kind of color model?

8. What is a gamut warning in Illustrator?

9. What tool can take a sample of color in an image?

10. Describe complementary colors.

exploring on your own

1. Access the Help > Illustrator Help menu option. Under Contents, read the section "Color." For more advanced information on working with color in Illustrator, read the section "Color Management."

2. Practice your color chords with the color theory lesson. Examples of the completed lesson are provided in the **chap5_lessons/samples** folder: **chords1.jpg** and **chords2.jpg**. See also Figure 5–48 and Figure 5–49.

Instructions:

- In Illustrator, open the file **colortheory.ai** in the folder **chap5_lessons/samples**.

- In the box for each labeled color chord, use the following tools to create a motif (design) for each chord:

  a. *Dyad:* Ellipse tool

  b. *Monochromatic:* Rectangle tool

  c. *Achromatic:* Star tool

  d. *Analogous:* Polygon tool

  e. *Warm hues:* Any tool

  f. *Cool hues:* Any tool

- Color each motif with the appropriate characteristics for each chord.

> **Note:** Review the characteristics of each chord in the section "Color in Design."

3. You can learn a lot about color theory and design by surfing the Internet. Do a search for "color theory" or "color design" and plenty of information is bound to pop up. For more information on color in design, see also the next section, "Adventures in Design: The Moods of Color."

4. Create and publish your own color schemes using Adobe Labs dynamic color selector program at *http://kuler.adobe.com/*.

ADVENTURES IN DESIGN

the moods of color

Certain colors and the way they come together can produce a visceral response from a viewer. Colors can be representative of a thought or idea, or evoke an emotion. Green brings visions of nature or money. Blue is calming or corporate. Yellow is happy, bright, illuminating. Advertisers know this fact all too well—a set of golden yellow arches, for example, reminds most of french fries, shakes, and Happy Meals.

As you have learned, there are guidelines for choosing appropriate color combinations—color modes, color chords, the color wheel. Moreover, colors chosen for a particular piece of artwork or layout directly relate to a design's look and feel. This is a deeper and more subjective aspect to the color-selection process—it involves the sense of "mood."

What is the mood you (or your client) want to convey in the artwork? Is it to appear classic and professional, warm and inviting, or playful and light? What color combinations will work best to achieve each mood? By identifying a mood for your design, the sometimes nightmarish task of picking colors can be more easily carved out. Let's introduce to you a scenario of choosing colors with mood in mind, and then it is your turn to give it a try.

Professional Project Example

In Chapter 1, you recreated from a sketch a logo for an actual real estate broker company called Stratton Buyer Brokerage (SBB) in Vermont. See Figure A–1. The company owner, Andrea, also requested a color version of the logo that can be used for both print and the Web. To avoid the endless decision process that can occur when choosing colors, it was important to try and hone in on some colors

Stratton Buyer Brokerage
(original logo)

Stratton Buyer Brokerage
(logo 1)

Stratton Buyer Brokerage
(logo 2)

Stratton Buyer Brokerage
(logo 3)

figure A–1 Sample colored versions of the SBB logo.

continued

ADVENTURES IN DESIGN

continued

Andrea envisioned for the logo. First, she used adjectives to describe what her company represents, providing a better idea of where to begin when selecting colors for her logo. It was learned that SBB is a small company; it is professional in a friendly, personalized way. With this in mind, certain color combinations could easily be eliminated: bright or neon colors were out—not professional looking enough. So were bold colors like navy blue and red (too corporate). It was decided that subtle, warmer colors were better—more inviting and homey. After several versions of the logo with different color combinations were created, a logo with deep greens and purples was the eventual choice. Various color versions are shown in Figure A–1. (To view samples, see the **aid1_example.ai** in the folder **aid_examples**.)

Your Turn

Now it is your turn to play with different color combinations on Andrea's logo. It is important to remember the identity of the company: personalized, professional, based in rural Vermont. Just as important, use what you learned about color in design in Chapter 5 to more easily blend combinations of colors. A sample file with four black and white duplicates of the SBB logo is provided in **aid_examples/ aid1.ai**. Use the duplicates to explore different stroke and fill color combinations on the logo shapes.

Color Mood Project Guidelines

1. Assume the logo will eventually go to print, so be sure the **aid1.ai** document is saved in the CMYK color mode.

2. To more easily and independently adjust different hues, saturation, and brightness levels when determining your color combinations, use the HSB Color panel. See Figure A–2. For example, select one part

of the logo and adjust the hue slider of the HSB panel to a color you like. Begin to adjust the S and B sliders to modify the color in saturation and brightness to what might seem appropriate to Andrea's description of the company's look and feel. (Here is where some subjective decision making comes in.)

3. Select another item on the logo and take a sample of the color you just created to fill the selected shape. Leaving the S and B sliders in the HSB Color panel the same, adjust only the H slider to another color of your liking. By adjusting the same component of the HSB color model for each color—in this example, just the H (hue) component—you can quickly create colors that have a similar tone, making for more compatible color combinations.

4. Try this method on another of the logo duplicates, using perhaps a lighter or darker set of colors on each logo shape.

5. For one of the other logo examples, use another technique for quickly choosing like colors with the Complement or Invert commands available in Illustrator. See Figure A–3. These options offer variations on a color, based on the complement (opposite) or inversion of it in a standard color wheel. First, fill a logo shape with a color. Take a sample of that color to fill in another selected shape on the logo. Then, from the Color panel options menu, choose Invert or Complement.

6. Make sure the colors you have chosen are within the CMYK color gamut. If they are not part of the CMYK color gamut, the print gamut warning—the alert triangle icon in the Color panel—pops up. If the warning comes up, click on the triangle icon to adjust the color to its nearest CMYK equivalent. See Figure A–4.

7. Save your color selections in the Swatches panel.

figure A–2   The HSB color panel.

figure A–3   Select the Complement command in Illustrator.

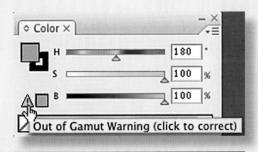

figure A–4   The CMYK warning icon.

8. Do a color test by printing your logos on a color printer. Compare how the color looks printed versus on the screen. As you have learned, color can vary depending on the device in which it is viewed.

Things to Consider

Here are some tips to consider when working with color.

-   As a starting point for picking colors, use color chords as described in the section Chapter "Color in Design."

-   If available, pick colors from a swatch book—a book of printable color examples that is usually available for viewing at your local printing bureau. Swatch books will also give you a sense of how colors might look printed on various types of paper.

-   Limit the number of colors used on a logo design or document. Work with only about two to four colors at a time.

-   With colored pencils, sketch out various color combinations on paper, then attempt to tackle the colors in Illustrator.

-   Remember the moods of color and how they reflect on your overall design objectives.

Explorer pages

BROOKE NUÑEZ

Fruit by Brooke Nuñez.

Chase by Brooke Nuñez.

About Brooke Nuñez

Brooke Nuñez was an artist from time she could first hold a pencil. She drew on everything: notebooks, tabletops, walls, napkins, furniture, skin, etc. While growing up, she spent endless hours drawing portraits and murals, and she had her first paying gig in elementary school. At 17, she took on a full-time job as an art instructor for her town's art center, which inspired her to major in graphic design in college. It was there she learned the limitless potential of computer graphics and also where Lifeinvector.com was born, her personal online portfolio showcase (*http://www .lifeinvector.com/*).

After graduating from a small design school in Arizona, she moved to New York City where she landed a job as one of four senior illustrators for the Toys'R'Us corporation. Two years later she moved to Savannah, where she began her full-time freelance career out of her home office. A year later, as work and clientele increased, she made another big move, this time to Chicago, where she currently resides as a successful freelance illustrator/designer. Brooke's clients over the years included companies like Coca-Cola, Nintendo, Dr Pepper, and Yahoo! Slowly but surely, she is branching out into several other areas of the creative field, including interior and landscape design.

To see more of Brooke's work, visit *http://www.lifeinvector.com/*.

About the Work of Brooke Nuñez

Brooke shares her process in creating the Santa illustration: "In general, there's not a whole lot to reinvent when it comes to Santa Claus," she said. "But in vector, the process was a fairly big challenge. Round after round of initial sketching was required before even touching the computer. Once the sketches were brought into Illustrator, though, more challenges arose than expected. What style-direction should I go toward? What kind of light should be used and where should it come from? What could I do to distinguish him? The decisions were uncovered as I went along.

"Section by section, I worked my way through the illustration," she continued. "I began with the beard, and all I have to say is: Bezier, Bezier, Bezier! I used a combination of both layering shapes and using my Divide tool in the Pathfinder panel. Colors were chosen based on several beard references I found on the Internet and in books I scanned. (Same process for his skin tones and the golds in his belt and buttons—tons of research beforehand.) The pieces that were intended to stand out were lighter, while the darker shapes created the depth it needed. And it wouldn't quite be Santa without a big, round stomach tucked tightly into his black belt, so the exaggeration was achieved by layering simple shapes on one big bumpy shape. The final details were the simple swirls in the edges of his outfit, which mimicked the wildness of his beard and created more flow throughout the whole piece. And voila! The portrait came together by adding a complementary background color and a burst for friendly emphasis."

Santa by Brooke Nuñez.

Fame by Brooke Nuñez.

Sumo by Brooke Nuñez.

| value and texture |

charting your course

What brings life to an illustration is the use of value and text, the last two components in our study of the fundamental building blocks of visual art. (For a review of these elements, see Chapter 3.) This chapter defines value and texture in art and introduces you to value and texture on strokes and fills, including brushes, patterns, filters, effects, and graphic styles. You will learn that the strokes and fills that comprise an Illustrator graphic can be further modified to take what is initially a flat colored illustration and transform it into one that appears to have more tactile characteristics.

goals

In this chapter you will:

- **Differentiate between the use of value and texture in illustrative art**
- **Get a handle on the various attributes of strokes and fills**
- **Master the use and modification of Illustrator brush types and the Paintbrush tool**
- **Explore the differences and uses of filters, effects, and graphic styles**
- **Understand the steps for creating and applying patterns**

IMPLYING SURFACE

Take a look at the row of flower images on the first page of this chapter. The flower on the left is the original image—a print of a drawing Annesa did when she was a young child, which now hangs in her office. Can you see, maybe even feel, the roughness of the paper on which it was printed? Is the tablecloth smooth or rough? Is the flower pot old or new? Now look at the flower in the middle. This is a trace of the print done in Illustrator using only solid, flat colors. The image has a completely different look and feel, very one-dimensional.

Finally, check out the flower on the right. This is the same Illustrator image, but with value and texture added. It looks a lot more like the original print with varied paint strokes and implied surface characteristics, but it is completely digitized and easily altered.

What are value and texture in art? What does it mean to add value and texture to a digitized image? *Value* is the relationship of light and dark parts within an image, sometimes referred to as *tone*, *shade*, or *brightness*. You experienced the use of value in the previous chapter when you worked with varying fill colors and with gradients, which are blended values of color. There is also value in line—a stroke in Illustrator has different weights (thicknesses), as do brushes. Value in line is what you learn mostly about in this chapter. Value can also imply a sense of space, which you encounter in Chapter 9. A good example, however, is the illusion that appears when you put a lighter copy of an object below its original, resulting in a shadow effect. See Figure 6–1.

Texture implies surface—how an object might feel if we were to touch it. It informs us of our surroundings, tells us about the nature of objects—smooth, rough, soft, hard. Textures in our environment are represented by how light hits a surface—depths of lights and darks. In Illustrator, the textures you create are simulated, meaning the texture is flat by touch but tricks the eye into thinking it is not. A filter or effect in Illustrator can produce simulated textures, brushes, and patterns—all of which are covered in this chapter.

figure | 6–1 |

The shadow of the word *shadow* is created by changing the value of the text to a lighter gray and adding a slightly blurry texture.

STROKE AND FILL ATTRIBUTES

By now, you should know the difference between a stroke and a fill. A stroke is the defined outline or path of an object, and a fill is the area enclosed by the path. In the previous chapter, you applied the attribute of color to strokes and fills. Lucky for us, strokes and fills have other attributes and appearance effects besides color. See Figure 6–2 and Figure 6–3.

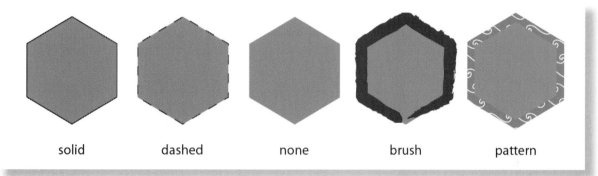

solid   dashed   none   brush   pattern

figure |6–2|

Stroke variations.

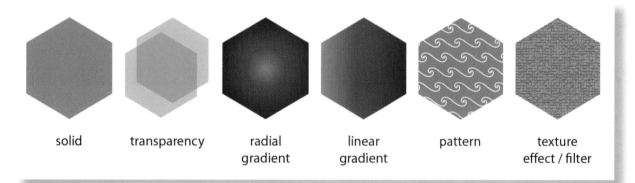

solid   transparency   radial   linear   pattern   texture
                         gradient   gradient   effect / filter

figure |6–3|

Fill variations.

Stroke Variations

Stroke variations include color, weight (line thickness), solid or dashed lines, line caps and joins, and brush styles. You can change the color of a selected stroke, or fill, in four areas in Illustrator—the Control panel, the Color Picker (accessed by double-clicking the stroke, [or fill] box in the toolbox), the Color panel (accessed by single-clicking on the stroke or fill box

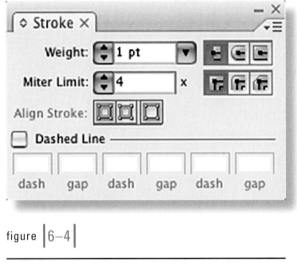

Choose Window > Stroke to open the Stroke panel.

in the toolbox), or the Swatches panel. To change the attributes of a selected stroke, such as the weight, line type, or line caps and joins, choose Window > Stroke or select the underlined word *stroke* in the Control panel and open the stroke properties. To access brush and pattern types, choose Window > Brushes and/or Window > Brush Libraries.

About Stroke Attributes

Stroke attributes for a selected object are located in the Stroke panel (Window > Stroke). See Figure 6–4. In the Stroke panel, you can alter a stroke's weight, cap, join, and miter limit. You can also create varied dashed lines. By default, a stroke's weight is measured in points (pts). If you want a thin line, set the weight to .05 pts; for a thicker line, set it to 20 pts. See examples of stroke weights in Figure 6–5.

Note: You can change the unit measurement of a stroke (to inches, picas, or pixels) by going to Illustrator > Preferences > Units & Display Performance (Mac) or Edit > Preferences > Units & Display Performance (Windows).

figure |6–5|

Example stroke weights, measured in points.

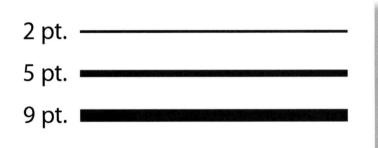

You can also add different caps to the ends of your strokes. Yes, "cap" might seem like such a funny name, but it makes sense—just like you might put a cap on your head for a stylish effect, you can do the same thing with strokes. To choose different caps, select one of three options in the Stroke panel. See Figure 6–6.

- *Butt Cap:* Stroked line with square ends.
- *Round Cap:* Stroked line with rounded ends.
- *Projecting Cap:* Stroked line with squared ends that takes the weight of the line and extends it equally in all directions around the line.

figure |6–6|

1. Butt Cap,
2. Round Cap,
3. Projecting Cap.

Another stylish effect is the line join options. Joins determine the look of a stroke at its corner angles. There are three types of joins. See Figure 6–7.

- *Miter Join:* Creates stroke lines with pointed corners. The miter limit controls when the program switches from a mitered join with a high value (pointed) to a beveled (squared-off) join with a low value. See Figure 6–8.

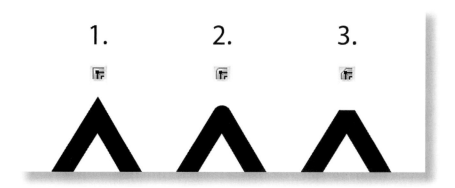

figure |6–7|

1. Miter Join,
2. Round Join,
3. Bevel Join.

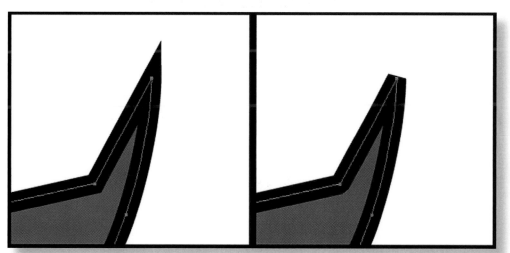

figure |6–8|

Miter of a stroke set at 4x and at 1x.

- *Round Join:* Creates stroked lines with rounded corners.
- *Bevel Join:* Creates stroked lines with squared corners.

From the Stroke panel, you can also create custom dashed lines. To do this, select a stroke and specify a sequence of dashes and the gaps between them. See Figure 6–9 for an example. You can also combine cap styles with different dash patterns, resulting in either rounded or squared dash ends.

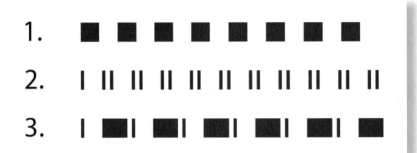

About Brushes

Another very popular stroke variation is the use of brushes. With Illustrator brushes you can mess around with the texture and value of your drawn paths without having to wash the brushes when you are done. You can apply Illustrator brush types to selected strokes or paint new strokes with the Paintbrush tool. There are four basic brush types (see Figure 6–10):

- *Calligraphic:* Calligraphic brush strokes resemble the angled strokes produced from a calligraphic pen.
- *Art:* Art brush strokes resemble sketched or painterly strokes, such as those created with chalk and watercolors. The brushes also include objects, such as arrows, that when drawn stretch evenly along the length of the path.
- *Scatter:* Scatter brushes randomly disperse objects along a path.
- *Pattern:* Pattern brushes produce a repeated pattern—derived from individual tiles—that repeat evenly along a path.

To find these brush types, choose Window > Brushes to open the Brushes panel. By default, some calligraphic and art brushes are provided. To find more, choose Window > Brush Libraries from the menu bar or Open Brush Library from the Brushes panel options menu. See Figure 6–11. You can also create and modify your own brush styles and libraries—and how wonderful is that?

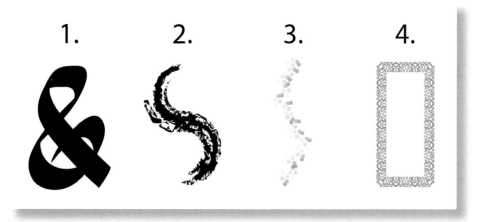

figure |6–10|

The four brush types:
1. Calligraphic; 2. Art;
3. Scatter; 4. Pattern.

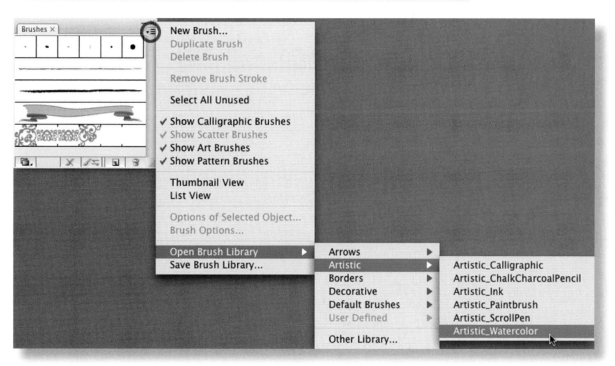

figure |6–11|

There are lots of brush libraries to choose from.

To draw a path and create a brush stroke at the same time, use the Paintbrush tool in the tool-box (see Figure 6–12). Painting with this tool can sometimes bring unwanted results, unless you adjust the tool's settings in its preferences box. To open the Paintbrush tool's preferences, double-click on the tool in the toolbox. See Figure 6–13.

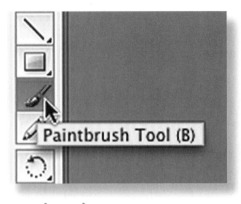

figure |6–12|

The Paintbrush tool.

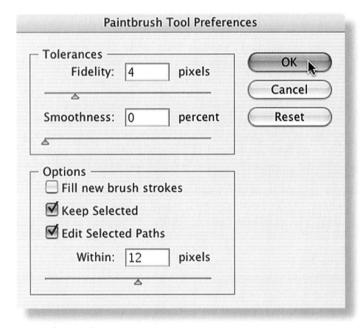

figure |6–13|

Double-click on a tool in the toolbox to open its options or preferences settings.

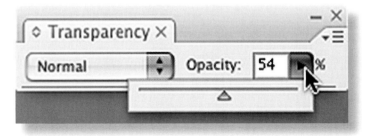

figure |6–14|

Adjust the transparency slider.

Note: "Double-clicking" on a tool as a way to bring up a tool's options or preferences applies to other tools in the toolbox. You might be surprised by the many options lurking under those tools.

You will experience painting with brushes and adjusting brush preferences in "Lesson 1: The Fish Painting."

Fill Variations

As demonstrated in Figure 6–3, fills have attributes other than solid colors. Linear and radial gradients were introduced in the previous chapter. You can also apply transparency to fills. Simply select the filled object, choose Window > Transparency, and in the Transparency panel adjust the opacity setting from 100 (no transparency) to **0** (full transparency). See Figure 6–14.

Note: To see the transparency effect on an object, it helps to put another object behind it.

Patterns are also a great way to have fun with fills. You can apply, create, and transform patterns—and save them in the Swatches panel. See Figure 6–15. Patterns are useful if you want a repeated tile effect or mosaic. Take a look at the fabric patterns at your local textile or clothing store. You will get to play with patterns in "Lesson 2: Playing with Custom Brush Styles and Patterns."

Another way to create fills with varied textures is to use the filters and effects available in Illustrator. At first glance the Filter and Effects menus seem the same. For instance, from the menu bar you can see the option for Artistic from the Filter menu and also from the Effects menu. What is up with that?

An effect (versus a filter) is a live overlay. When you apply an effect to an object, it is as if you are laying a cover, or covers, over the object. It changes the appearance of the object, but not its original characteristics. When you reshape the original characteristics of the object, the effects applied will readjust accordingly. The Appearance panel (described in the section "Using the Appearance Panel) lists your effect(s) and enables you to modify, expand, duplicate, delete, or save them as a graphic style.

A *graphic style* is a named set of appearance attributes (what comprises an effect) that can be stored in a Graphic Styles panel or library. Illustrator comes with many pre-made graphics styles (Window > Graphic Style Libraries). However, you can create your own. You can apply graphic styles to individual fills, strokes, grouped objects, and layers. See Figure 6–16.

Filters, on the other hand, alter an underlying object and cannot be modified or removed after the filter is applied. The filters in Illustrator work much the same way as those in Photoshop. In fact, Photoshop-compatible filters can be applied to objects that have been rasterized (Object > Rasterize) in Illustrator.

Initially it might be difficult to understand what filters and effects apply to what types of objects. In the filters menu, the items at the top of the list can be used on vector-based graphics (Illustrator Filters), while the items at the bottom are primarily used for bitmap (or rasterized) objects (Photoshop Filters). Options available in the effects menu can be applied to any kind of object, even text.

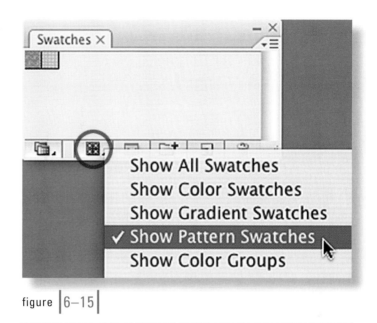

figure |6–15|

Select to view patterns saved in the Swatches panel.

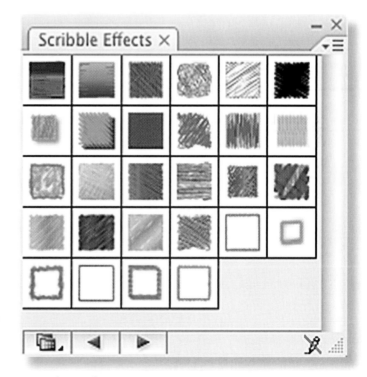

figure |6–16|

The Scribble Effects graphic styles library.

Some filters and effects are available only for documents in RGB mode. To identify what filter or effect works on what type of image, select the image, choose the Filter or Effect menus, and any filters or effects that are highlighted in black (versus gray) can be applied to that particular image, or in that particular document mode.

You will have the opportunity to work hands-on with filters, effects, graphic styles, and their many quirks in Lesson 1.

Using the Appearance Panel

Once you start applying multiple brushes, patterns, and effects to strokes and fills, you might find it difficult to remember what steps you took and modify all the variations. The Appearance panel comes to the rescue; it is your guide to what fill and stroke variations you have applied to a particular object(s). Let us say you applied a brush called *Splash* (yes, there is a brush style by that name) and a solid fill to an object. It would look

figure | 6–17 |

Filled object with the *Splash* art brush outline.

like Figure 6–17. When you open the Appearance panel (Window > Appearance), it will list the stroke and fill attributes of the selected object. See Figure 6–18. Furthermore, when you double-click on, say the word *Splash* in the Appearance panel, the options for that particular brush stroke will appear. See Figure 6–19.

If you have a complicated effect or graphic style assigned to an object, such as the Tissue Paper Collage in Figure 6–20, the Appearance panel shows a breakdown of the ingredients (per se) that comprise the object's "look," so you can modify individual parts. For example, see Figure 6–21 on the next page for the list of ingredients that produces the Tissue Paper Collage effect.

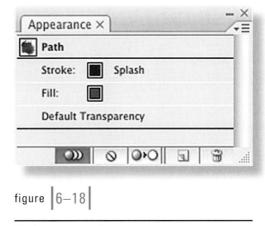

figure |6–18|

The Appearance panel.

Another great thing we like about the Appearance panel is that in its options box (see Figure 6–22 on page 129) you can do some crazy things like add a new fill or stroke, reduce the object to its basic appearance (theoretically, peel off its covers), or, when things get really messy, clear its appearance effects completely.

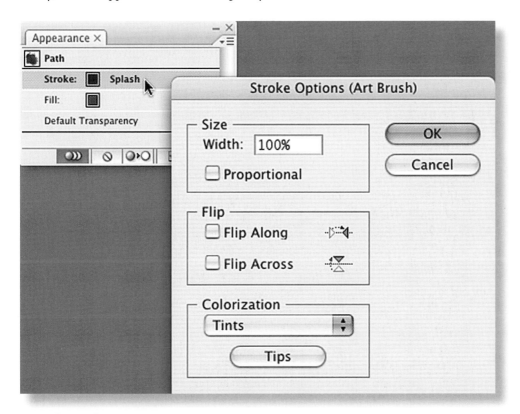

figure |6–19|

Using the Appearance panel to alter brush stoke options.

figure |6–20|

A complicated effect.

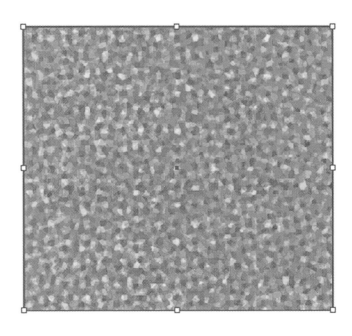

figure |6–21|

View the parts of an object's effects in the Appearance panel.

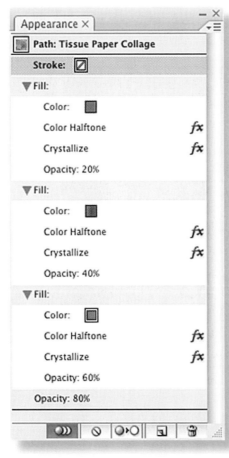

Lesson 1: The Fish Painting

Once you learn how to apply brush styles on drawn paths, paint directly with the Paintbrush tool, and use graphic styles and effects—all good things covered in this lesson—there is no turning back your inner artist. See Figure 6–23.

Setting Up the File

1. In Illustrator, open **chap6L1.ai** in the **chap6_lessons** folder.

2. Choose Window > Workspace > [Basic].

3. Choose Shift-Tab to hide any open panels/docks.

4. Choose View > Fit In Window.

5. Choose Window > Swatch Libraries > Other Library (located at the bottom of the list).

6. Browse for the custom library called **fish_ colors.ai** in the **chap6_lessons/assets** folder. Choose Open to open the swatches in the document.

Applying Brush Styles

1. Select the body outline of the fish. For easier reference, all the paths of the fish are labeled in the Layers panel. Open the Layers panel, then expand the layer called **fish** and select the desired path name. See Figure 6–24.

2. Click on the orange swatch in the **fish_colors** Swatches panel to apply the color to the fish's body. (Be sure the Fill box option is selected in the toolbox.)

3. Change the stroke color of the body outline to **None**.

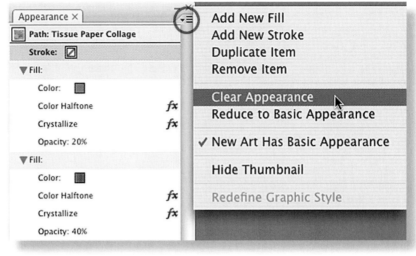

figure | 6–22 |

The Appearance panel's options.

figure | 6–23 |

The finished Lesson 1 file.

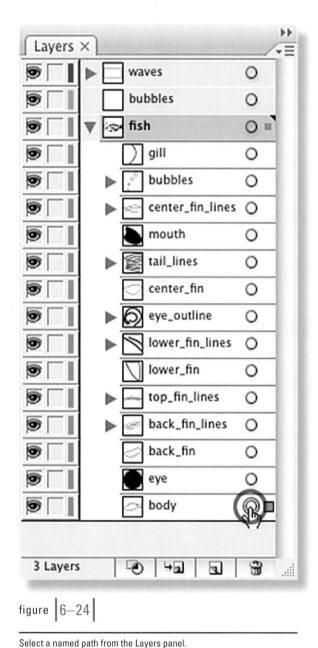

figure |6–24|

Select a named path from the Layers panel.

figure |6–25|

Select the *bubble* swatch. When you roll over a swatch, its name will appear.

> **Note:** To do this, select the Stroke box option in the toolbox, then choose None in the Fill options of the toolbox. If you forget to select the Stroke box before changing the color, your orange fill will change to transparent.

4. Select the bubbles of the fish with the Selection tool or by using the target icon in the bubbles sublayer. (The bubbles are grouped, so you can select them all at once.) In the custom Swatch panel, choose the swatch called **bubble.** See Figure 6–25.

5. Change the stroke color of the bubbles to **None.**

6. Select the **top_fin_lines** of the fish. See Figure 6–26.

7. Apply an art brush to the lines. In the Control or in the Brushes panel (Window > Brushes), choose the Thick Pencil art brush. See Figure 6–27. The brush stroke is applied to the selected paths.

8. Select the grouped lines of the fish's tail (**tail_lines**), and apply the Thick Pencil art brush. Hint: If you are using the Direct Selection tool, hold down Option-Alt to select an entire group.

9. Select the **gil, lower_fin_lines, back_fin_lines,** and **center_fin_lines** and apply the Thick Pencil brush.

10. Save your work in your lessons folder. Name it **chap6L1_yourname.ai.**

11. Select the **eye_outline** and choose the Rough Charcoal art brush (first one in the horizontal brush list). Notice that the width of the Rough Charcoal brush is a bit thick for the eye outline. We need to fix this.

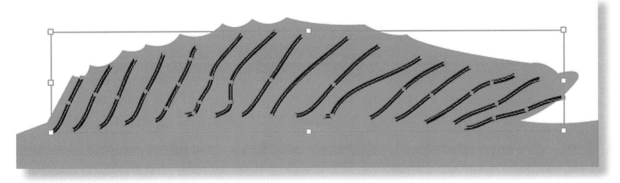

figure |6–26|

Select the **top_fin_lines** of the fish.

12. Double-click on the Rough Charcoal brush style in the Brushes panel. This brings up the Art Brush Options for that particular brush. See Figure 6–28.

13. Select the Preview option to see your changes updated on the object.

14. Change the width setting to **20%**, and press Tab to update the change on the object. Ahh, much better.

15. Click OK to close the options box. A dialog box will pop up asking if you would like to apply the new change to the currently selected brush strokes. Select Apply to Strokes. See Figure 6–29.

16. Select just the eye object. From the **fish_colors** Swatches panel choose the Predator Eye style.

17. Save your file again.

Applying Graphic Styles

1. Select the **center_fin** of the fish (the outer line, not the lines inside).

2. Choose Window > Graphic Styles to open the Graphic Styles panel.

figure |6–27|

Select the Thick Pencil art brush in the Brushes panel.

figure  6–28 |

Change the brush style
settings.

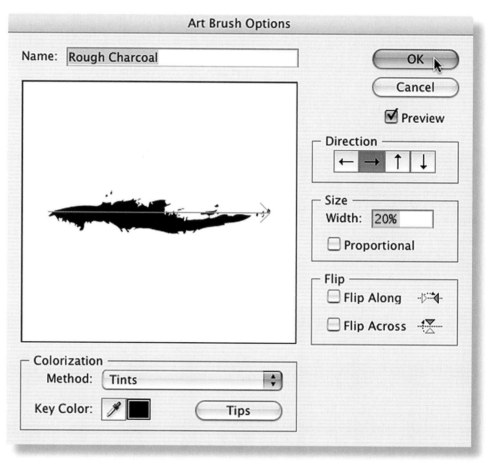

figure | 6–29 |

Select Apply to Strokes.

3. Some graphic styles are provided. To find more, open the Graphics Styles panel and, from the options menu in the upper-right corner, choose Open Graphic Style Library > Image Effects.

4. Select the effect called Chiseled in the Image Effects panel to apply it to the object. See Figure 6–30. (OK. We know you are itching to try the other graphic styles. Because they are so cool looking, we say, "Go for it." But save your file beforehand, and when you are done doodling, please come back to the next step.)

5. Assign the Chiseled effect to the **back_fin** and **lower_fin**.

6. Check out this graphic style in the Appearance panel. Select one of the fins and choose Window > Appearance. Notice the many stroke and fill variations that comprise this effect. See Figure 6–31.

7. You can change parts of the effect in the Appearance panel. Move the scroll bar of the panel down to find the Fill attributes. See Figure 6–32. Double-click on the Fill line to bring the Color panel forward. Select a new color in this panel for the Fill. Notice the color updates right away on the selected fin.

8. Notice there is a drop shadow and opacity setting for the Fill of the effect. Double-click on the Drop Shadow line to open its options. Click the Preview options box and choose **0.02 in** for the Y Offset. Press Tab to see the change on the fish fin without closing the options box. Click OK.

9. Double-click on the Opacity setting for the Fill. The Transparency panel will come forward. (Note: The panel is probably grouped with the Stroke and Gradient panels— look carefully). Change the opacity setting in the Transparency panel to **100%** to darken the fin effect color.

10. Let's assume you are the indecisive type, and you do not like the effect changes you just made. From the Appearance panel drop-down menu, choose Clear > Appearance to remove the appearance effect. See Figure 6–33.

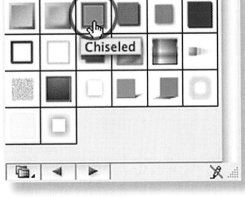

figure | 6–30 |

Select the Chiseled graphic style.

figure | 6–31 |

What a list of ingredients for just one effect!

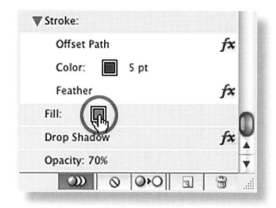

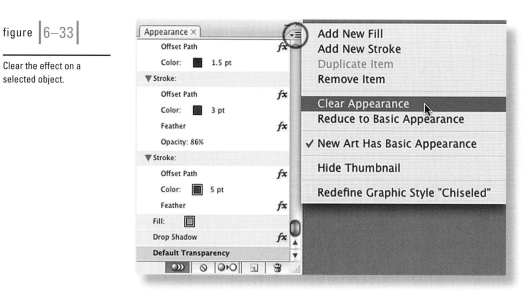

figure | 6-32 |

Double-click on an effect attribute to edit it.

11. The effect has now been removed from the selected fin. In the Graphic Styles panel, reapply the original, unmodified effect called Chiseled to the object.

12. Save your file.

figure | 6-33 |

Clear the effect on a selected object.

Applying an Effect

1. Choose Effect > Document Raster Effects Settings. Indicate the following settings (see Figure 6–34):

- *Resolution:* **Screen (72 ppi)**
- *Background:* **Transparent**

Click OK.

2. Select the fish's body outline (titled **body** within the Layer called **fish**).

3. Choose Effect > Photoshop Effects > Effect Gallery. In the gallery window, choose Artistic, then Rough Pastels. See Figure 6–35. Enter the following settings (or try out some of your own):

- *Stroke Length:* **29**
- *Stroke Detail:* **4**
- *Texture:* **Canvas**
- *Scaling:* **90**
- *Relief:* **28**
- *Light Dir:* **Top Right**

Click OK to apply the effect.

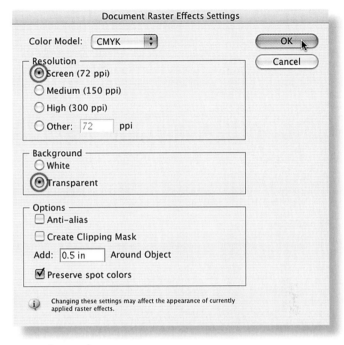

figure | 6–34 |

Choose Effect > Document Raster Effects Setting.

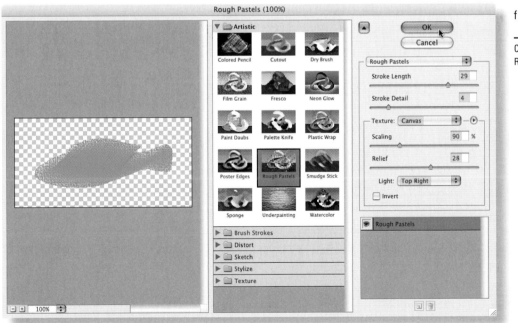

figure | 6–35 |

Choose settings in Rough Pastels.

Note: If you want to edit the effect, select the object with the effect, and in the Appearance panel double-click on the effect name (in this example, "Rough Pastels") to bring up its options box again.

Note: If you want to permanently apply the effect, select the object with the effect and choose Object > Rasterize. Once you have rasterized an object it is no longer editable in the Appearance panel.

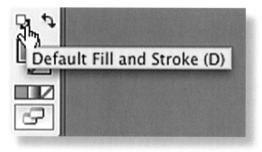

figure | 6–36 |

Change the Fill and Stroke to the default colors.

Applying a Scatter Brush

1. Choose View > Actual Size to see the whole document.

2. Choose Select > Deselect to deselect any objects in the document.

3. Set the Fill and Stroke colors to their defaults. See Figure 6–36.

4. From the menu bar, choose Window > Brush Libraries > Decorative_Scatter.

5. Select the Bubbles scatter brush (second in second row).

6. Double-click on the Paintbrush tool in the toolbox to bring up its preferences. In the Options, be sure the following are deselected:

- Fill new brush strokes
- Keep selected
- Edit Selected path

Click OK.

Note: By default, several of these options are selected. However, we like them deselected, especially Edit Selected path, which automatically edits the shape of your paths as you draw over them. On your own, try drawing with and without these options selected to see the varying results.

7. Highlight the **bubbles** layer in the Layers panel. With the Paintbrush tool, paint a single stroke of bubbles across the lower part of the document. See Figure 6–37.

8. With the Selection tool, click on the bubbles path to select it. Go to the Appearance panel. Double-click on the Stroke variation called Bubbles to open the Bubbles scatter brush options. See Figure 6–38.

figure | 6–37 |

Paint with the Bubbles scatter brush.

9. In the options window, set the following:

- *Size:* **500%** to **110%, Random**
- *Spacing:* **75%, Fixed**
- *Scatter:* **6%, Fixed**
- *Rotation:* **0%, Fixed**
- *Rotation relative to:* **Page**
- *Colorization:* **None**

Click OK to apply the changes.

10. Select the bubbles, and move them up so it appears as if the fish is swimming above the bubbles. Save your file.

Making Water and Waves

figure | 6–38 |

Modify the scatter brush options.

1. Choose View > Actual Size. Select the large, unfilled rectangle that surrounds the fish (it is the layer called **waves**).

2. Locate the **fish_colors** swatches you opened at the beginning of this lesson. (Window > Swatch Libraries > Other Library > chap6_lessons > assets > **fish_colors.ai**.)

3. Select the swatch called **water** (a blue gradient).

4. Adjust the linear direction of the gradient. Select the Gradient tool in the toolbox.

5. Position the cursor of the Gradient tool at the top part of the gradient-filled rectangle. Click and drag down to the bottom of the rectangle. The direction of the gradient is altered, with the dark blue color on the bottom and the light blue color on the top.

6. In the Opacity setting of the Control panel or by choosing Window > Transparency, set the opacity of the gradient anywhere between 50% and 80%, depending on how clear or muddy you want the water to appear.

7. Select None for the stroke color of the gradient-filled rectangle.

8. Double-click the Paintbrush tool to open its preferences. Select the Fill new brush strokes option. Click OK.

9. Choose Window > Brush Libraries > Artistic_Watercolor.

10. Choose the Light Wash-Thick art brush (the first one in the row).

11. At the top of the water you just created, paint some foamy waves. See Figure 6–39.

12. Save your file.

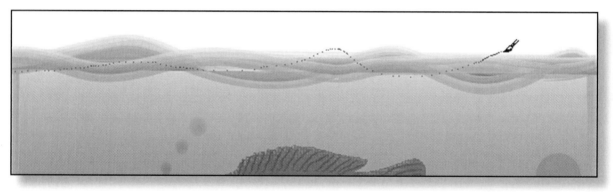

figure |6–39|

Paint waves using a watercolor art brush.

Lesson 2: Playing with Custom Brush Styles and Patterns

Creating custom brush styles and patterns in Illustrator requires a special lesson. In the first part of the lesson, you will learn how to design your own brushes and patterns and save them in libraries. Then, like a fashion designer, in the second part you apply and transform your custom patterns on clothing illustrations. Once you get the hang of designing and modifying brush styles and patterns, you will find them quite versatile in the quest to create more tactile looking imagery.

Setting Up the File

1. Open the file **chap6L2a.ai** in the **chap6_lessons** folder.

2. Choose Window > Workspace > [Basic].

3. Choose Shift-Tab to hide any open panels/docks.

4. Choose View > Fit In Window. This will be your working document for creating new brushes and patterns.

Creating a Custom Brush

1. Let us create a simple object—a smiley face—as your first custom brush stroke. In the first drawing area of the template called **My Custom Brush Styles**, draw a smiley face. See Figure 6–40 for an example. Keep your smiley face simple—you cannot use gradients, blends, other brush strokes, mesh objects, bitmap images, graphs, placed files, or masks in objects you intend to use in a brush. Also, art and pattern brushes cannot include type. However, there is a way around that, which you will learn about in the next chapter on type.

2. Select all parts of your drawing and choose Window > Brushes to open the Brushes panel. (If the panel is docked to other panels, click on its title tab to separate it from the group. Then close the other panels.)

3. Click on the arrow with three horizontal lines in the upper-right corner of the Brushes panel to open its options dropdown menu. Choose New Brush. (Or, alternatively, choose the New Brush icon at the bottom of the Brushes panel. See Figure 6–41.)

4. For brush type, select New Scatter Brush and click OK. In the Scatter Brush options box, enter a name for your brush. (Ours is called smiley_face.) You can determine your own settings for how the scatter brush will work, or try ours. See Figure 6–42. Once you have determined your settings, click OK. Notice your new brush is available in the Brushes panel. See Figure 6–43.

figure |6–40|

A smiley face.

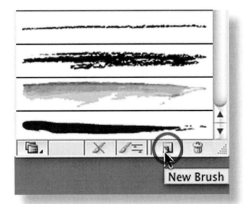

figure |6–41|

Select the New Brush icon.

figure |6–42|

Our settings for the scatter brush.

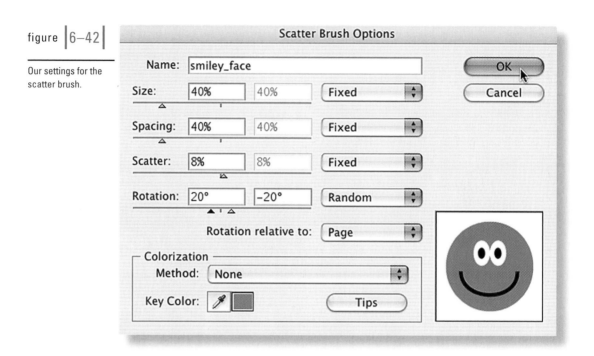

5. Choose Select > Deselect.

6. Select your new scatter brush in the Brushes panel.

7. Select the Paintbrush tool. Create some smiley-face paint strokes in the second drawing area of the template. See Figure 6–44.

> **Note:** To adjust the settings for your paintbrush, double-click on the Paintbrush tool to open its preferences. We turned off Fill new brush strokes in our example.

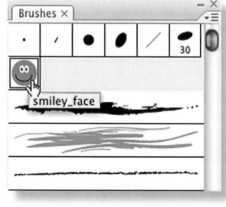

8. To modify your new smiley-face strokes, select a stroke and double-click on the **smiley_face** brush in the Brushes panel. The options for that brush pop up. Adjust the settings to your liking and click OK.

9. To save your brush stroke, choose Save Brush Library, from the Brushes panel drop-down options menu.

10. Give your new brush library a descriptive name and save it in your lessons folder.

11. Feel free to use the above steps to create other custom brushes to put in your custom brush library.

12. Save the document as **chap6L2a_yourname.ai.**

figure |6–43|

The new brush is made available in the Brushes panel.

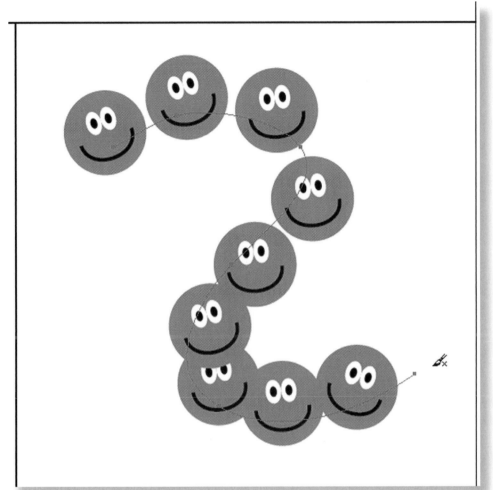

figure |6–44|

Adjust the settings for the paintbrush.

Defining a Regular Pattern

1. On the template, notice there are four boxes in the My Custom Pattern Fills area. These boxes are the required boundary areas for the patterns you create; they determine the bounding edges for where patterns begin to tile. A *bounding area* is a rectangle with the stroke and fill set to None. For visual purposes, the stroke and fill of the boxes are now set to the default colors. This will change when you go to save your patterns in later steps. Let us create a simple pattern in the first box. Select the Rectangle tool.

2. Draw a series of overlapping, colored rectangles within the box. See Figure 6–45 on the next page.

figure |6–45|

Create a pattern of overlapping rectangles.

My Custom Pattern Fills

Note: To align the rectangles perfectly, select all the rectangles, choose Window > Align, and in the Align panel select Horizontal Align Center and Vertical Align Center. See Figure 6–46.

figure |6–46|

Align the rectangles using the Align panel.

3. Select all the parts of your pattern. From the menu bar, choose Edit > Define Pattern. Name the pattern **rectangles1**, and click OK. See Figure 6–47. Open the Swatches panel to see your new pattern in the panel window. Feel free to test your new pattern. Create a new object and apply your pattern to it. We will also apply these patterns in the next part of the lesson.

4. Save your file.

Creating an Irregular Pattern

1. Creating an irregular pattern takes finesse. Select the Ellipse tool (hidden under the Rectangle tool in the toolbox) and draw a colorful circle that overlaps the top part of the second bounding box in the template. See Figure 6–48.

2. Choose View > Snap to Point (if not already selected).

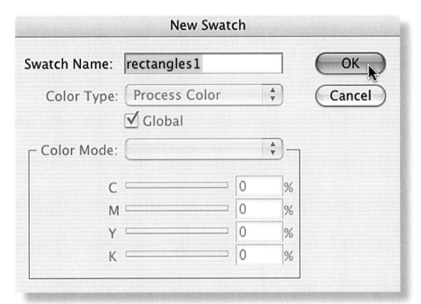

figure |6–47|

Define the pattern.

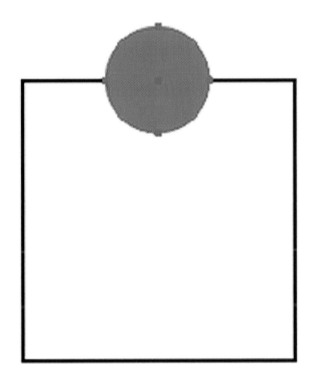

figure |6–48|

Start the creation of an irregular
pattern.

3. Select both the circle object and the bounding box.

4. Drag the rectangle down then press Option-Shift (Mac) or Alt-Shift (Windows) to create a copy and constrain the move. When the top of the duplicate rectangle overlaps the bottom of the first rectangle, release the mouse button, then release the keys. See Figure 6–49.

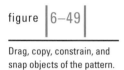

figure 6–49

Drag, copy, constrain, and
snap objects of the pattern.

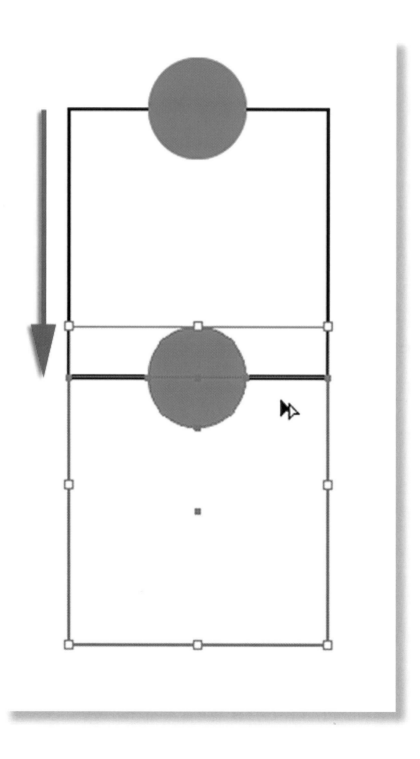

Note: Do not worry if you find it challenging to drag, copy, constrain, and snap objects all in one fell swoop. Usually we have to Edit > Undo a few times before we get it just right.

5. Click outside the rectangle to deselect it.

6. Select the bottom rectangle (not the duplicate circle) and delete it.

7. Create another set of colorful circles on the left side of the bounding box.

8. Select these side circles and the bounding box (but not the top and bottom circles) and follow the technique in Step 4 to drag, copy, constrain, and snap the objects to the right side of the bounding box. See Figure 6–50.

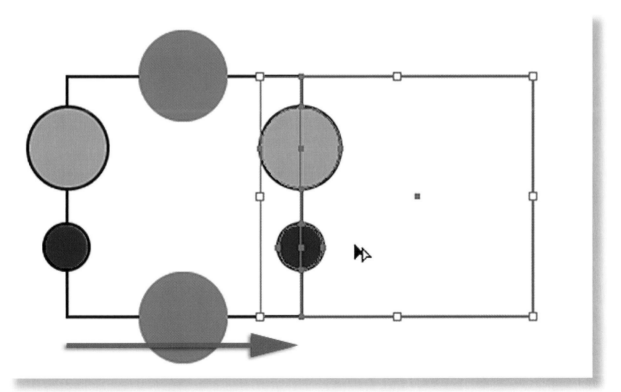

figure | 6–50 |

Finish the side portions of the pattern.

9. Click outside the rectangle to deselect all or choose Select > Deselect.

10. Select the right side rectangle (not the duplicated circles) and delete it.

11. Draw a couple more circles in the center of the rectangle area. Your final pattern will look something like Figure 6–51.

figure | 6–51 |

An example of the final pattern.

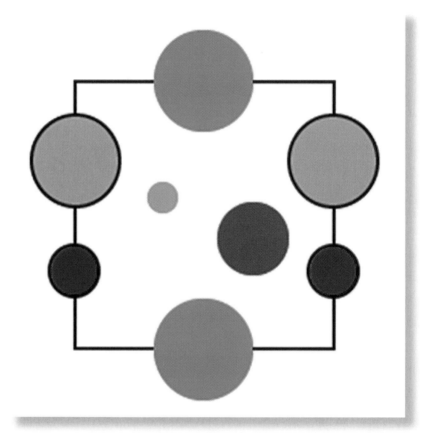

12. Select the bounding rectangle. Choose None for both its fill and stroke. This is a required step to get the pattern to work; Illustrator can only define a pattern when there is an invisible rectangle as the bottom-most shape in the design.

13. Select all the parts of the new pattern, including the now invisible bounding area (see Figure 6–52), and choose Edit > Define Pattern. Name it **polka_dots** and click OK. The new pattern appears in the Swatches panel.

14. Save your file.

15. Create two more patterns in the other bounding boxes provided. Define them in the Swatches panel.

16. Once you have all your patterns created and defined in the Swatches panel, choose Save Swatch Library as IA from the Swatches panel drop-down menu.

17. Name your new Swatch Library **my_patterns.ai** and save it in your lessons folder.

18. Close this file.

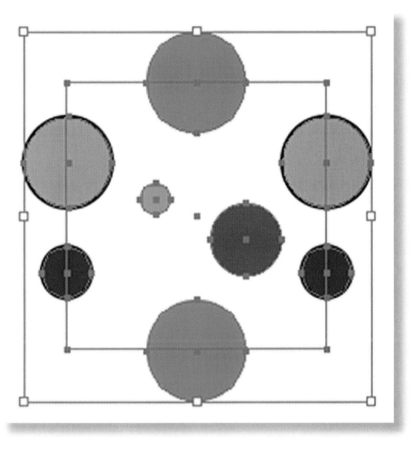

figure |6–52|

Applying and Transforming Patterns

1. Open **chap6L2b.ai** in the folder **chap6_lessons**.

2. Choose View > Fit In Window to see the clothing illustrations.

3. Choose Shift-Tab to hide unneeded panels.

4. Choose Window > Swatch Libraries > Other Library (at the end of the list). Browse for and open the custom library you created in the last section called **my_patterns.ai.** (Alternatively, you can find our version in the folder **chap6_lessons/assets**.)

5. Select one of the lapels of the tuxedo illustration. Then select one of your patterns in your custom library to apply it to the lapel. See Figure 6–53.

6. Let us transform this pattern; scale the pattern smaller. Select the Scale tool in the toolbox. See Figure 6–54.

figure | 6–53 |

Apply the polka dot
pattern.

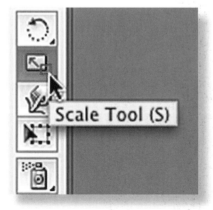

Scale Tool (S)

figure | 6–54 |

Select the Scale tool in the toolbox.

7. To scale only the pattern and not the selected object, hold down
the tilde key (~), place your cursor over the pattern, and drag your
cursor down and/or across to scale the pattern. A yellow bounding
box appears as you scale in this mode. To keep the pattern in proportion, hold down Shift as you drag diagonally. See Figure 6–55.

> **Note:** You can also use the Transform panel to transform a
> pattern. Choose Window > Transform. From the Transform
> panel drop-down menu, select Transform Pattern Only. Enter
> new values for the selected pattern in the W and H fields. Click
> the chain icon if you want to scale your pattern in proportion.
> If you choose this option, you must remember to change the
> settings back when you choose to transform only the object
> and not the pattern with the same object. If you select another
> object, it changes back to "both."

8. Select other parts of the tuxedo and sports jacket, and practice applying and transforming patterns.

> **Note:** To copy modified patterns to various parts of the clothing (such as from one sleeve to the other), select the object without the pattern, and with the Eyedropper tool take a sample of the modified pattern you want to copy. Or, Shift-click all the clothing parts you want to apply a pattern to and apply and transform them as a selected group.

9. Save this file in your lessons folder. See Figure 6–56 for an example of the completed lesson.

figure | 6–55 |

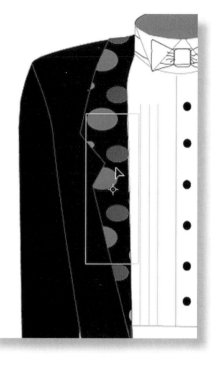

Adjust the scaling of just the pattern.

figure | 6–56 |

An example of the completed lesson.

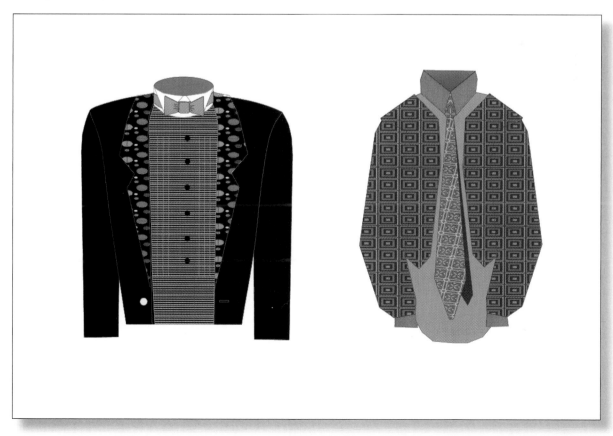

SUMMARY

Let us guess. After this chapter you are hooked on painting with Illustrator—so many brushes, patterns, and effects to fool around with, so little time and digital screen space. As you learned with every stroke and fill, your drawing can suddenly come to life with variations on value and texture. These variations can be modified again and again with the Appearance panel, and used over and over in custom libraries.

in review

1. Define *value* in drawing and painting.

2. Define *texture* in drawing and painting.

3. What are *caps* and *joins*?

4. What are the four brush types and their characteristics?

5. What is the main difference between an effect and a filter in Illustrator?

6. How can the Appearance panel enhance your workflow?

7. What are the steps to edit brush styles applied to a particular stroke?

8. What is *opacity*?

9. What does the Document Raster Effects Settings do under Effects in the menu bar?

10. What is so important about a bounding box when creating custom fill patterns? How do you make a bounding box?

exploring on your own

1. Access the Help > Illustrator Help menu option. Under Contents, read the section called "Painting."

2. As you explore the world of brushes, you may wish to add additional brushes to your toolset. One great location for brushes is the Adobe Exchange (*http://www.adobe.com/cfusion/ exchange/index.cfm*). In the Adobe Exchange, navigate to the Illustrator Exchange and choose Brushes from the categories menu. Here you will find a variety of brushes to choose from. Note: You may be required to create and/or login to the Adobe site to download the brushes.

Once the files have been downloaded from the Illustrator Exchange, access your new brushes by choosing Window > Brush Libraries > Other Library and locate your downloaded brush files. Now, you have more fuel for your creative fire!

3. Practice applying value and texture variations on Annesa's flower illustration. Open **chap6_ lessons/samples/flower.ai.** Or make your own flower image, starting with a flat colored version, then adding value and texture to the strokes and fills. An example of Annesa's original, digitized flower can be viewed on the first page of this chapter.

4. Complete the Runway Pattern Project. Similar to Lesson 2, develop your own patterned blouse, shirt, coat, dress, pants, or a whole outfit that can be complemented with a patterned accessory, such as a tie, ascot, scarf, sash, belt, or purse.

    First, draw your clothing fashions using the Pen tool with a basic black stroke color and no fills. Next, using the techniques in this chapter, design a variety of patterns (geometric, regular, irregular for both brushes and fills). Save them in a custom library (brushes in a Brush Library, fills in a Swatch Library). Then apply your patterns and transform, if necessary, on your fashion drawings.

ADVENTURES IN DESIGN

going live

Illustrator CS3 has two features worthy of an Adventure in Design experience—Live Paint and Live Trace. Live Paint simulates a more natural, intuitive way to create colored drawings while allowing the flexibility inherent in Illustrator's painting tools. When Live Paint is applied to selected areas of a drawn object, the faces and edges comprising the object can be selected with the Live Paint Bucket or Live Paint Selection tool and be quickly updated and easily edited. When you move or adjust a path's shape (with the Selection or Direction Selection tools), the paint attributes previously applied are automatically reapplied to the new regions formed by the edited paths. Live Trace automatically converts rasterized images, such as photographs, into detailed vector graphics for editing, resizing, and coloration. For example, instead of the painstaking task of retracing a bitmapped logo image by hand to produce a resolution-independent, editable vector version, the Live Trace tool can do it for you.

Live Paint and Live Trace can work well together in your Illustrator painting projects, as you will explore here.

PRACTICE PROJECT EXAMPLE

The Live Paint and Live Trace features can take a little getting used to. So before you try them on your own, let us introduce an example of how they might be used.

Live Paint works well when you have a drawing with many contiguous areas you want to color and/or modify, like patches on a crazy quilt, for example. See Figure A–1.

Begin by selecting a collection of paths. Click on the paths with the Live Paint Bucket (see Figure A–2), or choose Object > Live Paint > Make.

figure A–1   Example of a crazy quilt.

figure A–2 The Live Paint Bucket and the Live Paint Selection tool in the toolbox.

In Live Paint mode, the edges and faces are editable. Use the Live Paint Selection tool (below the Live Paint Bucket in the toolbox) to select groups of faces or edges to apply swatch colors, patterns, and graphic styles to the areas or remove those areas. Edit the anchor points with the Direct Selection tool, as you do for any point in an Illustrator drawing. You can also add and subtract points using the Add or Subtract Anchor Point tools. What makes this so unique (this is the "live" part) is that when you move an anchor point, the paint attributes applied to that area automatically readjust for the new region. See Figure A–3.

Once the features of Live Paint have been used, you select the live paint object and choose Object > Live Paint > Expand from the menu bar. The object returns to its original state, preserving the live paint modifications made to it, but removing the option to intuitively edit faces and edges on the drawing. To go back to Live Paint, choose Object > Live Paint > Make from the menu bar.

On the crazy quilt example, further modifications were made to paths and shapes using the Live Trace tool. To make detailed adjustments to the patterns applied to some of the quilt's patches, the object was selected and then rasterized (Object > Rasterize). Keep in mind that Live Trace's job is to make vectored outlines from bitmapped (rasterized) images based on the settings you make in the Live Trace Options. The Live Trace options are accessed

figure A–3 Adjusting points, edges, or faces on the Live Paint object automatically updates the paint attributes assigned to the adjusted area.

from Objects > Live Trace > Tracing Options or from the Control panel of the selected object. See Figure A–4.

There are also many presets for various trace effects that you might want to achieve, such as a Hand Drawn Sketch or Inked Drawing. See Figure A–5. Once traced, the object is composed of anchor points and paths. Choose the Expand option in the Control panel to make the points and paths editable, and to allow the use of Illustrator's many vector manipulation tools. See Figure A–6.

YOUR TURN

Now it is your turn to create a crazy quilt—digital style—and practice the Live Paint and Live Trace features.

continued

ADVENTURES IN DESIGN

continued

1. Create a new file in Illustrator.

2. Draw a large, filled rectangle shape as your quilt area.

3. With the Line tool, divide the rectangle into patch areas. See Figure A–7.

4. Select the quilt and convert to Live Paint. Click inside the quilt with the Live Paint Bucket or choose Object > Live Paint > Make.

5. Open the swatches panel. (Show all swatches, including patterns and gradients.)

6. Select patch areas of the quilt with the Live Paint Selection tool and apply the swatches. You can also select edge areas (stroke lines) and apply stroke attributes to those areas.

7. Edit the vector lines and points with the Direct Selection tool, or add and subtract points with the Add or Subtract Anchor Point tools. With each edit, notice how the paint attributes are automatically readjusted to match the modified region.

8. Select and delete any edges or faces you do not want.

9. Select the quilt and expand it to release the Live Paint mode.

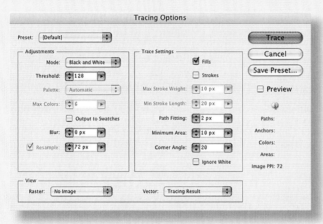

figure A–4
Adjust Live Trace Tracing Options for optimal performance.

figure A–5
Choose a tracing preset for a quick trace effect.

10. Optional: Choose Object > Rasterize and apply Live Trace options to the quilt. Alternatively, explore Live Trace using a placed photograph of your choosing.

Things to Consider

Working with Live Paint and Live Trace can be computer-memory intensive. It takes significant effort to calculate the readjustment of edited paint attributes and/or the conversion of an image from pixels to points and lines. With this in mind, be sure to save your work often and avoid overtaxing the Preview mode in the Live Trace options, especially if you notice the computer performance is slowing down. Also, with Live Trace, the more detailed the photo or image being converted, the longer the conversion process will take. If necessary, in the Tracing Options, lower the amount of colors being calculated (threshold), or increase the minimum area, path fitting, and corner angle areas that are being sampled.

figure A–6 Left image: Rasterized object. Middle image: Live Trace applied, converts areas (based on trace settings) to vectors. Right image: Object is expanded and modifications are made using Illustrator's vector manipulation tools.

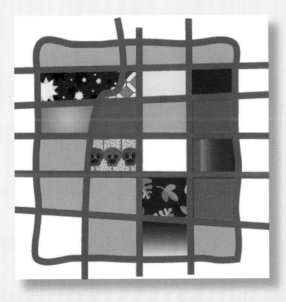

figure A–7 With the Line tool, divide the image into patch areas.

Explorer pages

REGGIE GILBERT

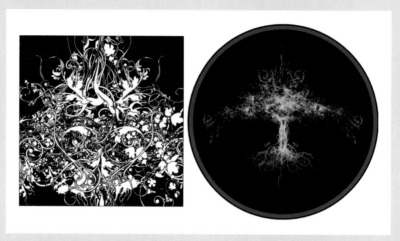

Illustration by Reggie Gilbert, showing close-up line and full-color versions.

About Reggie Gilbert

Reggie Gilbert spent most of his teen years in Los Angeles skateboarding and wrecking shop on trains and dark alleyways, so art was always something he was thinking about—paint on his shoes and screen print on the fat laces—some people thought he was a kook at the time for that ... now people are getting rich off it.

During the healing process after breaking his leg in a snowboarding stint, he learned Illustrator. Every day he sat and scanned in doodles and cleaned them up in Illustrator since he could not move around much. After a few months of not taking his new Illustrator skills too seriously, a local audio cables manufacturer caught wind that he was drawing exclusively vector images and asked if he could draw some technical illustrations for the company. "Sure," he said, and his professional illustration career started.

What are Reggie's predictions for the future? Cars are going to be belching out water instead of carbon, he is going to be killing it (illustrating) for several more years. Then his computer is going to melt down and—due to the fact he never backs up—he will lose everything he has ever done. He will then move to Costa Rica or Ecuador to surf and chill in a hammock, never to be heard from or use the Pen tool again.

Enjoy Reggie's work and his other exciting projects at TechVector, freestyle illustration and design at *http://www. techvector.com/*.

Illustration representing Reggie Gilbert's signature, freestyle illustration. Compliments of Reggie Gilbert.

Illustration of a spray can from sketch to 3D rendering using only Illustrator. Compliments of Reggie Gilbert.

Botanical vector set, for purchase, among others, at mighty TechVector (*http://www.techvector.com/*) and YouWorkForThem (*http://www.youworkforthem.com/*).

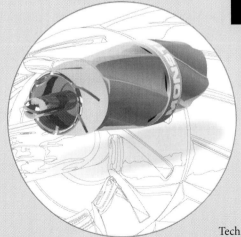

" *As an artist, don't ever lose sight of how lucky you are to be able to do art and make money from it. I've done it all … dug ditches, flipped burgers, so I recognize how fortunate I am with what I'm doing.*"

 Learn more about this artist via podcast at *http://www.designexploration.com/podcasts*.

Technical illustration by Reggie Gilbert.

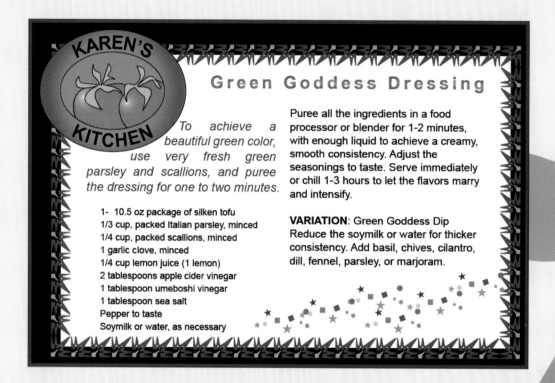

Green Goddess Dressing

To achieve a beautiful green color, use very fresh green parsley and scallions, and puree the dressing for one to two minutes.

1- 10.5 oz package of silken tofu
1/3 cup, packed Italian parsley, minced
1/4 cup, packed scallions, minced
1 garlic clove, minced
1/4 cup lemon juice (1 lemon)
2 tablespoons apple cider vinegar
1 tablespoon umeboshi vinegar
1 tablespoon sea salt
Pepper to taste
Soymilk or water, as necessary

Puree all the ingredients in a food processor or blender for 1-2 minutes, with enough liquid to achieve a creamy, smooth consistency. Adjust the seasonings to taste. Serve immediately or chill 1-3 hours to let the flavors marry and intensify.

VARIATION: Green Goddess Dip
Reduce the soymilk or water for thicker consistency. Add basil, chives, cilantro, dill, fennel, parsley, or marjoram.

| working with type |

charting your course

For the novice graphic designer, selecting fonts and working with type are often neglected—an afterthought to the overall image or layout. But type can become a design in itself and provides a vital role in communicating your illustrative message from business cards, to logos, to party invitations. The skill and talent of designing with type, or simply working with the appearance of printed characters, is called typography. This chapter is an opportunity to put on your typographer's hat, introducing you to the methods for creating, formatting, exporting, and importing type in Illustrator. Also provided are basic design techniques for making appealing and readable type layouts, turning you into a type guru or font aficionado in no time.

goals

In this chapter you will:

- **Practice the three methods of creating type in Illustrator—type at a point, type in an area, type along a path**

- **Discover the quirks of fonts, font families, and font formats**

- **Format type with ease**

- **Get an overview of what to know when importing, exporting, installing, and embedding fonts**

- **Learn basic design techniques when choosing and working with fonts and type layouts**

- **Become familiar with typographic terms**

WORKING WITH TYPE

CREATING TYPE IN ILLUSTRATOR

There are three methods for creating type in Illustrator:

- Type at a point
- Type in an area
- Type on a path

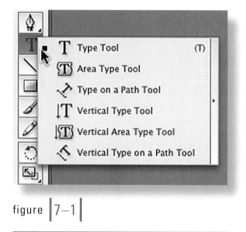

figure |7–1|

The Type tool and its expanded options.

Typing at a Point

Not unlike typing in any basic word processing program, to type at a point you click in a document with the Type tool and start typing. The Type tool, located on the toolbar, has a big T on it (no chance of missing that!). When you expand the tool, you get several more tools, which we will investigate soon enough. In general, the first three tools listed create horizontal type, while the last three create vertical type. See Figure 7–1 and Figure 7–2.

To type at a point, follow these steps:

1. Create a new document in Illustrator.

2. Select the Type tool in the toolbox. The cursor changes to what is called an I-beam—this is your starting mark. The small horizontal line toward the bottom of the I-beam determines where the text rests, called the baseline.

3. Click anywhere on the document and start typing. See Figure 7–3.

4. Hit Return or Enter to start a new line. To insert a letter, word, or line within the existing text block, click between any two letters and start typing.

Horizontal Text

T
e
x
t

V
e
r
t
i
c
a
l

figure |7–2|

An example of horizontal and vertical text.

> ▶ **Don't Go There!**
>
> Do not click on an existing object with the Type tool. Otherwise that object converts to area type or assumes you want to type along its path.
>
> To be on the safe side, hide or lock any objects that might get in your way.

Click with the I-beam and start typing.
To type a new line you hit Return or Enter.
Notice the little blinking cursor, indicating
where you are located in the text line.

figure | 7–3 |

Some text typed at a point.
Notice the I-beam at the end
of the paragraph.

5. To select the block of text, use the Selection tool, or, alternatively, Command-click (Mac) or Ctrl-click (Windows) the text.

> **Note:** When you choose View > Show Bounding Box and select the text block, transform handles appear around it. This makes it easy to move, scale, and rotate text. See Figure 7–4.

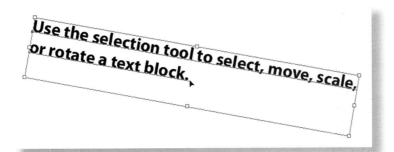

figure | 7–4 |

Transform a text block using
the Bounding Box.

6. There are several methods to select and modify individual characters, words, sentences, or paragraphs. Find which of the following methods that works best for you:

- If the text block or path is already selected, just double-click on the text to switch to the Type tool and get the I-beam cursor. With the I-beam, click in front of and then drag over the text you want to modify.

- Select the Type tool in the toolbox and with the I-beam, click in front of and then drag over the text you want to modify.

- If you want to select a single word, place the I-beam anywhere within the word and then double-click. If you are quick with your clicks, place the I-beam, then click three times to select a whole line.

Typing in an Area

There are two ways to type in a defined area. To define a rectangular area, click and drag with the Type tool or Vertical Type tool (see Figure 7–5), and then start typing within the area. To type within another kind of shape, click with the Type tool, Vertical Type tool, Area Type tool, or Vertical Area Type tool on any object's path, which converts it to a container for the text. See Figure 7–6.

If you type more than can fit in the defined area, a little red box with a plus sign shows up at the bottom of the text block, indicating the text is flowing outside of the space. See Figure 7–7. To fix this problem, you can either use a smaller point size for the font (see the section "Formatting Type"), or scale the text area larger. To scale, choose View > Show Bounding Box, then select the area and adjust the transform handles. When you scale a defined area, the area size changes but the size, or point size, of the text does not. This is different than scaling text at a point, which distorts the text. See Figure 7–8 and Figure 7–9.

There is also an Area Type Options box (see Figure 7–10), which includes options to numerically change the width and height of a text area, create rows and columns, and adjust offset and text flow. To get to this box, select some area type on the document, and either choose Type > Area Type Options from the menu bar or double-click the Type tool in the toolbox.

figure | 7–5 |

Drag with the Type tool to define an area.

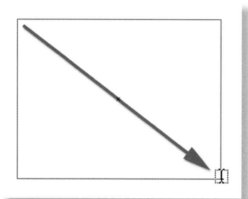

figure | 7–6 |

Create a text container out of an object.

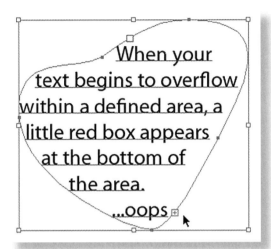

figure |7–7|

The little box with the plus sign in the corner of the text block indicates an overflow of text.

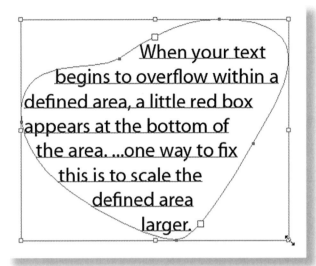

figure |7–8|

You can scale a text block larger to include overflow text.

figure |7–9|

Scaling text at a point distorts the text.

figure |7–10|

The Area Type Options box.

Using area type, you can also thread (or flow) type from one object to the next. On any selected type area there are two little boxes, called ports, on each side. To attach two blocks of text together, first click on the end port of one text block. Then click on the path of the next block to initiate the thread. See Figure 7–11 and Figure 7–12. If you want to release threaded text, select one of the linked boxes, and choose Type > Threaded Text > Release Selection or Remove Threading.

Typing on a Path

In Illustrator you can also create text that flows along an open or closed path. To do this, use the Type tool, Type on a Path tool, Vertical Type tool, or Vertical Type on a Path tool, depending on your preference. Click on any defined path and start typing. See Figure 7–13.

figure | 7–11 |

Click on an end port of a text area to initiate the threaded text option.

You click on a little box, called a "port", on either end of a block of area text to initiate the threaded text option.

figure | 7–12 |

Click on the edge of another object to continue the text thread.

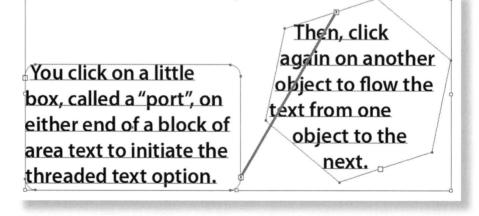

You click on a little box, called a "port", on either end of a block of area text to initiate the threaded text option.

Then, click again on another object to flow the text from one object to the next.

At some point you might need to move text along its path and adjust its orientation (i.e., bend text around an ellipse). To move text along a path, first select the path with the Selection tool. A bracket appears at the beginning, middle, and end of the path. Place your cursor over the middle bracket until a little icon that looks like an upside-down T appears. Click and drag on the middle bracket to move the path. See Figure 7–14 and Figure 7–15. The brackets on each end of the type line adjust the distance between the beginning and end of the typed line. See Figure 7–16 and Figure 7–17. Be aware that moving the brackets at the start and end points into type will make it disappear. If this occurs, pull the brackets back out to reveal the hidden type.

> **Note:** As you adjust the path using the brackets, avoid clicking on the little boxes, or ports, at each end of the line. This initiates the threaded area type option discussed in the previous section.

Of course, there are more goodies to tinker with in the Type on a Path Options box. Select some type on a path and choose Type > Type on a Path > Type on a Path Options, or double-click the Type tool in the toolbox. See Figure 7–18. We highly recommend selecting Preview in this box and exploring the different options available.

figure |7–13|

Create horizontal and vertical text on a path.

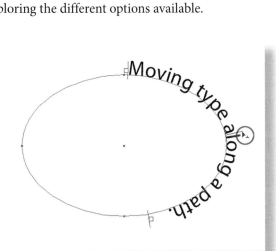

figure |7–14| and figure |7–15|

Select, then move, the middle bracket to adjust the text on a path.

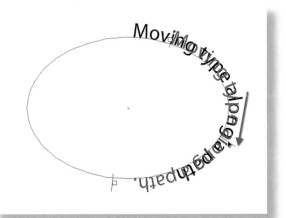

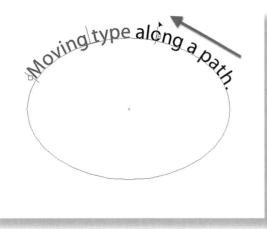

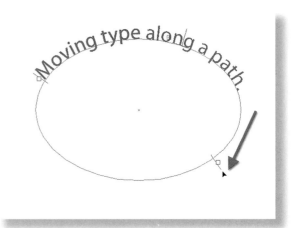

figure |7–16| and figure |7–17|

Select the end bracket and adjust the distance between the beginning and end of the text line.

figure |7–18|

The Type on a Path Options box.

Type on a Path Options

Effect:	Rainbow ⏶⏷	☐ Flip	(OK)
Align to Path:	Baseline ⏶⏷		(Cancel)
Spacing:	⏶⏷ 0 pt ⏷		☑ Preview

Type Tips

There are a couple miscellaneous things you should know about creating type. When we first learned how to create type in Illustrator, it seemed we could use either the Type tool or Area Type tool to create area type. Similarly, we could use either the Type tool or Type on a Path tool to create type on a path. Why have two tools for the same task? Well, we learned that the tool used depends on whether we are using an open or closed path. In the case of creating area type, we discovered that if the object to be used as the area is an open path, we needed to use the Area Type tool to define the bounding area. If we use the Type tool, it creates type on a path. In contrast, when creating type on a path, if the object to be used as the path is closed, we must use the Type on a Path tool. If we use the Type tool, it creates area type. Confused? See Figure 7–19 and Figure 7–20, or try the above scenario in Illustrator and you will understand what we mean.

figure | 7–19 |

If you use the Type tool on an open path, you get option #1; if you use the Area Type tool on the open path, you get option #2.

option #1   **option #2**

figure | 7–20 |

If you use the Type tool on a closed path, you get option #1; if you use the Type on a Path tool, you get option #2.

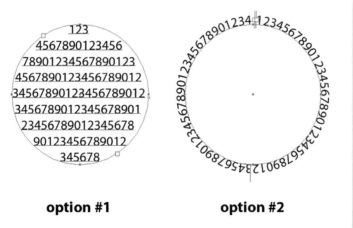

option #1   **option #2**

Another, somewhat odd, thing about creating type is that often (and usually inadvertently) empty type paths represented by an anchor point are created when you click the Type tool in the artwork area and then choose another tool. To clean up these stray type markings and containers, choose Object > Path > Clean Up and select the Empty Text Paths option. To delete all the anchor points in the file, choose Select > Object > Stray Points.

FORMATTING TYPE

You have probably formatted plenty of text in word processing programs—selected font styles and sizes, used the bold and underline options, copied, pasted, and justified paragraphs, and worked with letter and line spacing. These familiar formatting options are also available in Illustrator. (How convenient!)

To format specific characters, such as font style and size, leading, tracking, and kerning, choose Window > Type > Character to bring up the Character panel. To modify familiar paragraph options, such as paragraph justification and indentation, use the Paragraph panel, which is usually grouped with the Character panel. See Figure 7–21 and Figure 7–22. To access more options for both panels (by default they are hidden), click on the arrow with three horizontal lines in the upper-right corner of the panels and select Show Options. Additionally, most commonly used character and paragraph features can be found in the Control panel of any selected text object. Definitions for some of the formatting options, such as tracking, leading, and kerning, are provided in the section "Designing with Type."

Another kind of formatting that is somewhat specific to Illustrator is changing the appearance of type. You can change the basic fill color or stroke of type by selecting the text and changing the color, as you would any object, from the Control panel, Color panel or by double-clicking on the Fill or Stroke box in the toolbox. Using this same method, you can also change transparency, effects, and graphic styles. See Figure 7–23 and Figure 7–24.

figure | 7–21 |

The Character panel used to format type.

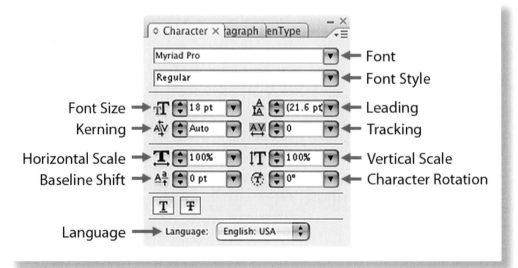

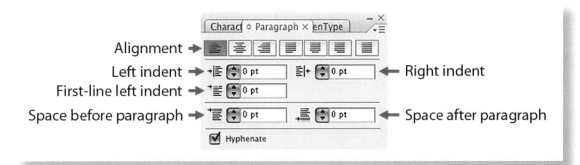

figure | 7–22 |

The Paragraph panel used to format type.

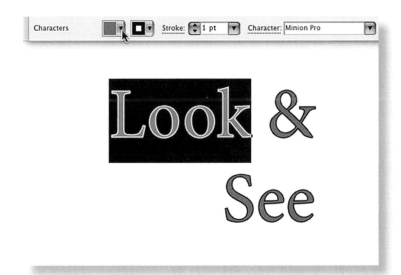

figure | 7–23 |

Select the text and change its fill and stroke color in the Control panel.

figure | 7–24 |

Play with graphic styles and transparency on text using the Effects menu and Transparency panel.

If you want to apply a gradient to some text, you must convert the text to outlines (the underlying path structure and shape of each letter) before assigning a gradient color to it. To do this, select the text path, choose Type > Create Outlines, and then apply the gradient blend. See Figure 7–25. Creating outlines is a necessary step if you want to manipulate the individual anchor points of a letterform, or need to use text in a custom-made art or pattern brush. However, be aware that once you have converted type to outlines, character and paragraph options for the type are no longer available. You will not be able to fix typos either, so make sure you proofread the text before converting to outlines. More on the characteristics of fonts and font formats in the next section.

THE STORY OF FONTS

Fonts are funky. If you have worked with type on a computer, you have experienced the quirks (or, rather, the frustration) of fonts. Suppose, for example, you find the perfect font, "Groovalicious," and use it extensively in a document. You send the document to a friend who tries to open it on his or her computer. However, a warning comes up indicating "Groovalicious" is nowhere to be found.

figure |7–25|

The top line indicates text when normally selected. Below is the text selected after converting it to outlines, then applying a gradient. Notice that the points that comprise the path of each letter shape are visible and editable using the Direct Selection tool.

Furthermore, unless otherwise specified, the missing font will be substituted with Times New Roman (or something like that), and . . . so much for design. This predicament occurs when one computer has a font installed that the other does not. To avoid this, designers often send their font files along with their documents, or embed (save) the fonts within the document.

Before we continue with this story about fonts, we should clarify what a font, or typeface, is. The dictionary supplied in an MS Word program defines fonts as follows: "A full set of printing type or of printed or screen characters of the same design and size." Fonts often come in font families—a group of similarly designed font sets. For a particular font within a font family, you can choose a font style, such as bold, italic, or medium. In Illustrator, you can select fonts using the Character panel (Window > Type > Character) or the Type menu (Type > Font). Each font family has a family name, usually derived from the artist who first created the font design. For example, Figure 7–26 shows some of the Helvetica font family.

figure |7–26|

Part of the Helvetica
font family.

Helvetica Regular
Helvetica Bold
Helvetica Neue Light Italic
Helvetica Neue Condensed Black

Font Copyright

Unless you use license-free fonts (freeware), fonts and font families are protected by copyright law. Using someone else's font requires permission, just as when you use someone else's image or photograph. Even though you have the ability in Illustrator to embed (save a font's outlines for viewing in other applications), select, and format any font installed in your computer system's font folder, that does not necessarily mean you have the right to showcase it in your Illustrator creations, especially if your work is designed for commercial purposes. You are reminded of this fact when you go to save your document and a font embedding notification pops up. See Figure 7–27. Play it safe, and contact the creator of the font to determine whether a given font can legally be embedded and used in your document. You can often find the font creator's information in the Read Me files or in documentation that accompanies the font before installation. You can also select the font's filename, and Ctrl-click > Get Info (Mac), or right-click > Properties (Windows) for information on that particular font.

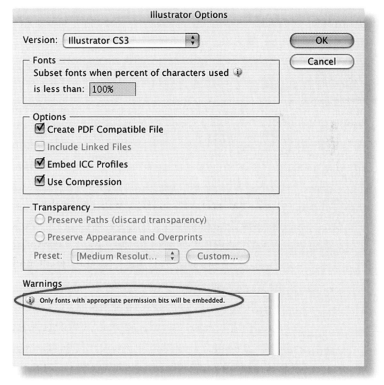

figure |7–27|

Note: Your font files are located in the \user\library\fonts folder (Mac) or the \Windows\Fonts folder (PC).

Depending on their license agreements, fonts used in your artwork might prompt the font embedding notification when you go to save the document.

Font Formats

Just as there are different ways in which a device, such as a computer or printer, renders a digital image (i.e., as bitmapped pixels or vectored outlines), so it is for fonts. A font's format, generally speaking, provides the instructions for how a digitized font is either printed on paper, presented on screen, or both. As is the nature of technology, font formats have evolved quickly over time, and it behooves us to have some understanding of the current font technologies.

Interestingly, in the 1980s it was Adobe Systems that made the most significant advancements in how computers handle text. It started out with PostScript, a page description language that stores objects or glyphs (character shapes on a page or screen) not as fixed resolution bitmaps, but as programmatically defined outlines or shapes. The nice thing about PostScript-derived glyphs is that they can be reliably recreated at the resolution of whatever PostScript-compatible device you use for output. In other words, it does not matter if you choose 12-point type or 72-point type; the document will always look crisp and clean when you print it.

> **Note:** Adobe PostScript® is still the worldwide printing and imaging standard. If you save a document in Adobe's Portable Document Format (PDF), you are using a form of the PostScript language.

To some extent, each of the three most common font formats uses Postscript. These are Type 1, TrueType, and OpenType.

- *Type 1:* A resolution-independent digital font type that can translate a font from the screen to a high-quality font in print. Adobe is the original designer and manufacturer of Type 1 and maintains its standards. However, other companies have designed and released their fonts using the Type 1 format. Type 1 fonts are commonly used by graphic designers whose work specifically goes to print.
- *TrueType:* The standard for digital type fonts. It was first developed by Apple Computer Corporation and subsequently licensed to Microsoft Corporation. Each company has made independent extensions to this format, some of which can be used on either or both Windows and Macintosh operating systems. Within a single font format, TrueType has the ability to translate fonts for print and screen, avoiding the bitmapped look when size and resolution quality are changed. TrueType fonts are great for graphic designers who create work for both print and screen (i.e., CD-ROM and Web).
- *OpenType:* This type was developed jointly by Adobe and Microsoft. It is currently the most sophisticated form of font technology. It is an extension of the TrueType font.

OpenType fonts have several benefits over previous font types. One, they are cross-platform compatible, meaning you can use a single font file for both Macintosh and Windows computers—no more font substitution issues. Also, they can support expanded character sets and languages, because they contain more variations of glyphs in a single font set, including nonstandard ones like old-style figures and fractions.

OpenType, literally, is opening new doors for typographers, providing better control over type layout and design. Illustrator CS3 has the expanded ability to support OpenType layout features on OpenType formatted fonts. A single character in the OpenType format can have several glyph (shape and symbol) variations to broaden its linguistic and typographic options. For example, variations on the number "2" in the font Myriad Pro (an OpenType font) could be alternated as you see in Figure 7–28, using the OpenType options box (Window > Type > OpenType).

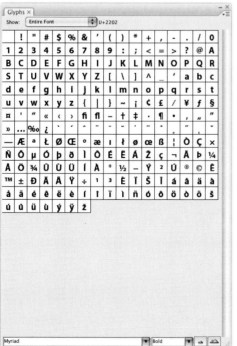

figure | 7–28 |

Example glyphs of the number "2" within the Myriad Pro OpenType font.

To view and choose glyphs for any currently selected font format, choose Type > Glyphs. For the glyphs available for the font Myriad Bold (a Type 1 formatted font) and Myriad Pro Bold (an OpenType formatted font), see Figure 7–29. The OpenType version has many more glyph variations.

figure | 7–29 |

Part of the glyphs list for Myriad Bold (Type 1) and Myriad Pro Bold (OpenType).

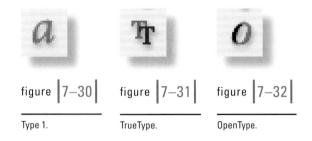

y

figure | 7–30 | figure | 7–31 | figure | 7–32 |

Type 1.   TrueType.   OpenType.

It is easy to identify a font's format, whether Type 1 (Figure 7–30), TrueType (Figure 7–31), or OpenType (Figure 7–32). When you go to select a font, choose Type > Font or Window > Type > Character. To the left of each font name you have installed on your computer is a small icon indicating the font type. See also Figure 7–33.

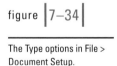

Ⓣ Bradley Hand ITC TT Bold
Ⓣ Brush Script MT Italic
O Brush Script Std Medium
a <Carta>   ○⊚△◇○
O Adobe Caslon Pro
Ⓣ Chalkboard
O Chaparral Pro
O CHARLEMAGNE STD BOLD
Ⓣ Cochin
Ⓣ Comic Sans MS

figure | 7–33 |

An example of part of the font list installed on Annesa's computer. Notice the icons next to the font names indicating the font's format.

Font Compatibility

As you encountered in the "Groovalicious" situation, fonts go a-missing when they are used in a document but are unavailable on a computer system. For easy identification, Illustrator automatically highlights missing fonts. You can then use the Find Font command (Type > Find Font) to replace the missing fonts with installed ones or identify the missing fonts so you can install them. You can also choose to highlight the substituted fonts or glyphs, as well as choose other global Type options under File > Document Setup. See Figure 7–34.

Another thing that needs mentioning, is the issue of legacy text. The term legacy in Illustrator refers

figure | 7–34 |

The Type options in File > Document Setup.

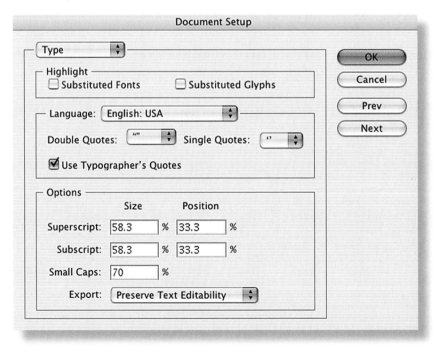

to earlier versions of an Illustrator file format. Thus, legacy text refers to text used in early versions of the program. Because Illustrator (since version CS2) has a more efficient way of dealing with text composition, called the Adobe Text Engine, legacy text must be updated before you can edit it. When you open an earlier version of an Illustrator file, a dialog box comes up asking if you would like to update any legacy text in the document. If you choose to update, slight variations in the text layout might occur; however, you can then edit the text. If you choose not to update, the legacy text will be preserved (indicated by an "X" in its bounding box when selected) and can be viewed, moved, and printed, but not edited.

Note: When an original font is not available, artists in the printing industry, for example, often will convert type to outlines before sending the file to someone else (see the earlier section "Formatting Type") or create PDFs (see Chapter 10) to help minimize the missing font problem.

Lesson: Recipe Card

In this lesson, you experience creating type and applying formatting options while constructing a graphically pleasing recipe card. Figure 7–35 is a visual reference of the completed file.

figure | 7–35 |

The completed Recipe Card lesson.

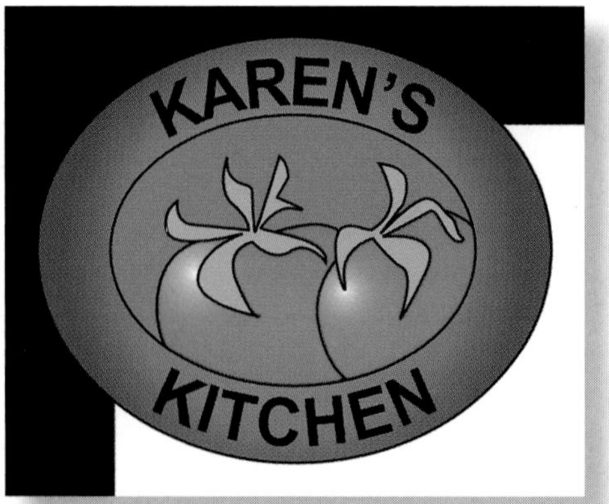

figure | 7–36 |

Karen's Kitchen logo is an example of type on a path.

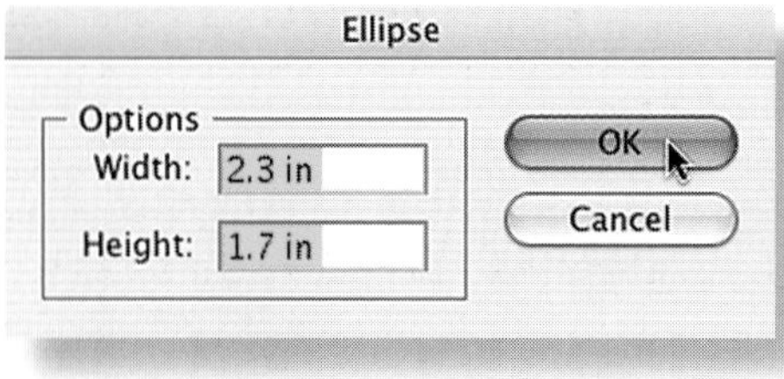

figure | 7–37 |

Specify an exact size for the ellipse.

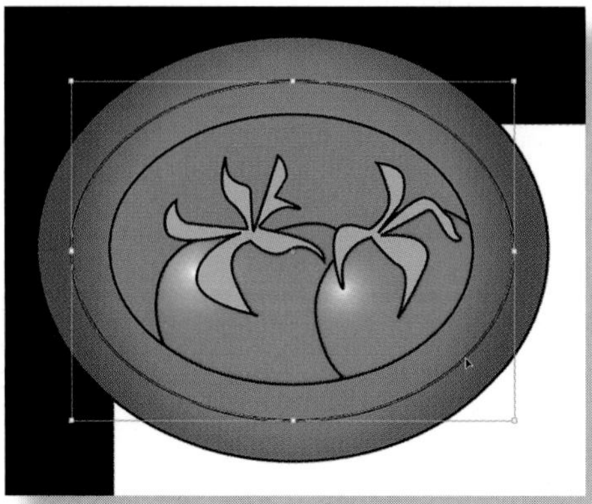

figure | 7–38 |

Fit the ellipse shape over the logo.

Setting Up the File

1. In Illustrator, open **chap7L1.ai** in the folder **chap7_lessons**.
2. Choose Window > Workspace > [Basic].
3. Choose Shift-Tab to hide any open panels/docks.
4. Choose View > Fit in Window.
5. Choose Window > Layers. Be sure the **type on path** layer is highlighted. Notice the other layers are locked (indicated by the lock icon to the left of the layer name), so you cannot accidentally select items in those layers.

Creating Type on a Path

1. Let us create some type on a path that looks like that shown in Figure 7–36. With the Zoom tool, zoom in on the tomato logo in the upper-left corner of the document.
2. Select the Ellipse tool in the toolbox. Click once over the logo to bring up the Ellipse tool options box. Type **2.3 in** for Width and **1.7 in** for Height. Click OK. See Figure 7–37. The ellipse shape will be created on the document.
3. Choose None for the fill color of the ellipse, then position the ellipse object so it fits over the tomato logo. See Figure 7–38. Remember that the ellipse object can be moved either by clicking and dragging directly on the outline or by using the up/down and left/right arrow keys.
4. Cut the ellipse shape into two sections: a top section to create one line of curved text and a bottom section for another line of curved text. First select your ellipse, then select the Scissors tool in the toolbox. See Figure 7–39.
5. Place the cursor over the anchor point on the left side of the ellipse shape and click to cut the path. Do the same on the anchor point on the right, breaking the shape into two halves. See Figure 7–40.

> **Note:** When you attempt to click over an anchor point to cut it with the Scissors tool, a warning box might come up as follows: "Please use the Scissors tool on a segment or an anchor point (but not an endpoint) of a path." This warning comes up when you have not directly clicked on a segment or anchor point on the selected path. Exit the warning box and try cutting the anchor point again.

figure |7–39|

The Scissors tool is used to cut paths.

figure |7–40|

Cut the ellipse in half using the Scissors tool.

6. Choose Window > Type > Character to open the Character options. For Font type and style, choose **Arial**, **Bold**. For font size, choose **24 pt**. See Figure 7–41.

> **Note:** If Arial Bold is unavailable, choose another font type to play with, such as Helvetica or Verdana.

7. Now you are ready to type some text on the defined paths. Select the Type on a Path tool in the toolbox. See Figure 7–42. Then click on the top line segment of the ellipse you just cut in half to convert the path into a text path. A blinking cursor will appear on the path line.

8. Type **KAREN'S**.

9. Adjust the alignment of the text. Select the Selection tool in the toolbox and select the text path. Click and drag on the middle bracket to the right or left until it is centered along the path. See Figure 7–43.

10. In the Control panel, click on the Align center icon next to the word *Paragraph* to center the text on the path. See Figure 7–44.

11. Choose Type > Type on a Path > Type on a Path Options. In the options box, choose Preview to view changes directly on the document. Take a moment to explore the Type on a Path Options. What does the 3D Ribbon Effect do? How about Align to Path, Descender, Spacing? Once explored, set the type to the following settings, then click OK to exit the options box:

- *Effect:* **Rainbow**
- *Align to Path:* **Center**
- *Spacing:* **0 pt**

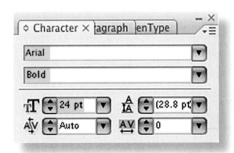

figure |7–41|

Format the type in the Character panel.

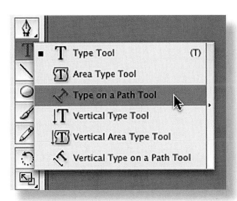

figure |7–42|

Select the Type on a Path tool.

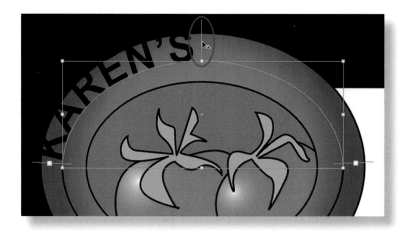

Center the text line on the path.

Choose the Align center option to center the text.

12. With the Type on a Path tool, click on the lower segment of the ellipse you cut in half.

13. Type **KITCHEN** along the path. Adjust the text alignment and type options of this lower segment the same way you did with the top segment of text. Refer to Figure 7–36 for an example of the final result.

> **Note:** You might need to use the Flip option in the Type on a Path Options box to fit the text upright on this lower path.

14. Save the document; name it **chap7L1_yourname.ai**.

Creating Type in an Area

1. Choose View > Actual Size to see the whole document.

2. Choose Window > Layers to open the Layers panel.

3. Lock the **type on path** layer. To do this, click on the blank box to the left of the layer's name and a lock icon will appear.

4. Unlock the **logo** layer. To do this, click on the lock icon to the left of the layer's name.

5. Select the **logo** layer. You are going to build a text block in this layer. The reason for doing this, rather than creating a new layer, is to prepare for a later step. Eventually you will wrap your text block around the logo image, and to do this you must have both objects on the same layer.

6. Select the Type tool in the toolbox.

7. Click and drag out a small text block in the center of the document. Do not worry about the exact size.

8. Choose Window > Transform to open the Transform options.

9. For width, type **7.153 in** (or 515 px), and for height, type **4.167 in** (or 300 px). Press Enter or Tab after each entry. Make sure the chain icon next to the width and height fields (used to constrain proportions) is off. See Figure 7–45.

10. Let us put some text in the text block. (Do not worry if it is off set.) Make sure a blinking cursor is indicated at the top of the text block. If not, choose the Type tool and click on the little white box in the upper-left corner of the text block to initiate the blinking cursor.

11. Choose File > Place from the menu bar. Look for **chap7_lessons/ assets** and select the **recipe.rtf** text file. Click Place, and leave the Microsoft Word options at their default. Click OK. The text should fill the defined area. See Figure 7–46.

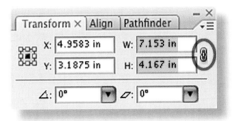

figure | 7–45 |

In the Transform panel, set the exact size of a text block.

> **Note:** RTF stands for Rich Text Format, a cross-compatible text format available in any popular word processing program. Illustrator will also import text in Microsoft Word formats (.doc) and plain text, ASCII, or .txt formats.

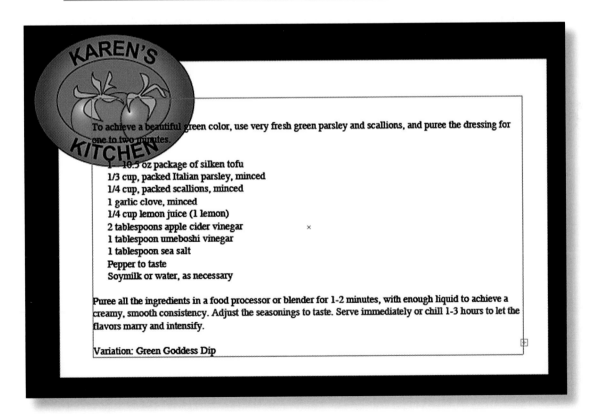

figure | 7–46 |

Imported text filling a defined area.

12. Select the text box with the Selection tool, then choose Type > Area Type Options. Enter **2** for Columns, Number, and click OK. See Figure 7–47.

figure |7–47|

Create two columns in the Area Type Options.

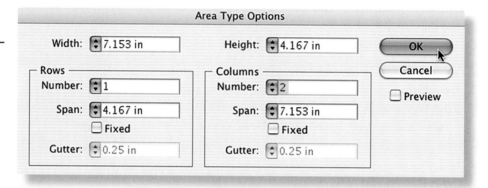

13. Position the text block in the center, lower part of the white space within the black border. See Figure 7–48. The text will overlap the logo image. You will fix this in the next exercise.

14. Save your file.

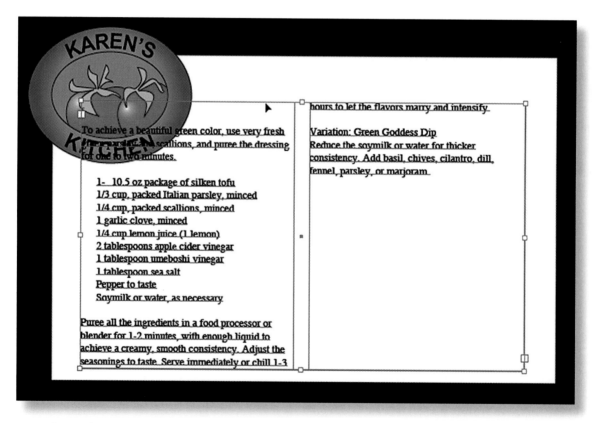

figure |7–48|

Position the text block.

Wrapping Text Around an Object

When wrapping text around an object, the text and object must be on the same layer. We anticipated this requirement in a previous step, so both the logo and the text block are located on the **logo** layer. In addition, the text block needs to be stacked below the objects you want it to wrap around. Let's fix this.

1. Open Window > Layers. Expand the **logo** layer. Select the sublayer with either no label or the words "To achieve a beautiful green color..." (this is the type you just placed), then click and drag it to the bottom of the list of logo sublayers. See Figure 7–49.

2. Select the logo image on the document or select the sublayer **Compound Shape** in the **logo** layer list.

3. Choose Object > Text Wrap > Make from the menu bar. Notice that the text now wraps around the logo. Choose Object > Text Wrap > Text Wrap Options and make Offset: **6 pts**. Click OK.

> **Note:** If the text does not wrap around the image, select the logo again, choose Object > Text Wrap > Release, then repeat steps 1 through 3. See Figure 7–50.

4. Save your file.

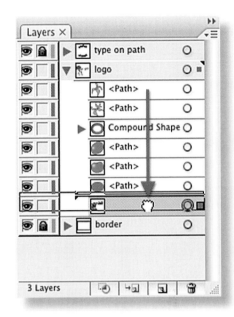

figure | 7–49 |

Move the text layer below the layers that make up the logo graphic.

figure | 7–50 |

The text block wraps around the edge of the logo graphic.

Formatting the Text

1. Select the two-column text block with the Selection tool. Then, with the Type tool, click in the text block and choose Select > All from the menu bar to select all of the recipe text.

2. In the Control panel or Character panel (Window > Type > Character), enter **Arial**, **Regular** for Font Type and Style and **12 pt** for Size.

> Note: You might be wondering why we are using such an unexciting (yet versatile and easily readable) font family such as Arial. It is mainly for compatibility purposes when working through this lesson. We are fairly certain that whether you are working on a Mac or PC, you will have the ever-so-common Arial font installed. If by chance you do not or prefer to use a different font for this lesson, that is perfectly legit. Just be aware that different font styles will vary in size and shape and might affect the text layout of this particular lesson. And you know what? That is OK. For now, it is all about exploring the tools.

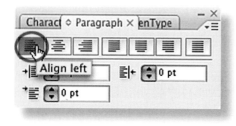

figure | 7–51 |

Align the text paragraph using the Paragraph panel.

3. Let us vary the different paragraphs of text in the text block. Select the text block. With the Type tool, highlight the first sentence of the text.

4. In the Control panel or the Character panel (Window > Type > Character), enter **Arial**, **Italic**, **15 pt**. In the Character panel, set the Kerning to **Auto** and Leading to **18**. Leave Tracking at 0.

5. Change the color of this selected sentence. In the Control panel, under the Fill option, click on any red colored swatch (We chose Crimson, a dark red), or create or select your own red from the Color panel or Color Picker.

6. In the Control panel, choose Window > Type > Paragraph. Make sure the first sentence is Align left. See Figure 7–51.

7. With the Type tool, highlight the list of ingredients—from 1–**10.5 oz. package of silken tofu** to **soymilk or water, as necessary**.

8. Open the Character panel, choose Window > Type > Character or click on the tab for the Character panel next to the Paragraph panel in the group. Enter **Arial**, **Regular**, **12 pt**. Set Kerning to **Auto**, and Leading to **16 pt**. Leave Tracking at 0.

9. Highlight the last section of the recipe (located in the second column). In the Character panel, enter **Arial**, **Regular**, **14 pt**. Set Kerning and Leading to **Auto**. Leave Tracking at 0.

10. Highlight the word *Variation*. In the Character panel, enter **Arial**, **Bold**. Open the Character options (arrow with three horizontal lines in the upper-right corner of the panel) and choose All Caps. See Figure 7–52.

11. Save your file.

figure | 7–52 |

Choose the All Caps option.

Adding a Headline

1. Choose Select > Deselect to deselect any items on the document.

2. Select the Type tool and click the I-beam to the right of the logo just above the two-column text block. Type in the recipe name: **Green Goddess Dressing**. See Figure 7–35.

3. Highlight the recipe name. In the Character panel, enter **Arial**, **Bold**, **22 pt**. Leave Kerning and Leading to Auto. Set Tracking to **200**. In the Character options (arrow with the three horizontal lines in the upper-right corner of the panel), click on All Caps to uncheck the option.

4. Select the recipe name with the Selection tool. In the Control panel under the Fill option, select any solid color to fill the text.

5. Choose a gradient swatch, such as Rainbow or Midday Sky, from the Swatches panel. Interestingly, it does not apply to the text. Let us remedy this.

6. Select the text with the Selection tool so the baseline is visible, then choose Type > Create Outlines (or Effect > Path > Outline Object) to convert the text to compound paths and shapes.

7. Select the gradient swatch called **New Leaf**. Then, deselect the headline. The text should be filled with the gradient color.

> **Note:** Once you convert type to outlines, it loses its instructions for character and paragraph adjustments. Therefore, it is advisable to set the formatting options for your type and spell check before converting to outlines.

8. Save your file.

Adding the Final Look

1. Choose Window > Layers and collapse the **logo** layer and lock it, then unlock the **border** layer.

2. Select the white rectangle on the document (the background for the two-column text block).

3. Choose Window > Brush Libraries > Borders > Borders_Decorative.

4. Select the Star Burst brush. (Roll over each brush to bring up a text-equivalent name for the brush. Hint: It is toward the bottom of the list.)

5. Choose Select > Deselect.

6. Choose Window > Brush Libraries > Decorative > Decorative_Scatter.

7. Select the Paintbrush tool in the toolbox.

8. From the Decorative_Scatter brush library, select the Confetti scatter brush (toward the top of the panel).

9. For fun, paint a couple strokes of confetti in the lower-right area of the recipe card.

10. Save your file. Your recipe card is complete.

DESIGNING WITH TYPE

Like color, type evokes a look and feel. And like designing with color, designing with type is an endless adventure into the creative depths of the subjective consciousness. Since we are not ones to be fooling around with an artist's inclination, let us just offer some common, general guidelines for honing your typography skills.

When given a visual comparison of what works "well enough" and what works "really well" in typography design, it is easy to see the difference between an amateur- and professional-looking document. See Figure 7–53 and Figure 7–54 to get an idea of what we mean. Making a few simple font style and formatting changes makes all the difference. Before reading on, identify your own typography likes and dislikes as you examine the two business card versions. What works for you? What does not?

figure | 7–53 |

A business card design that works "well enough," but could use some typographic improvement.

Andrea Linkin-Butler, Principal Broker
STRATTON BUYER BROKERAGE, LTD.

Exclusive Buyer Representative
802-824-4421 (800) 808-5917
www.strattonbroker.com
email: andrea@strattonbroker.com
P.O. Box 2036, S. Londonderry, VT 05155

When working with type, take into account the text's readability and visual impact, specifically the formatting and flow of the type for readability, and the use of type contrast and appropriate font selections for visual impact. Following is a modified list of typography tips to achieve readability and visual impact. Compare and contrast these suggestions with the two visuals of the Stratton Buyer Brokerage business cards (Figure 7–53 and Figure 7–54).

Spacing and Alignment

Line Length

Long lines of text are no fun to read, and short lines of text can break up the text flow, so you need to find the right balance. A general rule is that a line should have 55 to 60 characters, or approximately 9 to 10 words, for optimal readability. Of course, this suggestion applies to the creation of documents or layouts containing large blocks of text, and not so much to logo or stationery designs.

Leading or Line Spacing

Leading refers to the air—the distance of space—between lines of type. It is measured in points from baseline to baseline. Depending on the font type used, leading can vary for optimal readability. See Figure 7–55.

figure | 7–54 |

A business card design that works better—is more visually appealing and readable—when simple typographic design principles are applied.

figure | 7–55 |

Examples of leading (or line spacing).

Leading is the distance between lines of type.
If the line distance is too close, it's difficult to read.

If it's too far,

it's also difficult to read.

Adjust leading in the Character panel
to find just the right spacing.

Word and Letter Spacing

- **Tracking:** The process of adjusting the space between selected characters or entire blocks of text. See Figure 7–56. The spacing between individual words and letters is a subtle thing, but can really improve text legibility. Most typefaces available today are designed with correct spacing between characters. However, you might find yourself wanting to adjust these defaults if, for example, you want to work with ALL CAPS.

figure | 7–56 |

Tracking is the process of adjusting the space between selected characters.

space - too much space

space - too little space

space - just right for this font.

- **Kerning:** An even subtler variation of character spacing, kerning refers to how space appears between certain types of letters. For most letters, kerning is relatively uniform, but in some cases, such as with A and V, kerning must be adjusted so spacing looks consistent and more readable. See Figure 7–57. Kerning is also very useful when working with decorative type in a large headline.

> Note: Setting the kerning in the Characters panel to Auto often will work just fine. However, you should check what your text selection looks like using the Optical option. Optical kerning automatically adjusts the spacing between two selected characters based on their shapes. However, kerning and tracking manually are recommended for point sizes larger than 18 point for text such as titles and headlines.

figure | 7–57 |

Kerning is the process of adjusting the space between certain letter forms.

AVE - this text is not kerned. Note that there is more space between the A and the V.

AVE - this text is auto kerned. Note the reduced space between the A and the V.

> ▶ **Don't Go There!**
>
> The differences between tracking and kerning are so subtle that novice designers often get the two terms confused. Tracking provides a more global spacing of selected words and letters, whereas kerning works between two specific characters, depending on how they are placed next to each other.

Justification

Justification is the alignment of lines of text or text blocks. Documentation with lots of text is usually formatted with a left justification—aligned to the left margin (flush left) and ragged on the right. You can also choose to align text to the right margin (flush right) with the left side ragged, but the resulting text is not as easy to read. For a more formal look, all lines might be justified on both the right and left sides (no ragged edges), such as in this book. Often, newspaper or magazine articles have this type of look. Centered justification works well with small amounts of copy. See Figure 7–58.

Left justification example:
Justification is the alignment of lines of text or text blocks.
Documentation with lots of text is usually formatted with a left justification - aligned to the left margin (flush left) and ragged on the other end.

Right justification example:
You can also choose to align text to the right margin (flush right) with the left side ragged, but it's really not as easy to read.

Example of justification both right and left:
For a more formal look all lines might be justified on both the right and left sides (no ragged edges), such as this book. Often newspaper or magazine articles also have this type of look.

Centered justification works well with small amounts of copy.

figure |7–58|

Examples of justification.

Font Selection and Size

Proportional vs. Fixed Pitch

Fonts are distinguishable by their style and in the way in which their individual letters and characters are spaced. Spacing of a font can either be fixed pitch (mono-spaced) or proportional. A fixed-pitch font is usually what is defined as a typewriter font, where each character takes up the same amount of space and is representative of how old-style typewriters used to reproduce letterforms. Modern digital type and printable text is generally designed using proportional spacing, where each letter is given just the amount of space it needs to look visually appealing and legible. Proportional fonts can be formatted better on a page and actually improve readability over fixed-pitch fonts. See Figure 7–59.

figure |7–59|

Examples of fixed-pitch (mono-spaced) and proportionally spaced fonts.

Courier is a fixed-pitch font, often called a typewriter font.

Arial is a proportional font, so is Adobe Garamond Pro.

Serif vs. Sans Serif

It is important to know the difference between serif and sans-serif fonts because both types play a vital role in the readability of either print or Web-based documents. Serif fonts are letterforms with tails or cross lines at the ends of each letter stroke. Sans-serif fonts do not have these tails—evolutionally speaking, they have been removed. Serif fonts usually have a more formal look, whereas sans-serif fonts often look bolder and more modern. See Figure 7–60.

Times is a serif font - it contains serifs (tails) on the ends of each letter.

Arial is a sans-serif font, a font without tails. Other common sans-serif fonts are Verdana and Helvetica.

figure |7–60|

Examples of serif and sans-serif font faces.

For printed documents containing lots of text, serif fonts, such as Times New Roman, are easier to read. This is why newspapers traditionally use serif fonts for their copy. For screen-based text, like that on a Web site, sans-serif fonts are recommended, such as Arial, Helvetica, or Verdana. This is especially true when working with type sizes that are less than 12 points (the little tails of certain serif fonts get lost when the text is viewed on a lighted screen). Usually we like to use a combination of serif and sans-serif fonts in our designs, and stick with just two or three font families or typefaces (any more gets distracting). For Web page designs, for example, you might use a serif font family for the topic headings and a sans-serif font family for the body copy (main text areas). On the other hand, in the business card (Figure 7–54) example, which will be printed, notice that a sans-serif font (Berthold Imago) is used for the business title while a serif font (Georgia) is used for the address and contact information.

Contrast

To really put some "oomph" in your type design, the principle of contrast is a must-know. A contrast is something different from something else, and it is commonly used in design to heighten visual impact. Here are six characteristics of type that can be manipulated to create contrast; notice how these characteristics are used or not used to produce contrast in the two business card examples.

- **Size**: Big-size versus small-size type offers contrast, such as a 20-point headline above 10-point body text.
- **Weight:** Most font families and font formatting options come in varying weights for the purpose of providing contrast, such as medium, light italic, bold, or condensed versions. See Figure 7–61.
- **Structure:** Within a layout, a combination of serif and sans-serif fonts offers contrast.
- **Form:** Form implies a font's shape. For example, a good contrast of form would be an uppercase type set against lowercase type.
- **Color:** The color of type can make a huge impact on a design, especially how it might contrast with a colored background or other colored objects. Be sure there is sufficient contrast when working with colored copy, such as white text on a black background or dark blue text on a white background. Avoid combinations like yellow text on a white background, or dark blue text on a black background.
- **Direction:** As you experienced in the recipe card lesson, you can change the direction of text to provide contrast. For example, put text on a curved path, slant it, or send it vertically down a page.

COPPERPLATE LIGHT

COPPERPLATE REGULAR

COPPERPLATE BOLD

figure |7–61|

Provide contrast with variations of font weight.

SUMMARY

One of Illustrator's great strengths is its ability to work with type, offering you ample flexibility and versatility for creating, formatting, and managing type. With such control over these typography issues, you can better focus on the often-overlooked subtleties of type design, and watch your illustrative work transcend from amateur to professional.

in review

1. What tool do you use to type at a point? To type in an area? To type on a path?

2. What does the command Type > Create Outlines do? When would you use it?

3. Name three font formats and describe their characteristics.

4. What has happened when your document is missing a font?

5. What is legacy text?

6. When wrapping text around an object, the object and text must be on the same layer. Does the text need to be below or above the object in the layer stack?

7. What is an RTF file?

8. Define leading, kerning, and tracking.

9. Name at least four general design tips for working with type.

10. What should you do when you use someone else's font in your commercial artwork?

exploring on your own

1. Choose Help > Illustrator Help Menu. Under "Contents," read the topic Type.

2. Illustrator CS3 comes with an array of pre-made templates you can use for basic layout designs, such as cards and postcards, business sets, and stationery. In Illustrator, choose File > New From Template and explore the various templates provided. Some of them have pre-made designs, others are blank templates with common layout sizes you can build from. We used the **Business Card 2_Blank.ait** (.ait is the file format for Illustrator template files) found under Basic > Blank Templates to create the Stratton Buyer Brokerage business card shown in this chapter. Using your newfound typography skills, create your own logo design (or other layout design) using one of these templates.

> **Note:** To save your own layout designs for repeated use, choose File > Save As Template. You will work more with layout design in Chapter 8.

3. Adobe is a forerunner in digital type technologies, and it provides a wealth of information on type, such as type design, terminology, and typeface licensing and copyright FAQs, on its Web site *http://www.adobe.com/type*.

4. There are plenty of places online where you can buy fonts and font symbols (image glyphs such as Dingbats) in just about any style you can imagine. However, there are also many places that offer fonts for free use, usually with only a minimum requirement of crediting the font creator. Do a search for "free fonts" on the Web. Some of my favorite freeware font sites is *http://www.abstractfonts.com* and *http://www.dafont.com*. When you go to either site, do a search for the TrueType font "Groovalicious Tweak."

5. Explore the topic of "typography" and "typography design" online.

6. Open a magazine or a Web browser and put on your typographer's hat. Critique the text you see—analyze its design and visual impact and its legibility. What simple things would you do to improve text that is difficult or perhaps even "boring" to read? Adjust the leading (line spacing)? Change the font? Change the color? Make its size bigger or smaller? Become a type critic.

Online Learning Guidelines

OVERVIEW   ENROLLMENT   PREPARATION   HELP

Overview: What are online courses?

Welcome to ATW Online

What are online courses?

Is taking an online course for me?

How do I participate?

Online courses use the Web as the central environment for learning. At ATW Online we use a customized course management system that facilitates your class experience. As an online student you are no longer required to travel to campus to participate in a course or restricted to scheduling conflicts.

ATW Online offers:

- Over 500 course offerings, both credit and non-credit
- Online instructor office hours for personal support
- Flexible course scheduling for working professionals
- 24-hour technical help
- Asynchronous and synchronous discussion options

| object composition |

charting your course

You have learned the basic components of drawing in Illustrator—creating lines and shapes with the Pen tool, and then enhancing objects using value, texture, color, and type. The next step is to combine, group, and organize objects to produce more complex and complete illustrations or graphic layouts. This process is called composition. In this chapter, you explore features for combining paths and shapes, such as grouping, the Pathfinder panel, and clipping masks. You also explore the process for creating a design layout, which introduces you to the organization and elements of composition in design. In addition, you work with layers and layout tools, such as rulers, guides, and grids, and you get extensive information on importing content. Then you venture further and build a layout for a Web site home page.

goals

In this chapter you will:

- **Get a handle on grouping objects**
- **Create compound paths and shapes using the Pathfinder panel**
- **Reveal artwork through clipping masks**
- **Develop an understanding of design composition**
- **Learn workflow and organizational techniques for developing compositions and layouts**
- **Learn what works when importing content**
- **Gain practical experience working with layers**
- **Practice working with rulers and guides**

OBJECT COMPOSITION

COMBINING PATHS AND SHAPES

So far, you have been drawing simple paths and shapes. Now you will learn how to get more complex with your object construction through the process of combining (or compounding) paths and shapes. This is something Illustrator does very well through grouping, the Pathfinder panel, and clipping masks.

Grouping

Grouping objects is easy and something you might be familiar with from other programs. It is a common way to consolidate objects into a single unit so you can move, scale, or rotate them without affecting their attributes or relative positions. To create a group, select the intended objects and choose Object > Group. See Figure 8–1. To release a group, select the grouped object with the Selection tool and choose Object > Ungroup.

figure |8–1|

Create a group.

If you create a group from a series of objects each on a different layer, when you choose Object > Group the objects are combined into a single layer called <Group>. When you open the grouped layer, each individual item is stacked in sublayers. See Figure 8–2. The

Layers panel then allows you to select either the whole group layer or the individual sublayers. You can also select and modify individual objects within a group by choosing the Group Selection or Direct Selection tool in the toolbox. See Figure 8–3 and Figure 8–4. To modify the stacking order of a group—how objects are arranged in front of or behind each other—select an individual object using the Group Selection tool, and choose Object > Arrange. You can also arrange the stacking order of objects that are not grouped, but they must be on the same layer.

If you like to keep things organized, especially when you have lots of objects overlapping one another, you can group grouped objects (called nesting). For example, let us say you draw a face. First, you group the two eyes together so you can move them around easily. Then you choose the head, nose, mouth, and the grouped eyes and make them into a larger group that can then be selected as a whole. To practice this idea, complete "Lesson 1: Creating Groups" in this chapter.

Compound Paths, Shapes, and the Pathfinder Panel

Using the geometric shape tools and creating simple paths with the Pen tool are not going to cut it when constructing more complex objects. You need to be able to combine these simple paths and shapes into new and different objects. There are various ways to do this in Illustrator, which can get confusing. In fact, when constructing more complex shapes, you often do not get the result you want on the first try. It usually takes some experimentation with the available tools in Illustrator to get things right.

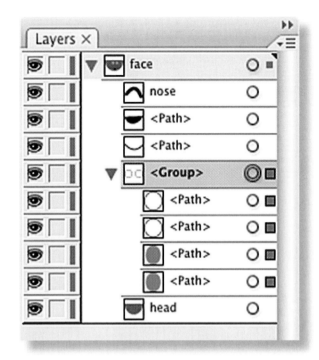

figure |8–2|

The individual parts of a grouped object are available in sublayers.

figure |8–3|

The Group Selection tool selects individual parts of a group.

As a point of reference, it is important to understand the difference between a simple path or shape in Illustrator versus compound paths and shapes. See Figure 8–5. Simple paths and shapes are what you have been working with up until now in this book. They are a single path or shape, either open or closed.

figure |8–4|

Select and arrange objects in a group forward or back of each other.

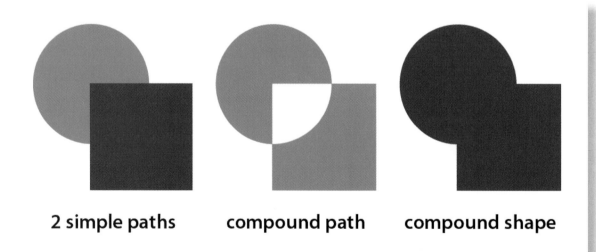

2 simple paths **compound path** **compound shape**

figure |8–5|

Identify simple paths and shapes versus compound paths and shapes.

A compound path is created when you take two or more simple paths and intercept them to create a new kind of path. To create a compound path, select two or more simple paths and choose Object > Compound Path > Make. To release the paths, choose Object > Compound Path > Release.

A compound shape is composed of two or more paths, compound paths, groups, blends, text, or other compound shapes that intercept one another to create new and editable shapes. To create a compound shape, select the desired paths, choose Window > Pathfinder, and in the submenu of the Pathfinder options choose Make Compound Shape. See Figure 8–6. To release, choose Release Compound Shape.

figure | 8–6 |

Make a compound shape.

Admittedly, it can be difficult to understand the difference between compound paths and compound shapes. Here is what we can tell you: Compound shapes are more editable. Although you can select parts of a compound path or compound shape with the Direct or Group Selection tools, only with compound shapes can you change appearance attributes or graphics styles on individual components or manipulate them individually in the Layers panel. This difference makes sense when looking in the Layers panel. Objects merged into a compound path create a single layer. Objects within a compound shape are contained in a single layer, but each part is editable in sublayers. See Figure 8–7.

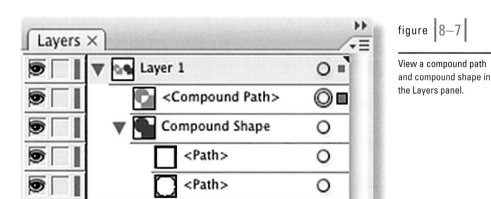

figure | 8–7 |

View a compound path and compound shape in the Layers panel.

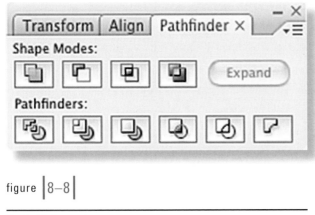

figure |8–8|

The Pathfinder panel.

Commands to combine compound paths and shapes are available in the Pathfinder panel (Window > Pathfinder) or in Effects > Pathfinder. The Pathfinder panel contains two sections of commands: Shape Modes and Pathfinders. Shape Modes allow you to add, subtract, intersect, and exclude objects. Pathfinders allow you to divide, trim, merge, crop, outline, and subtract objects. See Figure 8–8 and Figure 8–9, and the Pathfinder examples in Figure 8–24. The Expand option in the Pathfinder panel converts a compound shape into a path or compound path. Generally, expanding is useful when you have created an object that is native to Illustrator and need to import it to a different program, or if you are finding that the attributes assigned to the object (i.e., transparency, gradients, or blends) are having difficulty printing. For more details on each Pathfinder combination, choose Help > Illustrator Help and go to Index and look for information on Pathfinder effects. You also get to explore the Pathfinder exclusively in "Lesson 2: Hands-on with Pathfinder."

2 simple rectangle shapes

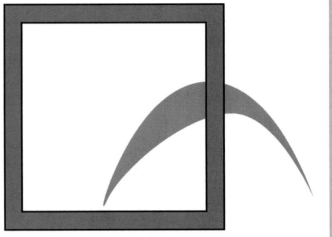

A compound shape
Subtracting one shape from another to create an empty space.

figure |8–9|

Create a compound shape using the subtract option in the Pathfinder.

The Pathfinders in the Pathfinder panel are filters, which do not allow editing in the Appearance panel. However, Pathfinder effects in the Effects menu do. To use the Pathfinder effects, first group your selected paths or shapes. Choose Object > Group, and then choose Effect > Pathfinder and whatever effect of your choice.

Clipping Masks

Masking is a universal concept in graphic design. A mask is an object that hides or reveals other objects. A mask in Illustrator is referred to as a clipping mask, which can be a vector object or group, whose shape becomes like a window that reveals other objects or artwork through it. See Figure 8–10 and Figure 8–11. You will make masks in "Lesson 3: Clipping Masks."

figure |8–10|

Before Object > Clipping Mask > Make is applied.

figure |8–11|

After Object > Clipping Mask > Make is applied. The flower photo is visible only through the text mask.

What you should know about clipping masks:

- Only vector objects can be masking objects, such as a path, a compound shape, a text object, or a group of these. However, they can mask any type of artwork, such as bit-mapped photographs or other vector objects.
- The masking object must reside above or in front of the object being masked.
- Masked objects are moved into the clipping mask's group in the Layers panel if they do not already reside there.
- When an object is converted to a clipping mask, it loses all its previous attributes and is assigned no fill or stroke.
- When using more than one vector object as a mask, the objects must first be converted into a single compound path.

Lesson 1: Creating Groups

This lesson will familiarize you with grouping and how grouped objects are indicated in the Layers panel. Your completed file will look like Figure 8–12.

figure |8–12|

The completed file.

Setting Up the File

1. Open **chap8L1.ai** in the folder **chap8_lessons**.

2. Choose Window > Workspace > [Basic].

3. Choose Shift-Tab to hide any open docks/panels.

4. Select the Zoom tool and magnify the funny face.

Grouping Face Parts

1. With the Selection tool, Shift-click both parts of the mouth. Do not select the head. See Figure 8–13.

2. Choose Object > Group to group the two pieces.

> **Note:** To test if the objects are grouped, move the mouth section around and see if both pieces move as one.

3. Deselect all by clicking on a blank area of the artboard or choosing Select > Deselect.

4. Shift-click the four parts of the two eyes (the right and left outer eyes and eyeballs). See Figure 8–14.

5. Choose Object > Group to group the parts.

> **Note:** If you made a mistake in your grouping, choose Object > Ungroup to release the grouped state.

6. Select the parts of the face, including the mouth group, eye group, nose, and head.

7. Choose Object > Group to consolidate the objects and groups into one larger group. This becomes a "nested group" or "groups within a group"—an even more nitpicky way to organize a file.

> **Note:** The shortcut key command to group is Command-G (Mac) or Ctrl-G (Windows).

8. Deselect all by clicking on a blank area of the artboard.

9. To maintain the "groupness" of the objects and yet select individual parts for modification or adjustment, choose the Group Selection tool (hidden under the Direct Selection tool). See Figure 8–15.

10. With the Group Selection tool, practice selecting individual parts of the face.

11. Save the funny face. Name it **chap8L1_yourname.ai**.

Examining Groups in the Layers Panel

1. Choose Window > Layers.

2. Open the layer named **face**. Then expand the sublayer named **<Group>**. Notice the groups within groups. See Figure 8–16.

3. Double-click on the topmost group title within the **face** layer (**<Group>**), and rename the whole group **face**.

4. Within the **face** group, rename the groups containing the eye parts and the mouth parts: name them **eyes** and **mouth** respectively. See Figure 8–17.

5. Collapse the subcategories of the **face** layer to save room in the Layers panel. See Figure 8–18.

figure |8–15|

The Group Selection tool.

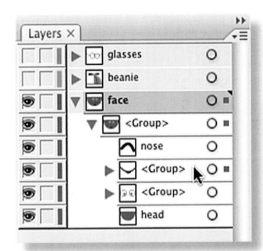

figure |8–16|

Groups within groups in the Layers panel.

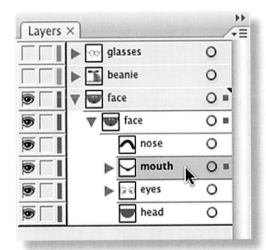

figure |8–17|

Name the layers.

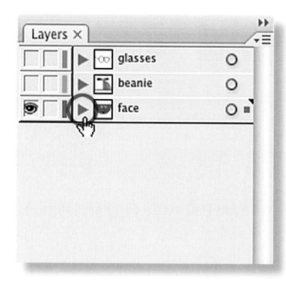

figure |8–18|

Collapse the subcategories of a layer.

Creating a Beanie Cap

1. Choose View > Fit in Window.

2. Unhide the layer named **beanie**.

3. Zoom in on the half-completed beanie cap drawing.

4. Select the three colored sections of the beanie cap (red, blue, orange). Do not select the black propeller or the green rim. See Figure 8–19.

5. Choose Object > Group.

6. Make a duplicate for the other side of the hat, and flip it in one step. Select the Reflect tool (hidden under the Rotate tool) in the toolbox. See Figure 8–20.

7. Double-click on the Reflect tool icon in the toolbox to open its options.

8. In the Reflect options box, choose Vertical and click the Copy button (not OK). See Figure 8–21. A flipped copy of the half-beanie is created on top of the other.

figure |8–19|

Select the colored sections of the beanie cap.

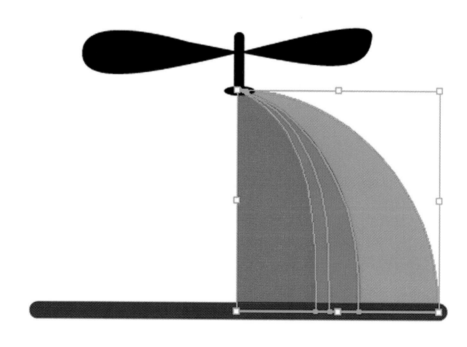

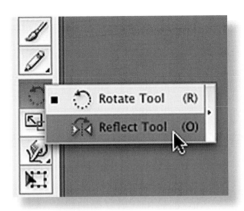

figure |8–20|

The Reflect tool.

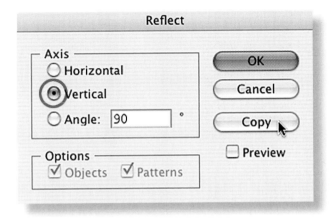

figure |8–21|

Create a flipped copy of an object using the Reflect tool.

9. With the Selection tool, place the new copy to the left of the first half. See Figure 8–22.

> **Note:** You can move the new copy into place incrementally by clicking the right/left or up/down arrow keys. To adjust the increment distance, choose Illustrator > Preferences > General (Mac) or Edit > Preferences > General (Windows) and enter an amount in the Keyboard Increment option.

figure |8–22|

Use the Selection tool to position the new copy to the left of the first half.

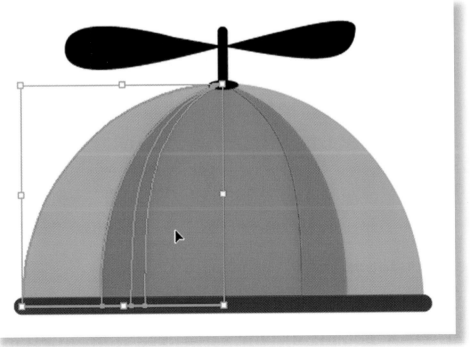

figure | 8–23 |

Select the target icons in the
Layers panel to select
the objects in the document.

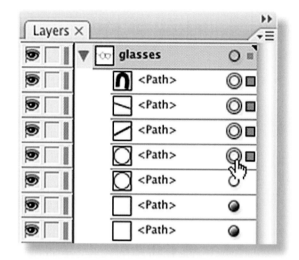

10. Select both halves, and choose Object > Group, or Command-G (Mac) or Ctrl-G (Windows).

11. Select the grouped halves, the propeller, and the green rim, and choose Object > Group to create one larger group.

Finishing the Character

1. Choose View > Fit in Window and position the beanie cap above the funny face.

2. To complete the character, unhide the layer named **glasses** in the Layers panel.

3. Let us group all the parts of the glasses. Expand the **glasses** layer to see the parts.

4. In the Layers panel, Shift-click each target icon of each layer (right-hand side) that is part of the glasses. Notice that each object is also selected in the document. See Figure 8–23.

5. Choose Object > Group to consolidate the pieces.

6. Save your file.

Lesson 2: Hands-on with Pathfinder

The best way to get a handle on what the options are for constructing compound paths and shapes is to try each shape mode and pathfinder variation in the Pathfinder panel. Here is your chance. For an example of this lesson, see the Pathfinder panel variations in Figure 8–24.

Setting Up the File

1. Open **chap8L2.ai** in the folder **chap8_lessons**.

2. Choose Window > Workspace > [Basic].

3. Choose Shift-Tab to hide any open docks/panels.

4. Zoom in on the first set of moths under the Shape Modes heading. See Figure 8–25.

Pathfinder Panel

Shape Modes

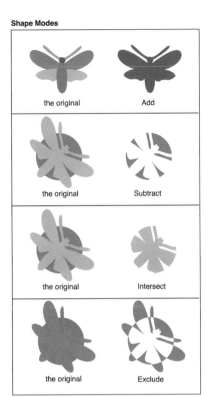

Pathfinders (pathfinder filters)

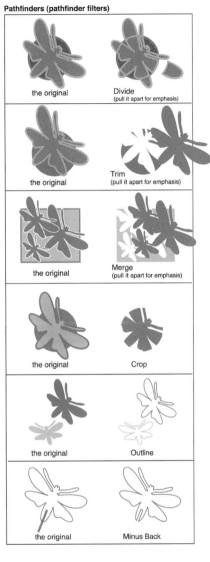

figure | 8–24 |

Variations of an image created using the Pathfinder.

Pathfinder Panel

Shape Modes

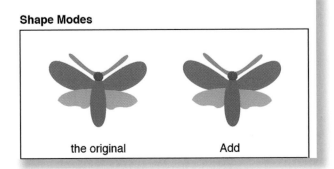

the original   Add

figure | 8–25 |

Zoom in on the first set of moths.

Exploring the Shape Modes

1. Select all the parts of the moth above the Add label.

2. Choose Window > Pathfinder. In the Pathfinder panel, choose the Add to shape area option. See Figure 8–26.

figure | 8–26 |

The Pathfinder panel options.

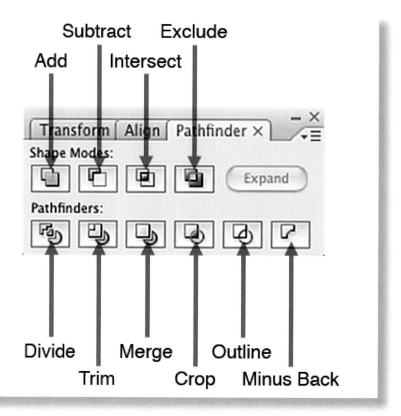

3. The moth parts merge. The Add variation joins the outer edges of selected objects into one compound path object. The paint attributes (stroke and fill) from the front-most object (the bug's head) are applied to the new object.

4. Select the moth above the Subtract label.

5. Choose the Subtract from shape area option in the Pathfinder panel. This option subtracts the front-most objects from the back-most object. Use this command to delete areas of an illustration. The paint attributes of front-most objects are applied to the new object.

6. Select the moth above the Intersect label.

7. Choose the Intersect shape areas option in the Pathfinder panel. This option deletes any non-overlapping areas from overlapping, selected objects. The paint attributes of front-most objects are applied to the new object.

8. Select the moth above the Exclude label.

9. Choose the Exclude overlapping shape areas option in the Pathfinder panel. With Exclude, areas where an even number of selected objects overlap become transparent; areas where an odd number of objects overlap are filled. The paint attributes of front-most objects are applied to the new object.

Exploring the Pathfinders

1. Choose View > Fit In Window.

2. Zoom in on the upper-right side of the document to see the first moths under the Pathfinders (Pathfinder filters) heading.

3. Select the moth above the Divide label.

4. Choose the Divide option in the Pathfinder panel. This option divides overlapping areas of selected paths into separate, non-overlapping closed paths or lines. The new objects will maintain their original fill and stroke attributes. To get a better idea of how the division works, select and pull apart the divided sections with the Group Selection tool.

5. Select the moth above the Trim label.

6. Choose the Trim option in the Pathfinder panel. With Trim, the front-most object is preserved, whereas parts of the object(s) behind it and overlapping it are deleted. Objects retain their original fill attributes, but stroke colors are deleted. Once again, pull the trimmed areas apart to see the effect.

7. Select the moth above the Merge label.

8. Choose the Merge option in the Pathfinder panel. With Merge, all the front objects are merged/united into a single element and subtracted from the background object (unlike Trim, where they are separate). Objects retain their original fill attributes, but stroke colors are deleted. Pull the merged areas apart to see the effect.

9. Select the moth above the Crop label.

10. Choose the Crop option in the Pathfinder panel. With Crop, the back object acts like a cookie cutter, eliminating any portion(s) of the front object that extend outside the edges. The front-most object is removed. Remaining non-overlapping objects retain their fill colors; strokes are removed.

11. Select the two moths above the Outline label.

12. Choose the Outline option in the Pathfinder panel. Nothing tricky here—objects turn into stroke lines. The fill colors of the original objects become stroke colors, and the fills are removed. If the shapes are overlapping, this option will divide them where they intersect.

> **Note:** If you cannot see the stroke lines, it is possible the stroke weight needs to be readjusted in the Stroke panel (Window > Stroke) or in the Control panel.

13. Select the moth and blue marker above the Minus Back label.

14. Choose the Minus Back option in the Pathfinder panel. This option subtracts the back-most selected objects from the front-most objects. Parts of objects that overlap the front-most objects are deleted. The paint attributes of the front-most objects are applied to the new object. The selected objects must partially overlap for this command to create an effect.

15. Save your file in your lessons folder.

Lesson 3: Clipping Masks

Clipping masks are commonly used and easy to create, as you will learn in this lesson.

Setting Up the File

1. Open **chap8L3a.ai** in the folder **chap8_lessons**.

2. Choose View > Actual Size.

3. Open the Layers panel (Window > Layers).

Creating the Mask Effect

1. Expand **Layer 1**. Notice there are two sublayers: **THINK PINK Group** and **flower photo**.

2. Expand the **THINK PINK Group** layer. Each letterform is in its own layer and recognized as compound paths, rather than type. To turn type into compound paths, like this example, select the type and choose Type > Create Outlines.

> Note: Creating compound paths out of type can be useful when you want to work with the type as an image, need it to be compatible with certain printers, or when you do not want to worry about whether the proper font is installed to render the type correctly. Be aware, however, that once you convert type to outlines, you can no longer use the type formatting options, such as font size, style, and spacing. It is not necessary to convert type to outlines when working with clipping masks; we just did it in this lesson in case you did not have the correct font on your computer.

3. Select the THINK PINK text on the document using the Selection tool.

4. Choose Object > Compound Path > Make to convert the letter forms into one compound path. This is necessary when you are using more than one object in a mask (i.e., each letter).

5. Select the THINK PINK text (now invisible) and the flower photo. To do this, either marquee with the Selection tool around the flower photo, or Shift-click each target icon of each layer in the Layers panel.

6. Choose Object > Clipping Mask > Make. The flower photo is revealed through the letters.

7. Notice in the Layers panel that both pieces are in a clipping group layer. See Figure 8–27.

8. Select the flower photo by clicking on its target icon in the Layers panel.

9. With the Selection tool, practice moving the flower photo on the document. Notice it stays behind the text mask.

10. Save this file in your lessons folder, and then close it.

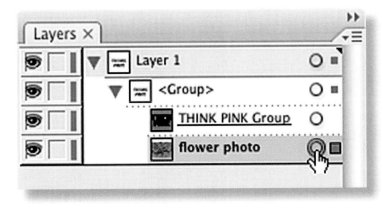

figure | 8–27 |

Both parts of the clipping mask are grouped under one layer.

Creating Another Clipping Mask

1. Open the file **chap8L3b.ai** in the folder **chap8_lessons**.

2. Choose View > Actual Size.

3. Select the Spiral tool (hidden under the Line Segment tool) in the toolbox. See Figure 8–28.

4. Press the D key to set the default fill and stroke options (white for fill, black for stroke) if they are not already selected in the toolbox.

5. Click and drag over the boy's face in the photo to create a spiral shape that covers his face.

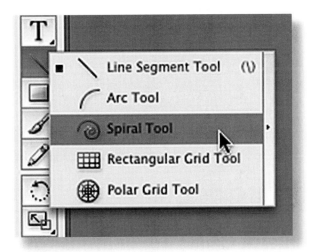

figure | 8–28 |

The Spiral tool.

6. Create two more spirals over the photo. See Figure 8–29.

7. Shift-click the spirals, and choose Object > Compound Path > Make to combine the three shapes into a compound group.

8. Select the compound group (the spirals) and the photograph, and choose Object > Clipping Mask > Make.

> **Note:** To release the mask, choose Object > Clipping Mask > Release.

figure | 8-29 |

Create spirals.

9. Select the Group Selection tool (hidden under the Direct Selection tool) and practice adjusting individual parts (spirals) of the mask or the photo underneath.

> **Note:** Selecting the spirals can be tricky, since there is no fill or stroke associated with them. You must click directly on a path edge to select it. See Figure 8–30.

10. Save the file in your lessons folder.

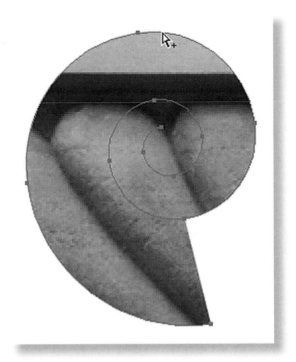

figure | 8–30 |

Click and drag directly on a path edge with the
Group Selection tool to move the individual
spiral.

ABOUT COMPOSITION

Author Otto G. Ocvirk and contributors define composition best in their book *Art Fundamentals: Theory and Practice*: "An arrangement and/or structure of all the elements, as organized by principles, that achieves a unified whole. Often used interchangeably with the term 'design.'"

Reflect for a moment on things in your life that seem compositionally complete—your car, your house, the flower in the vase sitting on your table, or your favorite TV commercial or song. These things came to being through the combination of some predefined elements of design. See Figure 8–31.

For us, as graphic or multimedia designers, the elements derived are from those in visual art, and they are what we have studied explicitly through the use of Illustrator—line, shape, value, texture, and color. How these elements are organized is what brings about the sense of completeness of a drawing or layout. In traditional art study, the principles of organization include concepts such as harmony, variety, proportion, dominance, movement, and economy. The study of these concepts and their effective interaction with one another is more than we can get into in a book about Illustrator, but is not to be overlooked in your own study of visual art and graphic design. In this section, we introduce a general process with which to organize and produce a compositionally sound design. We also share with you some of the tools available in Illustrator for organization and workflow.

figure | 8–31 |

Composition is everywhere—in the design of a temple, a fuel-efficient car, a mosaic of ceramic tiles.

The Layout Process

The creative process comes to fruition in many ways. When Annesa designs a Web page or print layout, her process is well mapped out. It is mostly stuff she learned from experience and quickly adopted to streamline production and reach a compositionally whole design. Generally, her process breakdown is as follows: start with an idea, make an initial mock-up, gather content, assemble content, and fine-tune.

Starting with an Idea

A design always starts with a vision or idea. Sometimes the idea is perfectly realized in your mind, and it is simply a matter of getting it into a tangible form. Other times, the idea is further fleshed out as you go through the design process. Either way, you have to start with an idea—something that drives you to make it "real."

Making a Mock-Up

Once you have got the idea, the next step is to put it into some tangible form or mock-up. Mock-ups help to envision what an over-all design(s) will look like before you begin the development stages. Often it starts as a series of cursory sketches (called thumbnails), then it is reproduced into a more detailed drawing. Many artists will sketch ideas on paper first, scan them, then use the most realized sketch as a template for constructing a final, digital version. See Figure 8–32. Others construct the thumbnails, the draft mock-up, and the final version digitally, utilizing the flexibility of undo and redo.

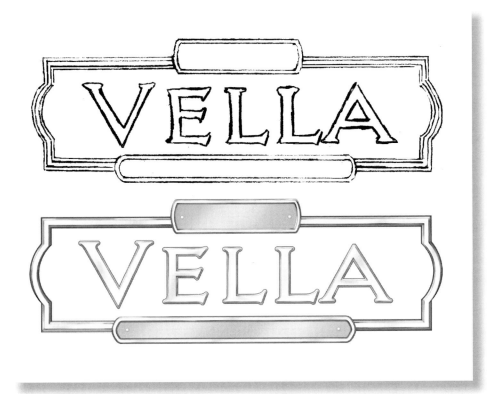

figure | 8–32 |

Before and after of the Vella logo design for Gallo Winery. It starts with a sketch.

When it comes to page layout design, setting up what Annesa calls "content zones" within a grid structure works successfully. Content zones are designated, blocked-out areas where information will be placed, such as images, copy, and logo treatments. Using the grid mapping idea, an initial mock-up for a Web page might look something like Figure 8–33, with each content zone labeled for easy reference.

If you are creating multiple pages of a similar look, keep the positioning of content zones consistent from page to page. For example, in the creation of a Web page design—something you will practice in "Lesson 4: Practicing the Process—Building a Web Page Design"—it is important that the positioning of text to images to navigational (button) elements is both visually appealing and consistently easy to use as you click from page to page. After all, a Web page is not a static design—it is an interactive experience.

After identifying content areas, Annesa begins the most creative and interesting part of the process: applying design elements and principles to get the "look and feel" she wants. Usually this is done in a very malleable fashion, knowing that the final version will be completed once there is client approval of the design idea (if that is the case), and the final content pieces are gathered. Figure 8–34 and Figure 8–35 are two design layouts Annesa created for a client; you will build the second one in Lesson 4.

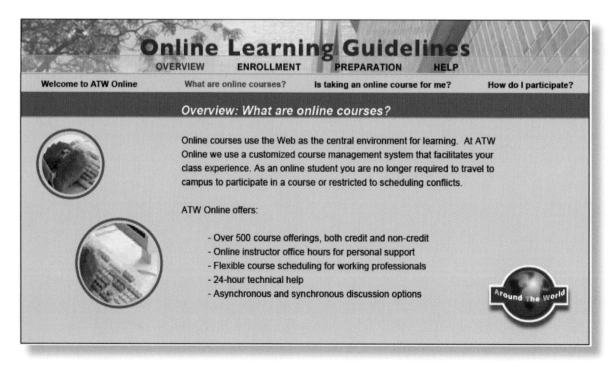

figure | 8–33 |

Each content zone is assigned within a grid.

figure | 8–34 |

Web page design No. 1.

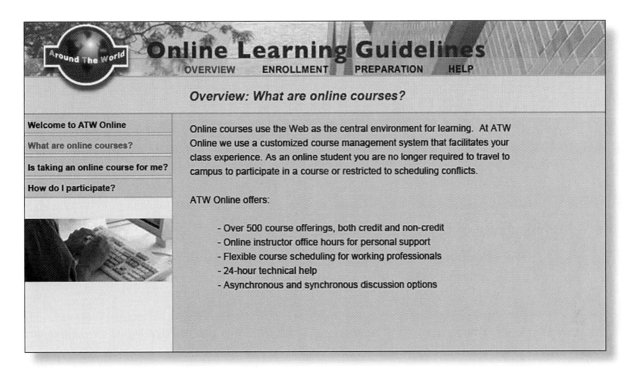

figure |8–35|

Web page design No. 2.

▶ Don't Go There!

Many novice designers fall short on their designs because they do not take the time to create mock-ups. Experience shows that starting with an initial mock-up can alleviate many unwanted headaches and stalled deadlines later on.

Gathering Content

When you have your initial sketch, you have a better idea of what kind of content you need to fill each content zone area. Gathering content for your layout can be the most time-consuming and challenging part of the whole process. In some instances you might have to create all the content—images and copy—yourself, or procure the content from other sources (i.e., your client or an outside resource, such as another artist or writer, image, or font repository). This is where issues of copyright come into play. If you create your own content or use copyright-free material, there is no need to worry about the permission process. However, if you use others' materials, such as another company's logo or a photo of a famous person, you need the correct permissions for using them in your work.

Another aspect of content gathering is getting the content into the right format for your use. For example, if Illustrator is to be used as the medium for integrating your content (see next section), make sure the content can be successfully imported into the program. Are the images and photos you want to use in the correct file format for Illustrator to read? Is the written copy translatable in the Illustrator environment? We will not go into detail about each importable file format supported by Illustrator (you can review that information in the Illustrator Help files), but here is a quick list: EPS, Adobe PDF, Photoshop, SVG/SVGZ, PICT, WMF/EMF, DXF/DWG, Freehand, CorelDraw, CGM, raster formats (i.e., GIF 89a, JPEG/JPEG2000, PNG, TIFF, BMP), and text formats, such as plain text/ASCII (.txt), MS RTF (.rtf), MS Word 97, 98, and 2000 (.doc), MS Word 2007 (.docx).

Assembling Content

After content is gathered, you assemble it in your design program (i.e., Illustrator). There are two parts to integrating content into your final layout design: properly importing content from outside the program, and accurately positioning content in the intended composition using placement and organization tools.

Importing When you have the content in an appropriate format (see the previous section "Gathering Content"), you bring it into Illustrator in one of several ways—using the Open, Place, or Paste commands, or, if available, dragging and dropping.

- *Open (choose File > Open):* Opens artwork in a new Illustrator document. Vector artwork is converted to Illustrator paths, which you can modify with any Illustrator tool. Bitmap artwork can be modified with only some tools, such as transformation tools (scale, rotate, etc.) and image filters.

- *Place (choose File > Place):* Places artwork into an existing Illustrator document. You can place the artwork in one of two ways: linked or embedded. Linked artwork remains independent of the Illustrator document, which is good if you need to keep the document's file size down. However, if you move your Illustrator document to another spot on the desktop, the linked files must be moved, too, and possibly be re-linked to the Illustrator document. This is very similar to how fonts are read by Illustrator—the fonts must be available in your font folder, for Illustrator to find them. The other option is to embed the artwork, which is when Illustrator copies the artwork into the document, increasing the file size but keeping everything intact. The option to link or embed a file is available when you choose File > Place—select the link option if you want to link the artwork, or unselect the option to embed it. See Figure 8–36. To identify and monitor linked and embedded files, choose Window > Links. In the Link panel options box, you can also change a linked file into an embedded file (see Figure 8–37), or choose the Embed option in the Control panel of the selected image.

- *Paste (choose Edit > Paste):* Pastes copied artwork into the document. This method is useful when transferring content from one Illustrator document to another. Before pasting artwork into Illustrator, the copied artwork is saved on the Clipboard. You can think of a clipboard as a virtual holding place for copied information. It sits in

figure | 8–36 |

To link or not to link? That is the question when you choose File > Place.

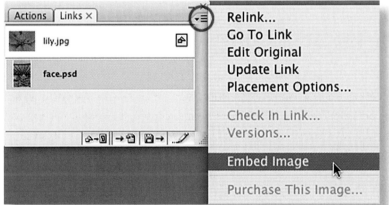

figure | 8–37 |

The Links panel lets you easily identify and modify your placed files.

this temporary space until you are ready to paste it. To specify copy and paste preferences, choose Illustrator > Preferences > File Handling & Clipboard (Mac), or Edit > Preferences > File Handling & Clipboard (Windows).

* *Dragging and dropping:* This option can also transfer artwork from one document to another, most commonly between different Illustrator files, or between Illustrator and Photoshop or InDesign. If you are a Mac user, you can also drag a copy of Illustrator artwork to the desktop, which converts the artwork into PICT format.

Problems can arise when importing content into Illustrator, or other programs for that matter. For example, when you try to import a CorelDraw file that is in a newer version than what the current Illustrator version supports. If the file is in a vector format (which, if it is CorelDraw, it will be), it often helps to save the file in the Encapsulated PostScript (EPS) format, rather than its native file format, then import it into Illustrator. EPS is a standard, cross-platform file format that recognizes both vector and bitmap information. Generally, when importing native file formats—such as Photoshop (.psd), CorelDraw (.cdr) or Flash (.fla)—from one program to another, it is a hit or miss proposition. Keeping files in more generic file formats—EPS for vector-based files, or TIFF for bitmap-based files—might prove a better solution, even if on occasion you lose some information in translation.

Another importing issue might arise when you attempt to import a newer version of an Illustrator file into an older version (i.e., CS3 into version 10). In this case, you usually get a dialog box that says something like Figure 8–38. The conversion will probably work, but you might lose some information. One other thing: When you go to import artwork and you can't access the file you want to import, it's your clue that the file has been saved in a format Illustrator cannot read.

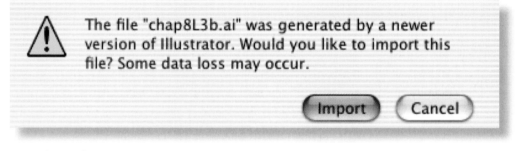

⚠ The file "chap8L3b.ai" was generated by a newer version of Illustrator. Would you like to import this file? Some data loss may occur.

Import   Cancel

figure | 8–38 |

This is the screen you will see if you attempt to import an Illustrator CS3 file into Illustrator 10.

Organizing After you have imported the content into Illustrator, or created it directly in the program, you should organize it. We emphasize the word *should* here because this is optional, However, we highly recommend it, especially to those of you who would rather close the door of a dirty bedroom than clean it up. You cannot leave all your content in one, unnamed layer and expect to find what you need quickly and without frustration.

The Layers panel will come to your rescue. This panel is your organizational mecca. In the Layers panel, for example, you can name, select, move, categorize, hide, and link elements on your document. You have already worked a lot with layers in previous lessons, such as the Adam's Eye lesson in Chapter 3. You will also get to work with layers in Lesson 4 of this chapter. To see what the Layers panel can do for you, see Figure 8–39 through Figure 8–43.

For more details about layers, choose Help > Illustrator Help and do a search on "layers."

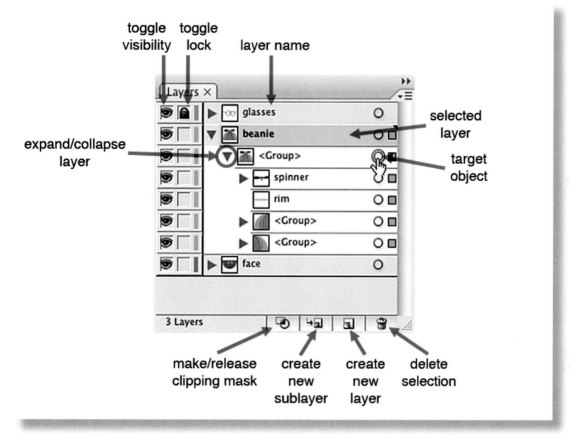

figure | 8–39 |

Basic layer options.

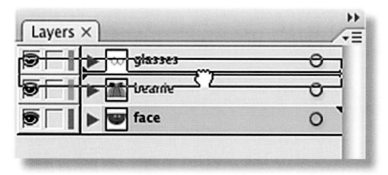

figure | 8–40 |

Click and drag a layer to a new location in the layer stack.

figure | 8–41 |

More layer options are available in the Layers panel drop-down menu.

figure | 8–42 |

From the Layers panel drop-down menu, choose Options for… to open the specific options of a selected layer.

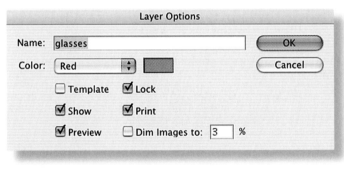

figure | 8–43 |

From the Layers panel drop-down menu, choose Panel Options… to adjust how you view layers in the panel.

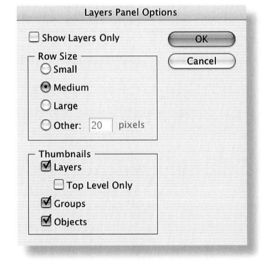

Other features that keep your work organized while integrating content in a document include the Align panel, Rulers, Grids, Guides, Smart Guides, and Snap to Grid or Point. The Align panel is located under Window > Align. You can find the other features under the View Menu.

- The **Align panel** aligns selected objects horizontally right, left, or center or vertically top, bottom, or center either in relation to themselves or the artboard. It also horizontally or vertically distributes selected objects evenly, using either the objects' edges or anchor points as the spatial reference. See Figure 8–44 and Figure 8–45.

figure |8–44|

The Align Panel.

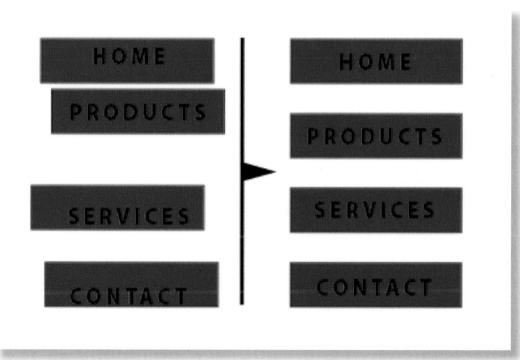

figure |8–45|

Before and after example of using the Align tool. The buttons and text on the right are horizontally centered, with a vertically centered distribution of space between each object.

- **Rulers** are designed to accurately measure and place objects on the artboard. To turn the rulers on, choose View > Show Rulers. To turn them off, choose View > Hide Rulers. Both a horizontal and vertical ruler appears along the top and left edges of the document. To change the measurement of the rulers, Ctrl-click (Mac) or right-click (Windows) on a ruler and select a new measurement from the drop-down menu. See Figure 8–46. Alternatively, you can go to Illustrator > Preferences > Units & Display Performance (Mac) or Edit > Preferences > Units & Display Performance (Windows). In the upper-left corner of the document, where the vertical and horizontal rulers meet, you can set what is called the Ruler Origin. Setting the ruler origin is useful when, for example, you are working on an object that is 2 by 3 inches on an 8 1/2-by-11-inch document. You can set the ruler origin at 0, 0 in the upper-left corner of the 2-by-3 area, rather than the 8 1/2-by-11 area for more precise positioning. To set the ruler origin, place the cursor in the upper-left corner of the document where the rulers intersect, then click and drag the crosshair to the new origin edge. See Figure 8–47. To restore default settings, double-click on the upper-left corner where the rulers intersect.

figure |8–46|

Set the measurement of the rulers.

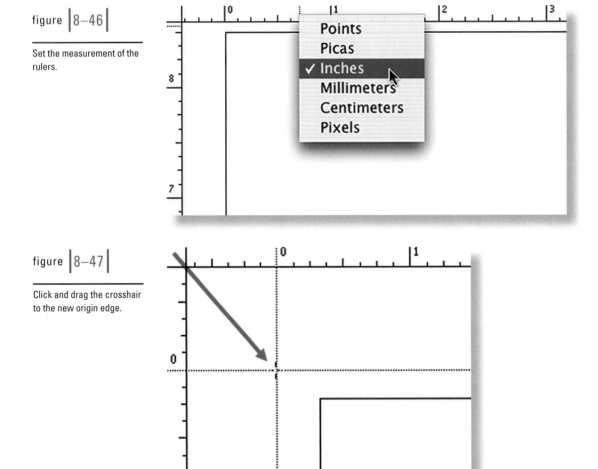

figure |8–47|

Click and drag the crosshair to the new origin edge.

- The **Grid** in Illustrator is located under View > Show Grid. A grid of lines or dots appears behind your artwork, and it can be used to symmetrically position objects. Grids do not print. To adjust Grid settings, such as color, style, and subdivisions, choose Illustrator > Preferences > Guides & Grid (Mac) or Edit > Preferences > Guides & Grid (Windows).

- **Ruler Guides** and **Guide Objects** are useful for aligning your work. To create ruler guides, choose View > Show Rulers and drag guidelines from the horizontal and vertical rulers on the edges of the document (see Figure 8-48). Guide Objects can be any vector object(s) you decide to turn into a guide. To create a Guide Object, select the object and choose View > Guides > Make Guides. To hide, lock, release, and clear guides, choose View > Guides. Guides do not print. To adjust guide colors and style, choose Illustrator > Preferences > Guides & Grid (Mac) or Edit > Preferences > Guides & Grid (Windows).

- **Smart Guides** (see Figure 8–49 and Figure 8–50) have a "snap-to" ability, which helps you create, align, edit, and transform objects relative to other objects. With Smart Guides turned on (View > Smart Guides), your cursor is like a magnet; it becomes an identifier for object edges, anchor points, and intersections. If you prefer to use Smart Guides without the color lines and information, choose Illustrator > Preferences > Smart Guides and Slices (Mac) or Edit > Preferences > Smart Guides and Slices (Windows) and uncheck the display options.

- **Snapping** allows for even more precise positioning by snapping objects to the Grid (when visible) or anchor points. Choose View > Snap to Grid or Snap to Point.

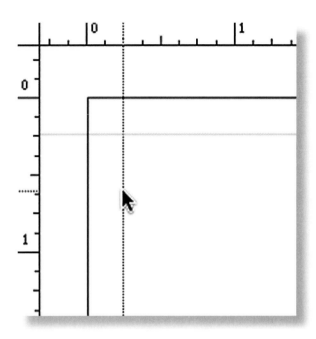

figure |8–48|

Drag ruler guides from the horizontal and vertical rulers.

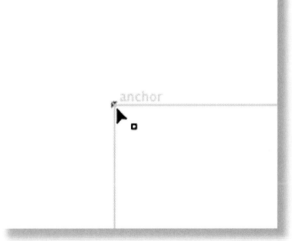

figure |8–49|

Use Smart Guides to snap to anchor points.

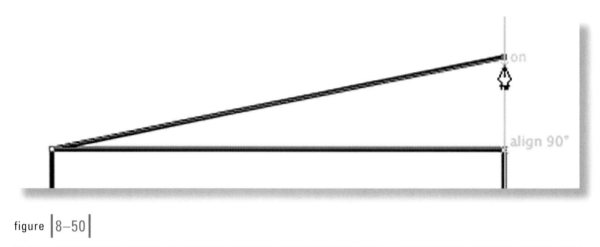

figure |8–50|

Use Smart Guides to align paths and shapes.

Fine-Tuning

Fine-tuning involves fixing the fine details of your layout: adjust colors, incrementally align items, play with subtle formatting of text, like line and character spacing. In this phase, you also prepare your final work for its intended output, such as set the proper color mode and settings for either screen or print and export into the desired file format.

Lesson 4: Practicing the Process—Building a Web Page Design

Put the creative process into action. In this lesson, you will construct a Web page. See Figure 8–51.

Setting Up the File

1. In Illustrator, choose File > New.

- *Filename:* Name it **chap8L4_yourname.ai**
- *New Document Profile:* **Custom**
- *Size:* **Custom**
- *Units:* **Pixels**
- *Width:* **760 px** (Standard dimension for a Web page layout.)
- *Height:* **420 px** (Standard dimension for a Web page layout.)
- *Color mode:* **RGB Color**, since this is eventually to be viewed onscreen. If Color Mode is not visible, click on the arrow next to Advanced to reveal more options. Click OK.

2. Choose File > Place and browse for the **page_template.jpg** in the **chap8_lessons/assets** folder. Unchecked the link option in the Place dialog box, then click Place.

> **Note:** When you uncheck Link, you are choosing to embed the image into the document.

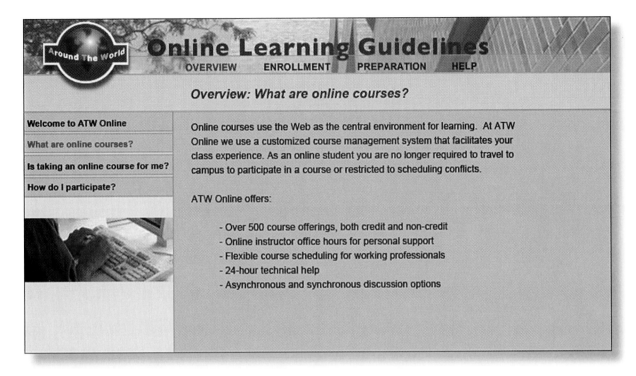

figure |8–51|

Completed Web page design.

3. Choose View > Actual Size. This is a pre-made template based on a grid layout we constructed for purposes of this lesson. We color-coded and labeled content zones for easy reference. When you create your own layouts, consider doing something similar.

4. Position the template precisely within the artboard area.

5. Choose Window > Workspace > [Basic].

6. Choose Window > Layers. In the Layer options drop-down menu, choose Options for "Layer 1".

7. For Layer name, type **page_template**. Select the Template option, and dim the image to 40%. Click OK. Notice in the Layers panel, in the visibility column, a Template layer is indicated by a series of geometric shapes rather than an eye icon, it is automatically locked, and the layer name is italicized.

8. Save the file in your lessons folder.

Creating Guides

1. Click the Create New Layer icon at the bottom of the Layers panel to create a new layer above the template layer.

2. Double-click on the name of the new layer (**Layer 2**) to open the layer's options. Name the layer **guides**. Click OK. See Figure 8–52.

figure |8–52|

Create and label a layer.

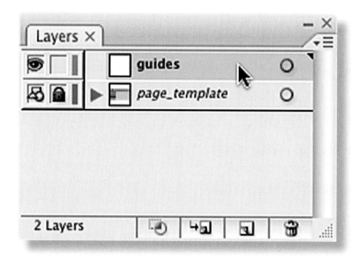

3. Choose View > Show Rulers.

4. Ctrl-click (Mac) or right-click (Windows) on the ruler at the top of the page and select Pixels.

5. Place the cursor on the top, horizontal ruler then click and drag down to create a guide. Position the guide at the top edge of the document.

6. Create another horizontal guide for the bottom edge.

> Note: To move guides, first unlock them. Go to View > Guides > Lock Guides to toggle the lock option off. Then, with the Selection tool, click and drag right over the guide you want to move. Remember to relock them so you do not move anything accidentally.

7. Continue creating horizontal guides along the horizontal edges of each colored rectangle of the template. See Figure 8–53.

> Note: For precision placement of the guides, zoom in on the document.

8. Place the cursor over the left side ruler and click and drag to create a vertical guide. Place the guide on the leftmost edge of the template.

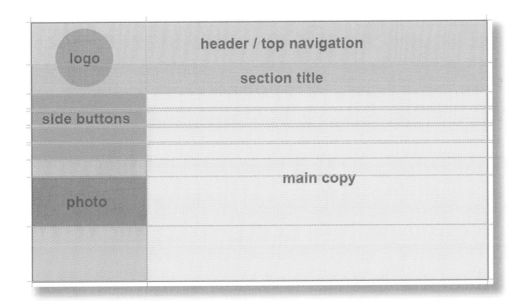

figure |8–53|

Use the template to accurately place horizontal guides.

9. Create another vertical guide for the rightmost edge.

10. Place a third vertical guide between the side buttons and main copy areas. See Figure 8–54.

figure |8–54|

Final guide placement.

11. Expand the **guides** layer in the Layers panel. Notice that each guide is indicated in this layer. Collapse and lock the layer.

12. Save your file.

Importing and Creating Content

1. Click the Create New Layer icon at the bottom of the Layers panel to create a new layer above the **guides** layer.

2. Double-click on the name of the new layer (**Layer 3**) to open the layer's options. Name the layer **header_and_top_navigation**.

3. Choose File > Place and browse for the **header.jpg** in the **chap8_lessons/assets** folder. Uncheck Link and click Place.

4. Position the bitmap image into the upper area of the template labeled **header/top navigation**.

5. Choose Select > Deselect.

6. Create a new layer and name it **section_title**.

7. Select the Rectangle tool.

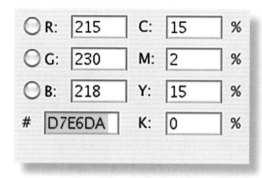

figure |8–55|

Enter a hexadecimal color in the Color Picker.

8. For fill color, double-click on the Fill box in the toolbox. In the hexadecimal box of the Color Picker, for the fill color type **#D7E6DA** (a very light green), then hit Tab to update the color. Click OK to exit the picker. See Figure 8–55.

9. Double-click the Stroke icon in the toolbox and type **#999999** (gray) for the stroke color.

10. Choose View > Smart Guides.

11. Click and drag the Rectangle tool from the upper-left corner of the purple section title area to the lower-right corner. Note how using Smart Guides allows you to draw and position elements very precisely. When you have Smart Guides turned on, drag objects from the edges to ensure accuracy.

12. Choose Select > Deselect.

13. Create another new layer and name it **side_buttons**. If the Layer panel is not open, choose Window > Layers or press F7.

14. Select the Rectangle tool.

15. For the fill color, type **#C3CFE6** (a very light blue) in the hexadecimal area of the Color Picker. Click OK.

16. Zoom in on the four side buttons to the left of the template.

17. Create a rectangle shape for each blue side button. Look closely at the template or the original Web page design (Figure 8–51 or **chap8L4a_final.ai** in the lessons folder) to accurately place the buttons. Notice that the buttons do not bump up right next to each other, but have a horizontal space between each one.

18. Zoom out.

19. Create another layer and name it **main_copy**. If the Layers panel is not open, press F7.

20. With the same color attributes as the side buttons, create another, large rectangle to cover the **main copy** area.

21. Create a new layer and name it **photo**.

22. Choose File > Place and browse for the **typing.jpg** in the **chap8_lessons/assets** folder. Embed the file, do not link it. Click Place.

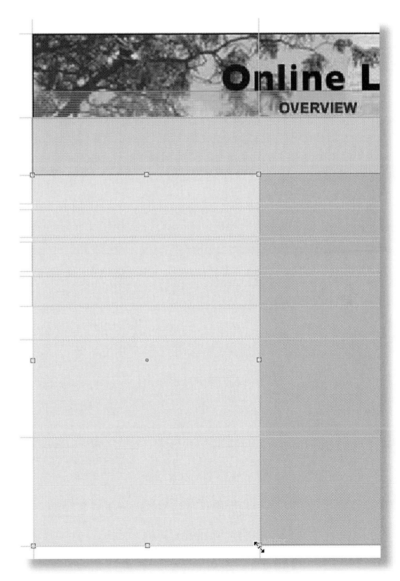

23. Position the photo into the photo area of the template.

24. Create a new layer and name it **side navigation background**.

25. Choose Select > Deselect.

26. Select the Rectangle tool. Type **#E8E9EA** (a very light gray) for the fill color, no stroke.

27. Create a rectangle that covers the remaining orange-colored area to the left of the template—from the top of the side navigation buttons, over the photo, to the bottom of the page. See Figure 8–56.

28. So you have a problem. The rectangle you just created is covering the buttons and the photo. Fix this by reordering the layer stacks. In the Layers panel, click and drag down on the **side_navigation_background** layer and place it below the **side_buttons** layer, but above the **section_title** layer. See Figure 8–57. Ahh, much better. While we are here, click and drag the **photo** layer between the **side_buttons** layer and **side_navigation_background** layer.

figure |8–56|

Add a light-gray rectangle to the left side of the template.

figure |8–57|

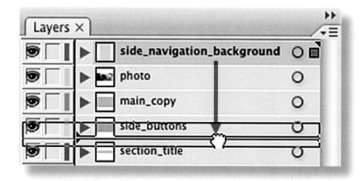

Move a layer below
another layer.

29. Choose View > Guides > Hide Guides, and check out your work.

30. Lock all your current layers.

31. Save the file.

Adding the Text

1. Choose View > Guides > Show Guides to toggle the guides on.

2. In the Layers panel, unlock and highlight the **guides** layer.

3. Drag a vertical guide from the left side ruler and place it between the *R* and the *V* of the word *Overview* in the header. This guide will be used to align your copy text.

4. Lock the **guides** layer and highlight the **main_copy** layer.

5. Create a new layer above the **main_copy** layer and name it **main_text**.

6. Choose File > Place and select the **overview.rtf** in the **chap8_lessons/assets** folder.

7. If the Microsoft Word Options come up, deselect all the Include options and the Remove Text Formatting option.

8. If you get a Font Problems warning, click OK.

9. A text block is placed into the document. Align the text along the guide you created within the **main_copy** area. Refer to Figure 8–51 for reference.

10. Choose Window > Type > Character and change the text to **Arial Regular**, **12 pt**. Set Kerning to **Auto**, Leading (line spacing) to **18 pt**, and Tracking (character spacing) to **10**.

11. Create a new layer above the **main_text** layer and name it **title_text**.

12. Select the Type tool in the toolbox. On the document, click just above the **main_copy** in the light-green area, and type **Overview: What are online courses?**

13. Select the Overview text and, in the Character panel, choose **Arial Bold Italic**, **16 pt**. For Kerning and Leading, choose **Auto**.

14. Position the title along the same vertical guide as the main copy block.

figure | 8–58 |

The Web page with text added and aligned.

15. Choose View > Guides > Hide Guides, and check the alignment of your work. See Figure 8–58.

16. Create a new layer above the **title_text** and name it **button_text**.

17. Create a text line that says **Welcome to ATW Online**.

18. Select the text line and set the characters of the text to **Arial**, **Bold**, **11 pt**, and position it over the first blue side button on the left of the page.

19. With the Selection tool, Option-Click (Mac) or Alt-click (Windows) and drag down to create a copy of the text line. Make two more copies, one below the other.

20. Change the text on one of the copies to **What are online courses?**

21. Change the text on another copy to **Is taking an online course for me?**

22. Change the final text copy to **How do I participate?**

23. Position *Welcome to ATW Online* in the center of the first side button.

24. Position *How do I participate?* in the center of the fourth (last) side button.

25. Roughly place the other two text lines in the second and third button areas.

26. Shift-click the four text paths.

27. Choose Window > Align to open the Align tool. Choose the Horizontal Align Left option, and Vertical Distribute Center to align the text paths.

28. Position the text paths so they fit properly over the side button area. See Figure 8–59 and Figure 8–60.

figure |8–59|

Before text alignment.

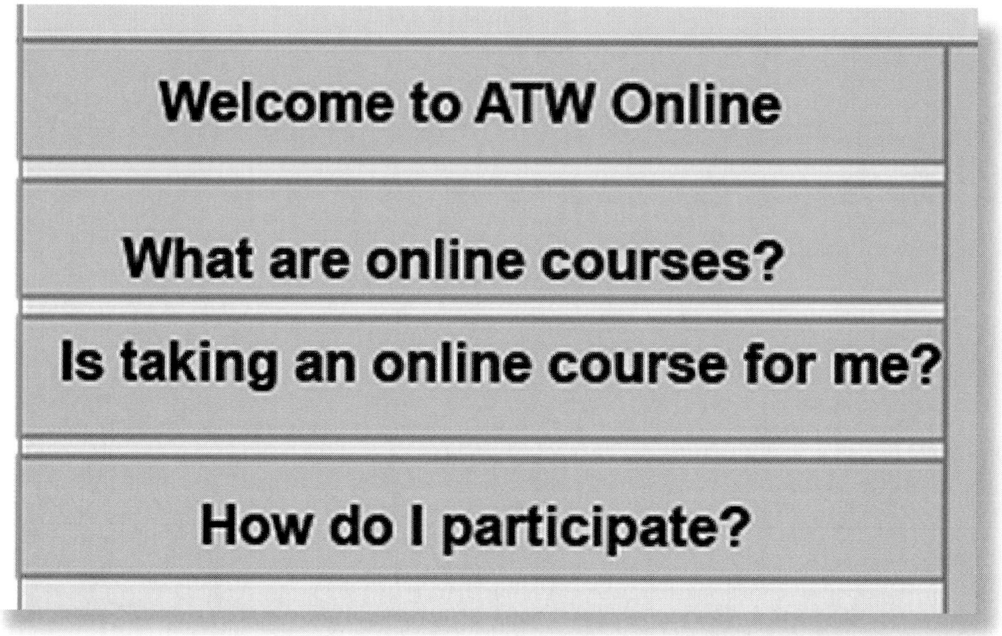

figure |8–60|

After using the Align tool.

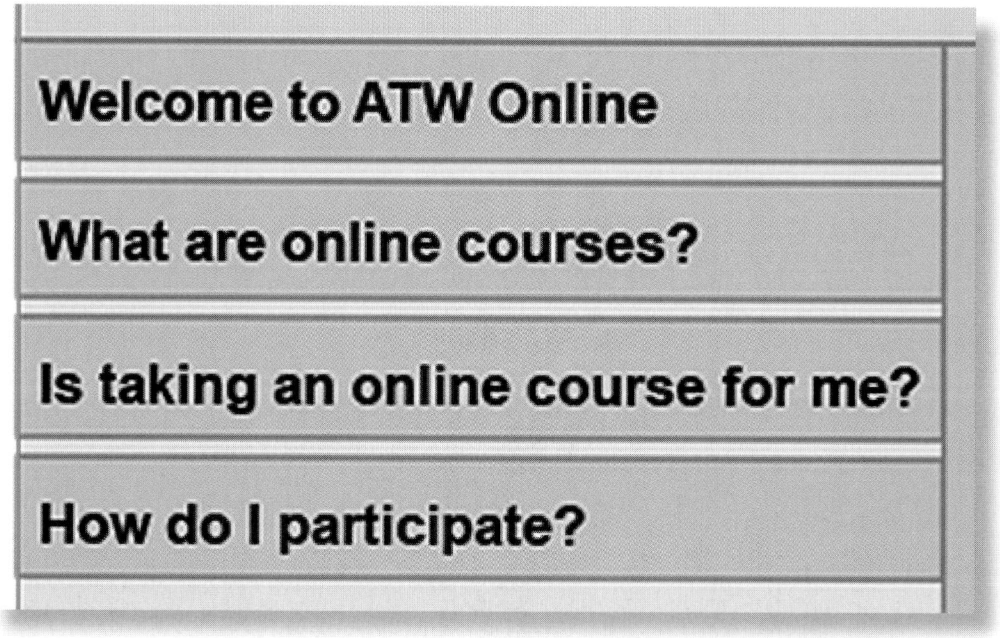

29. Select *What are online courses?* In the Swatches panel, choose a dark red color swatch.

30. Save the file, but do not close it.

Adding the Logo

1. Choose File > Open and open up the file **chap8L4b_final.ai** in the folder **chap8_lessons**. This is a completed logo file for ATW Online.

2. Open the Layers panel, expand the **ATW_logo** layer and **<Group>** sublayer and notice the compound shapes that were created. Also notice that the logo parts are grouped.

3. Copy and paste the logo into the Web page design. First, select the logo on the artboard.

4. Choose Edit > Copy.

5. Go to your Web page design, **chap8L4_yourname.ai**.

6. Go to the drop-down menu of the Layers panel and choose Paste Remember Layers. See Figure 8–61. This command ensures that when you paste the logo into the document, the layers and their order will stay intact.

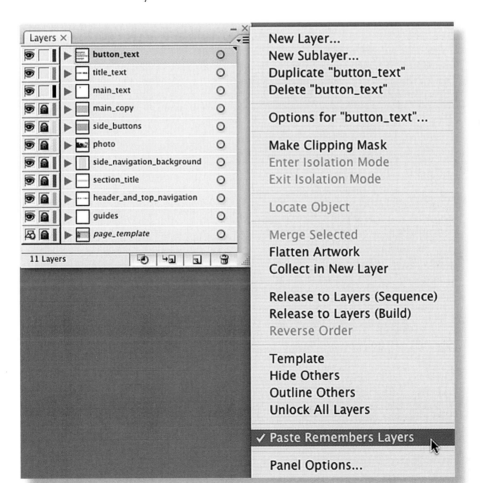

figure | 8–61 |

Select the Paste Remember Layers option before copying the logo.

7. Choose Edit > Paste In Front. (Notice in the Layer's panel, a layer is automatically created for the logo.) Position the logo in the upper-left corner of the document. See Figure 8–62.

Whew! You are done with the layout process.

figure |8–62|

Position the logo.

SUMMARY

After this chapter, hopefully your use of Illustrator has been bumped up to a whole new level. Constructing more complex shapes is no longer a mystery with the use of the Pathfinder panel, grouping, and clipping masks. And suddenly, the not-so-secret steps of producing compositionally complete layouts are within your grasp. Ideas that might have originally been lost can now be put into a tangible form with the importing, organizational, and workflow features of Illustrator.

in review

1. What is an important difference between a compound path and a compound shape?

2. What does the Expand command do and why would you use it?

3. What is the difference between pathfinders in the Pathfinder panel versus the Pathfinder effects (Effects > Pathfinder)?

4. Describe the steps for creating a clipping mask in Illustrator.

5. What tool do you use to select individual parts of a grouped object?

6. Describe the difference between linking and embedding artwork. Where would you go if you wanted to embed a linked file?

7. When you copy something, where does it go until you are ready to paste it?

8. Explain the EPS format and when it would be useful.

9. Name at least four features of the Layers panel.

10. How do you make ruler guides in Illustrator?

11. Where do you go to make a Template layer?

12. When would you use the Align panel?

exploring on your own

1. Choose Help > Illustrator Help. Under "Contents," read the topics Selecting and Arranging Objects, and Reshaping Objects.

2. Practice your layout skills by deconstructing a pre-made design. Cut out a magazine advertisement or newspaper article, or print a Web page, and with a pencil and ruler draw grid

lines to partition each section of the design. Label the sections as content zone areas, such as main copy, logo, header/title, photograph, artwork, etc.

3. Scan in a flattened drug box, bring it in as a template in Illustrator by selecting the Template option in the Place dialog window, and reproduce its design or create your own. Keep in mind that since you are reproducing someone else's design, this project can only be used for educational purposes and should not be presented commercially in any way without prior permission from the designer. To protect copyright of the original designer, the example of student work in Figure 8–63 has been slightly altered.

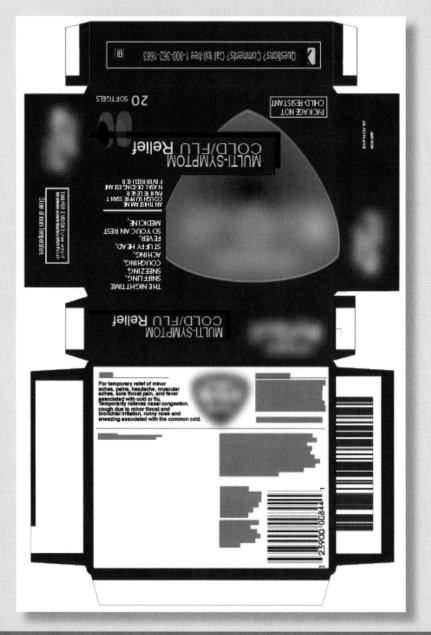

figure | 8–63 |

An example design reproduced from a flattened drug box.

making a wine label

In the world of graphic design, Illustrator and Photoshop go hand in hand. When working with a project where many elements must come together in a compositionally complete design, often the illustrative or textual elements are created in Illustrator and the photographic elements or effects are created in Photoshop. These separate elements are then combined—layered and arranged in a complete layout—in either Photoshop or Illustrator. As an example, we would like to share with you the development of a five-liter wine box label by Gallo Winery, Modesto, Calif. (Art direction: Dave Garcez. See Figure A–1). Then you can apply your own skills to first envision a wine label design and then create parts of it in Illustrator. If you know Photoshop, use that program, too, to recreate your vision.

Professional Project Example

A five-liter wine box label was created for Gallo Winery using a combination of Photoshop and Illustrator. First, a photograph was taken of a wine glass, a basket, and some grapes. See Figure A–2. Then they were layered together using Photoshop. See Figure A–3. The logo was created in Illustrator. A hand-drawn sketch was scanned and placed as a template into Illustrator. See Figure A–4. Then outlines were created for each letter shape.

The Offset command under the objects menu (Object > Path > Offset Path) was used to create additional outlines around each letter to produce a beveled effect. Colored

figure A–1   A five-liter wine box label was produced using Illustrator and Photoshop. (Used with permission of E & J Gallo Winery.)

figure A–2   Photographs were taken and layered in Photoshop.

continued

ADVENTURES IN DESIGN

continued

figure A–4   A hand-drawn sketch of the logo.

figure A–3   The photographs arranged in a complete image.

fill and stroke attributes were then added to the logo. See Figure A–5 and Figure A–6. The final logo design and photographic images were then arranged together in Photoshop, and saved and imported into Illustrator, where additional typographic elements were added and the whole file was prepared for print. See Figure A–1.

Your Turn

As you can see from the description of the wine label project, it is a common technique to start with a sketched drawing or template to help you reconstruct an artistic vision (a logo) in Illustrator. In several of the lessons in this book you also used pre-made templates to aid you in your digital drawing. Now it is your turn to develop an illustrative element using this technique.

Wine Label Project Guidelines

1. With sketchbook in hand, take a stroll through the wine section of your local grocery or liquor store.

2. Take note of the wine labels that catch your eye. What is appealing about the label to you? Its color? Its graphics? Its use of fonts? Its dimensions? Its shape?

3. Sketch your own wine label idea in the sketchbook. First determine the general size of the label. Make up a name for your wine. Start blocking out content zone areas. (Where will the title, the main graphic element, the copyright, ingredients, and alcohol content instructions go?) How will the graphics you create for the label reflect the title for the wine you have chosen?

4. Create a final sketch of the wine label in the sketchbook. Be as precise as possible with your drawing—measure the label, use colored pencils or markers to indicate the color scheme, and draw to the best of your ability what you envision the label will look like.

5. Scan a copy of your sketch into a digital format (a TIFF or JPEG image).

figure A–5 The stages of recreating the logo drawing using Illustrator.

figure A–6 The final logo design with value and texture. (Used with permission of E & J Gallo Winery.)

6. Import the image into Illustrator, and put it on a template layer.

7. Begin to construct the label, using the tools you have learned in Illustrator.

8. After you have read Chapter 10 you can prepare the label for print.

Things to Consider

We assume you will eventually want to do some of these adventures in design and actually get paid for your work, or at least recognized with high praise. Here are some things to consider when making your wine label or any other professional-type project.

- A design is never finished. Leave time to do revisions.

- Save often and back up your work. we suggest also saving different versions of your work, like "mylabel_v1," "mylabel_v2a," etc.

- Keep your document organized. In other words, use layers and name them intuitively.

- Show your wine label to a few trusted friends or colleagues. Ask them what they think. Is the information clear, easily readable? Are the graphics visually appealing?

- Print your design from a desktop printer to get a good idea of the size of the label. Cut out the label and superimpose it over an actual wine bottle to see how it looks.

- If you "borrowed" from someone else's work, or used an existing image as a template in the creation of the label, keep copyright issues in mind.

Explorer pages

JANET MCLEOD

"In this work, people skills are needed to listen to clients, respect their projects and negotiate good work processes with them so that jobs go smoothly and are financially worthwhile for both parties."

 Learn more about this artist via podcast at *http://www.designexploration.com/podcasts*.

About Janet McLeod

Janet McLeod is a Toronto-based illustrator with 15 years' experience. Working predominantly in Adobe Illustrator, her work is bold, colorful and graphic often with a strong sense of line. Frequent subjects include diversity in ethnic individuals, groups of people, activities, spirituality, technology, and world development. Her clients include design companies, marketing firms, and advertising. Originally from London, Ontario, Janet studied Visual Arts at The University of Western Ontario.

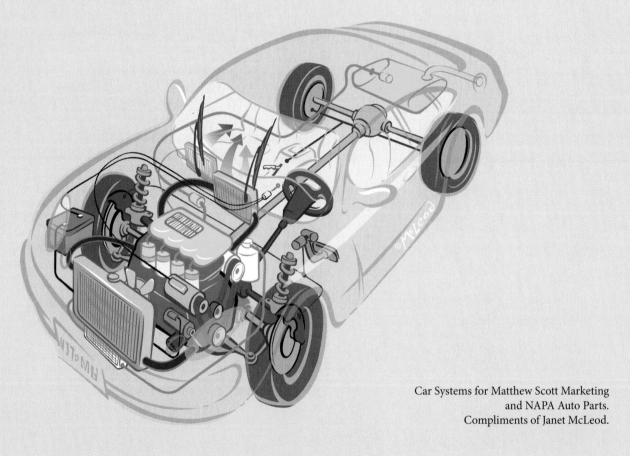

Car Systems for Matthew Scott Marketing
and NAPA Auto Parts.
Compliments of Janet McLeod.

"Basic art skills such as drawing skills, having an engaging concept and composition, mastering the medium and managing the dark and light shapes within the image, are the skills that ensure 95% of the success of any work of art."

Winter Wonderland for Scholastic Canada Ltd.
(Insert: linear detail for Winter Wonderland).

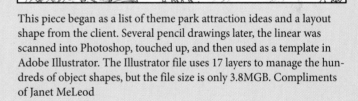

This piece began as a list of theme park attraction ideas and a layout shape from the client. Several pencil drawings later, the linear was scanned into Photoshop, touched up, and then used as a template in Adobe Illustrator. The Illustrator file uses 17 layers to manage the hundreds of object shapes, but the file size is only 3.8MGB. Compliments of Janet MeLeod

About the Work of Janet McLeod

Janet shares a bit about her creative process: "When I need to think up concepts I pull out a huge pad of paper and just start doodling, writing, and drawing. A key to creativity is to not self-censor; anything I think gets written down because stupid ideas often are the stepping-stones to great ideas. For each conceptual project, I like to develop about 12 to 15 ideas or approaches that could work, and then pick the best one to three ideas to present to the client. Original ideas are about pulling together disparate elements that together make sense. Often a gut feeling that an idea works is the best indicator of quality. Over thinking an idea often kills its creativity."

The Young Urban Professional, a personal work which emerged from a project for Ledden Design. Compliments of Janet McLeod.

spatial illusions

charting your course

Our world would be a flat place indeed without a sense of space. And so would your 2D artwork without the means of spatial illusion. In fact, the arrangement of objects into a whole—our definition of composition from the previous chapter—is really only the surface of what could be a more dimensional visual experience. With a little Illustrator magic, you can create an illusion of dimensionality, organic form, and space in your drawing and design. Obviously, we cannot show you all the methods for creating such spatial illusions, but we will cover some Illustrator tools and commands to help you get started. This chapter will explore the use of the blend and mesh commands, the Liquify reshaping tools, and 3D effects.

goals

In this chapter you will:

- **Discover the use of blends for producing subtle transitions of color and dimensional impact**

- **Distort and transform blended objects**

- **Reshape and distort objects with the Liquify tools**

- **Use envelopes to mold objects**

- **Precisely control the tonal detail of gradients with gradient meshes**

- **Use 3D effects to construct objects in the x, y, and z dimensions, simulating a 3D look.**

MAKING SPACE

Establishing a sense of space in 2D artwork involves the skillful application of the fundamental elements of design: line, shape, value, texture, and color. The way in which these elements might be sized, rearranged, and positioned trick our eyes into seeing and believing the illusionary effects of depth and dimension on flat surfaces. A simple example of this concept is one-point perspective drawing—the convergence of lines and shapes into a distant vanishing point.

> **Note:** The one-point perspective example shown in Figure 9–1 is an easy and actually quite fun task to recreate and expand on in Illustrator. Some suggestions: Turn on View > Smart Guides to accurately snap your lines into place. To identify lines that are in the back of the box shape, use the dotted lines option in the Stroke panel.

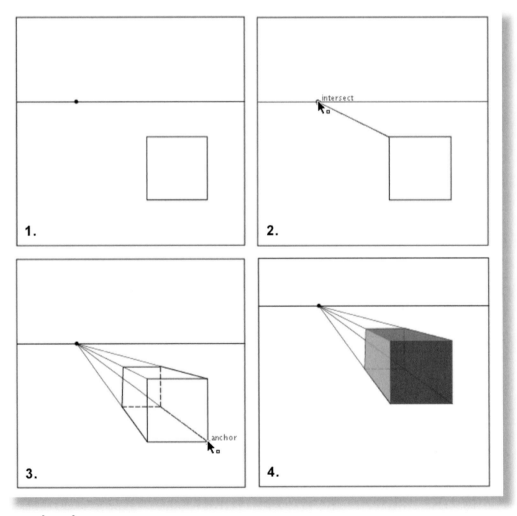

figure | 9–1 |

One-point perspective—placing lines and shapes in such a way that the feeling of space is achieved.

Another example of spatial trickery is the use of light and dark shades of color (or value) to achieve dimensionality. In Figure 9–2, a graphic artist we know, Gregory Sinclair, took his photograph, then drew a realistic self-portrait by identifying the light and dark areas in the photo and transposing them into filled light and dark colored shapes. Since you are drawing digitally with Illustrator, mastering the art of spatial illusion can be more manageable than doing it by hand. First, you have the luxurious feature of undoing and redoing. Also, as covered in this chapter, you get to use some specific tools and commands, such as blends, envelopes, liquify tools, gradient meshes, and 3D effects.

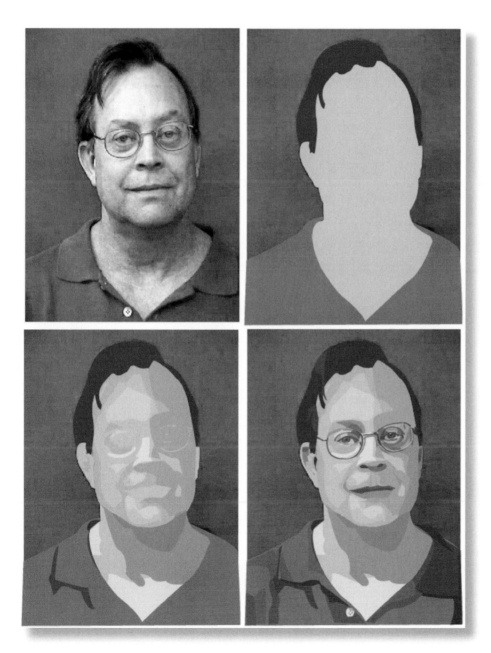

figure |9–2|

The stages of Gregory's self-portrait. Compliments of Gregory Sinclair.

Blends

With the Blend tool or the Object > Blend > Make command, you can create smooth transitions or distributions of color or shapes between objects. It is a great way to make anything from simple borders to morphed, organic shapes. To use the Blend tool, do the following (the sample file is provided in **chap9_lessons/samples/shells_blend.ai**):

1. Start with some shapes you would like to blend. If they have different fill colors, the colors will blend, too. See Figure 9–3.

figure | 9–3 |

Use a blend to create a border with the different color starfish objects on each corner of the artwork.

2. Without selecting anything, go to Object > Blend > Blend Options. See Figure 9–4. You can choose Smooth Color to space the blended objects smoothly, like a continuous gradient; Specified Steps, which distributes a specified number of morphed objects between the start and end objects; or Specified Distance, which controls the distance of objects within a blend. When blends are created, the objects are blended along a straight path, which can be adjusted with Illustrator's editing tools. The Orientation option lets you control how the objects are oriented to the path, either perpendicular to the x-axis of the page, or to the path itself. Try each option and see what happens. Click OK once you have made your choice. If you are using the sample file, choose **Specified Steps**, **6** for Spacing, and the **Align to Page** for Orientation.

3. Select the Blend tool in the toolbox. See Figure 9–5.

figure |9–4|

Set up the Blend options.

4. Click with the Blend tool on the top point of one of the star shapes, then click again on the same point of the next star to create the blend. If you have more than one object (i.e., more than one star), click on each object to continue the blend. Make sure you click on the same point on each object.

> Note: The order in which you select each object will affect the blending pattern. See Figure 9–6.

figure |9–5|

Select the Blend tool.

figure |9–6|

Click on each corner object to create the blend.

5. Select one of the objects in the blend to see how the blend is made. Notice the blend objects are connected by a path. If you adjust an original object in the blend with the Illustrator editing tools, the total blend will update. See Figure 9–7.

figure | 9–7 |

If you change the size of one of the original blending objects, it automatically adjusts the size of the objects created from the blend.

> **Note:** To remove a blend between objects, choose Object > Blend > Release. To create individual, editable objects out of each blend object, choose, Object > Blend > Expand.

Alternatively to the Blend tool, the Make Blend command makes blends between multiple objects in one step. To practice using this command, you can use the sample file **circles_blend .ai**, in the folder **chap9_lessons/samples**, or draw your own objects.

1. Select the objects you want to blend within one circle.

2. Choose Object > Blend > Blend Options to set your blend preferences. To produce the blend shown in Figure 9–8, we chose **Smooth Color**, **Align to Page**.

3. Choose Object > Blend > Make to produce the blend.

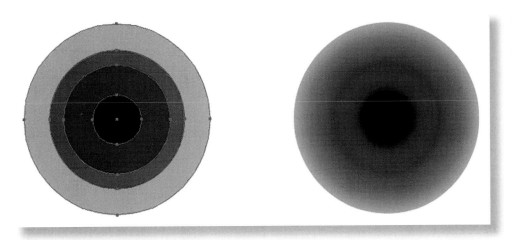

figure |9–8|

This visual shows the before and after using the Smooth Color blend.

4. To modify or transform individual, blended parts, use the Group Selection tool (hidden under the Direct Selection tool in the toolbox). See Figure 9–9. To modify individual anchor points of each part, use the Direct Selection tool. The blend readjusts automatically to your modifications.

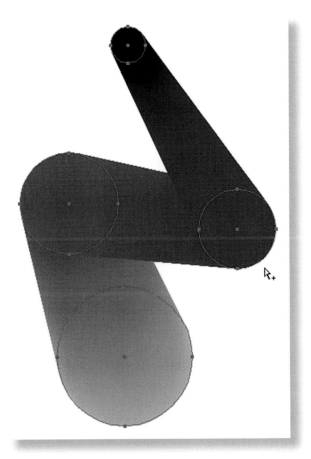

figure |9–9|

Each circle in the blend was pulled apart with the Group Selection tool. The blend readjusted automatically with the changes.

> **Note:** Be aware that creating blends plus adding effects to them can get file-intensive. The effect might take a while to render, and it might take a couple extra seconds for items to redraw on the artboard. This is normal; your computer has to think a lot to execute more complex imagery. Save often when things get slow. If necessary, use View > Outline to move around quicker or to select items in the document.

For kicks, add some Distort & Transform effects to blended objects. Use the **circles_blend.ai** to practice.

1. Select all the objects within a blended object.

2. Choose Effect > Distort & Transform and choose the Roughen effect. Choose the Preview option in the dialog box.

3. Set the size, detail, and point specifications to your liking. In Figure 9–10, we chose 10 and 10 for both the size and detail. Click OK.

figure | 9–10 |

Examples of the Roughen and Tweak effects on a blended object.

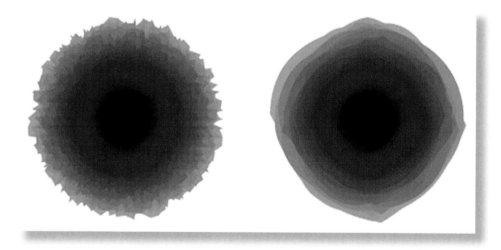

4. On your own, try other Distort & Transform effects on blended objects.

There is more to blending. You can blend not only shapes, but also paths, as shown in Figure 9–11 through Figure 9–14.

Try the following steps with the sample file **paths_blend.ai**, located in **chap9_lessons/ samples**, or make your own blended paths.

1. Select the paths you want to blend.

2. To set your blend options, choose Object > Blend > Blend Options. As seen in Figure 9–12, we chose **Specified Distance**, **4 pt**, which created blend lines equally four points apart between the two master paths.

figure |9–11|

Start lines—an arc and a spiral.

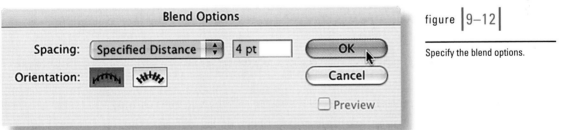

figure |9–12|

Specify the blend options.

3. To create the blend, choose Object > Blend > Make. See Figure 9–13. If you want to release the blend, choose Object > Blend > Release.

4. To modify individual anchor points of the blend, use the Direct Selection tool. See Figure 9–14.

figure |9–13|

Create a blend between the two lines.

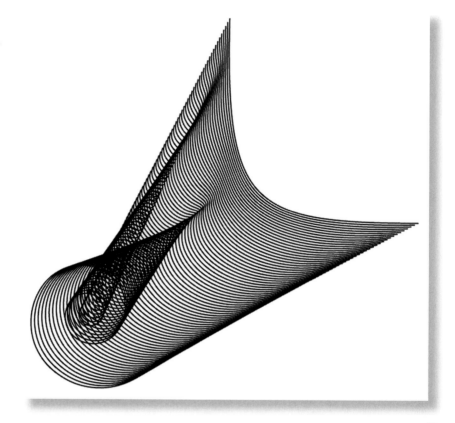

figure |9–14|

Modify the blend with the Direct
Selection tool.

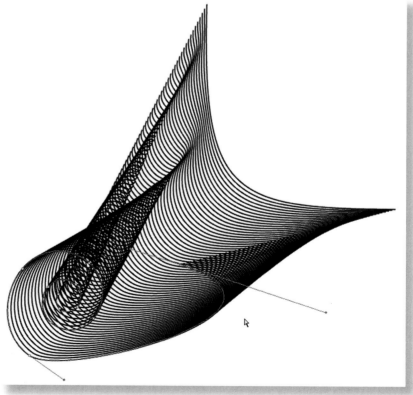

Liquify Tools

Seven playful tools for reshaping and distorting objects are located in the Illustrator toolbox. See Figure 9–15. These are the Liquify tools with fun names like Warp, Twirl, Pucker, Bloat, Scallop, Crystallize, and Wrinkle.

To use a Liquify tool, select it from the toolbox and then click or click and drag the tool over the object you want to reshape. If you double-click on a Liquify tool icon in the toolbox, the options for that tool appear. See Figure 9–16.

An example of what each Liquify tool does is provided in Figure 9–17. For you to experience each hands-on, a practice version of this file is located in **chap9_lessons/samples/ liquify.ai**.

1. Select an object you want to reshape or distort.

2. Select a Liquify tool in the toolbox.

3. Click or click and drag the tool over the selected object.

figure |9–15|

The Liquify tools.

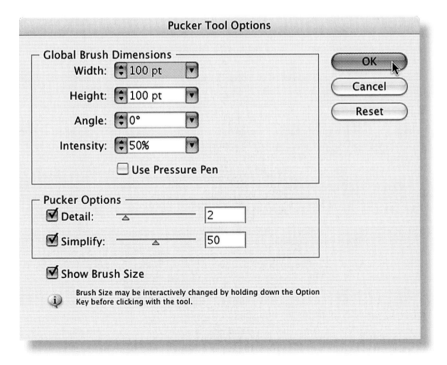

figure |9–16|

The options for the Pucker tool.

figure | 9–17 |

Examples of what each Liquify tool does.

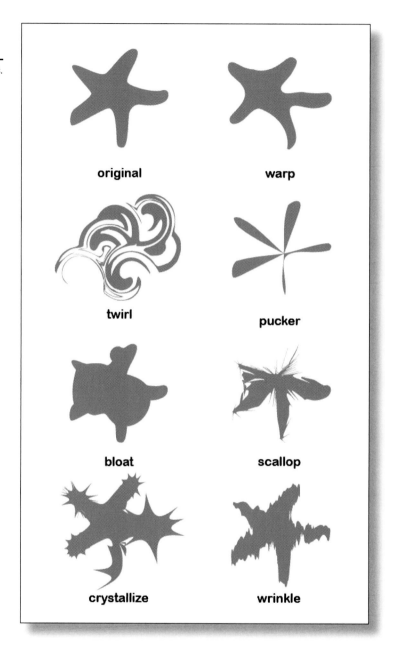

original   warp

twirl   pucker

bloat   scallop

crystallize   wrinkle

> **Note:** Liquify tools cannot be used on linked files or objects containing text, graphs, or symbols. To work with these objects, first outline the text, and ungroup and/or expand the graphs and symbols.

4. To modify the tool, double-click on the tool's icon in the toolbox to bring up its options box.

5. To interactively adjust the brush size of a Liquify tool, hold down Option—or Option-Shift to constrain it to a circular shape—(Mac), or Alt—or Alt-Shift—(Windows) as you click and drag with the tool.

Envelopes

Like the Liquify tools, envelopes allow you to reshape and distort objects, but in a more global way. Think of envelopes as elasticized molds that wrap around objects, making them bendable and malleable like in Figure 9–18. You can edit an envelope with Illustrator's editing tools, such as the Direct Selection, transform, and Liquify tools. Also, envelopes can be created from paths, compound paths, text, meshes, blends, and raster images, such as GIF, JPEG, and TIFF.

To make an envelope, choose Object > Envelope Distort and choose from one of three envelope types: warp shape, mesh grid, and with a different object. Let us show you how to create each kind.

Warp Shape

The Warp shape gives you a variety of choices for creating envelopes. See Figure 9–18.

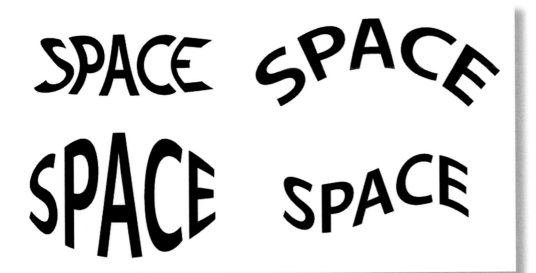

figure |9–18|

Here are examples of the Squeeze, Arc, Flag Warp, and Bulge envelopes (clockwise from top left). There are many more.

1. Select some text, a raster, or vector object.

2. Choose Object > Envelope Distort > Make with Warp.

3. From the Warp options window, select Preview.

4. Choose a Style, Bend amount, and the level of horizontal and vertical distortion. See Figure 9–19. Experiment with different settings and see what distortions are possible.

5. Click OK.

figure | 9–19 |

The Warp Options window—
so many warp styles to
choose from!

Warp Options

Style: ☼ Squeeze ▲▼

⦿ Horizontal ◯ Vertical

Bend: 50 %

— Distortion —

Horizontal: 0 %

Vertical: 0 %

OK

Cancel

☑ Preview

6. Modify the scale of the warp using the Free Transform tool, or individual anchor points with the Direct Selection tool.

> **Note:** To remove an envelope, choose Object > Envelope Distort > Release. To create individual, editable objects out of each blend object, choose Object > Envelope Distort > Expand.

Mesh Grid

The Mesh Grid, as shown in Figure 9–20, looks like a grid on graph paper, but this one is stretchable.

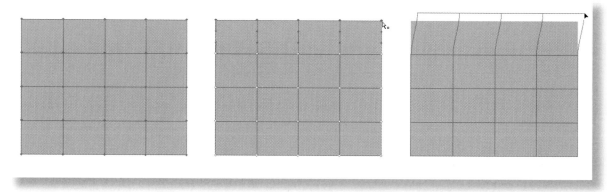

figure | 9–20 |

An example of a 4-by-4 Mesh Grid on a simple rectangle, which is then modified with the Direct Selection tool.

1. Select some text, a raster, or vector object.

2. Choose Object > Envelope Distort > Make with Mesh.

3. In the Envelope Mesh dialog box, choose the number of rows and columns you would like in the mesh. Click OK.

> Note: Depending on the shape you are trying to create from the mesh, you might want to experiment with more or fewer rows and columns. Keep in mind, more rows and columns produce more editable anchor points; however, the time it takes to redraw the mesh will increase.

4. Modify points on the mesh with the Direct Selection tool.

5. To add more rows and columns to the mesh, click on the grid lines with the Mesh tool. See Figure 9–21.

6. To delete a point, select the point with the Direct Selection tool or the Mesh tool and press Delete.

> Note: When a point is deleted, the mesh will become deselected.

figure |9–21|

The Mesh tool.

A Different Object

You can create an envelope of any shape to surround and reshape an object or group by using the Envelope Distort Command. See Figure 9–22.

figure |9–22|

An object stacked above another object (i.e., the transparent circle above the text) can become an envelope for the object below it (i.e., the text).

1. Select the object(s) you want to reshape and the object you want to use as an envelope. Very important: Make sure the object to be used as the envelope is above and in front of the object(s) you want to reshape. If both objects are on the same layer, select the object to be used as the envelope and choose Object > Arrange > Bring to Front. Another option is to place the envelope object on a layer (or sublayer) above the reshaped object in the Layers panel.

2. Choose Object > Envelope Distort > Make with Top Object. The two objects are grouped into an envelope mold.

3. Apply a fill or stroke to the selected envelope using the options in the Appearance panel. See Figure 9–23.

figure |9–23|

Change the fill color of the envelope object.

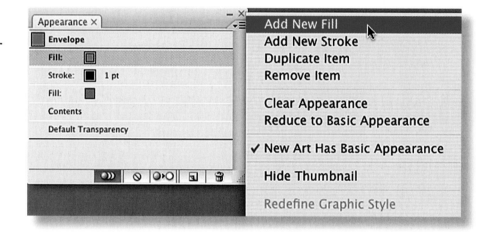

4. To adjust the envelope, choose Object > Envelope Distort > Edit Contents. Select the individual parts of the envelope with the Direct Selection or Group Selection tools, or in the Layers panel. See Figure 9–24. Any envelope type can be selected and modified from the Layers panel. Each envelope object is placed on its own layer. See Figure 9–25.

figure |9–24|

Adjust an individual section of the envelope.

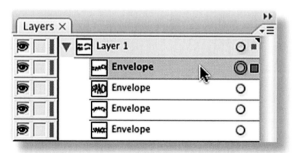

figure |9–25|

Envelopes are indicated in the Layers panel.

Gradient Meshes

Gradient meshes allow you to subtly and precisely control the application, coloring, and tonal detail of gradient blends. See Figure 9–26. There are two ways to create mesh objects: select the Gradient Mesh command (Object > Create Gradient Mesh) or use the Mesh tool. The Gradient Mesh command allows you to define a regular pattern of mesh lines and points. To create a customized mesh with a varied pattern of lines and points, use the Mesh tool. Here are some important things to know about mesh objects.

- Once a mesh object is created, it cannot be converted to a path object. You can, however, Edit > Undo a mesh if you made a mistake.

- Meshes can be created on any simple path object or bitmap image, but not directly on text (see note), compound paths, or linked EPS files.

> **Note:** Meshes can be created on text if it is first converted to outlines (Type > Create Outlines) and any compound paths within the text shape are released (Object > Compound Path > Release).

- Complex mesh objects can affect a computer's performance and the speed in which the graphics refresh on the screen. Keep your mesh objects simple. Create a few small mesh objects rather than a single complex one.

figure | 9–26 |

Use gradient meshes to create tonal detail and smooth transitions of color.

Of course, as with any tool you have been using, the best way to understand how it performs is to try it out. Using the sample file **balloons_mesh.ai** in the folder **chap9_lessons/samples** or with your own artwork, practice your mesh making skills with the following steps:

1. Select a filled object.

2. Choose Object > Create Gradient Mesh.

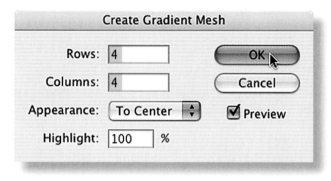

figure |9–27|

The Create Gradient Mesh options box.

figure |9–28|

The Mesh tool.

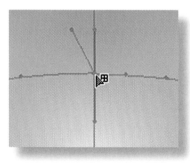

figure |9–29|

Select an anchor point of a mesh patch.

3. Set your gradient options in the Create Gradient Mesh dialog box. Choose Preview to see how each option affects the object. Keep your rows and columns to a minimum. We suggest four rows and four columns to start out. See Figure 9–27. Click OK.

4. Select the Mesh tool (see Figure 9–28) and click on a mesh patch, where an anchor point intersects a row and a column. See Figure 9–29.

5. Open the Swatches panel.

6. Choose a colored swatch to apply to the selected patch area.

7. With the Mesh tool, select another anchor point and apply a color. Notice how the colors subtly blend. See Figure 9–30.

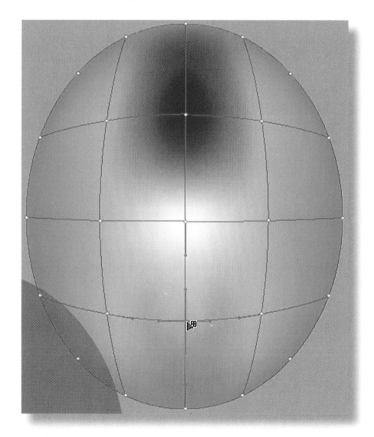

figure |9–30|

Apply a colored swatch to a mesh patch.

8. Click and drag on a mesh point or its tangent handles with the Mesh tool to modify the anchor points and how the colors blend. See Figure 9–31.

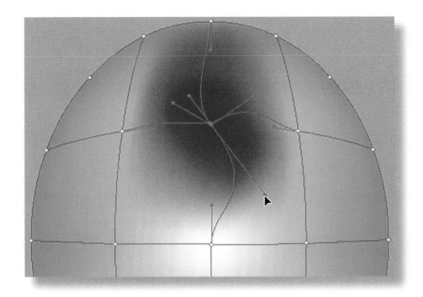

figure | 9–31 |

Modify an anchor point of a mesh patch.

9. Click between two anchor points on the mesh to add another mesh row or column. See Figure 9–32.

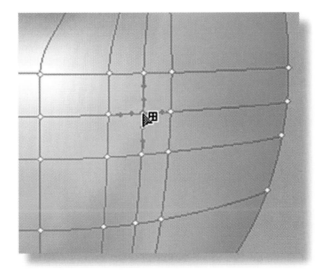

figure | 9–32 |

Add another column and row to the mesh using the Mesh tool.

10. To delete an anchor point, if necessary, select it and press Delete

> **Note:** Alternatively to choosing Object > Create Gradient Mesh, you can create a gradient mesh by selecting a filled object and then clicking directly on it with the Mesh tool, adding rows and columns as you like. Remember to use Edit > Undo if you make a mistake.

3D Effects

You easily get lost—in a good way—using the 3D Effects feature. Suddenly you are immersed into the third dimension, where paths and shapes can be extruded, rotated, and revolved around the x-, y-, and z-axes. See Figure 9–33, Figure 9–34, and Figure 9–35. You can also adjust the lighting and shading of the 3D objects, and place artwork on its dimensional surfaces (called *mapping*).

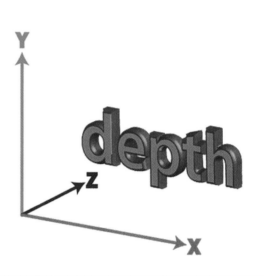

figure |9–33|

Extrude and bevel text in three dimensions.

figure |9–34|

Rotate and add perspective to text.

figure |9–35|

Revolve the profile of a
wine glass around the
y-axis.

3D Effects are located in the Effect menu (Effect > 3D), where you choose either Extrude & Bevel, Revolve, or Rotate. An options box appears where you interactively choose in which directions (x, y, or z) you would like your object to move and distort. To do this, click, then drag the cursor on a corner edge of the box model to affect a certain axis—the edges are color-coded for easy reference. See Figure 9–36. To adjust the box in the three axes combined, click and drag on a side of the box. See Figure 9–37. We suggest turning on the Preview mode so you can see how the changes affect your selected object—each alteration takes longer to render, but it gives you a better idea of the final look.

Expect to spend late nights captivated by the many options in the 3D Effects Options box. To get you started, the following steps describe how to use the 3D Revolve effect. Use the file **glass_3d.ai** in the folder **chap9_ lessons/samples** or draw your own paths.

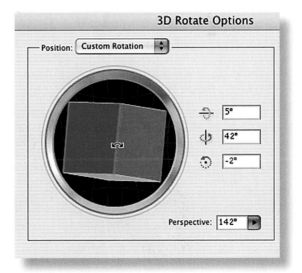

figure |9–36|

Adjust the y-axis of the object.

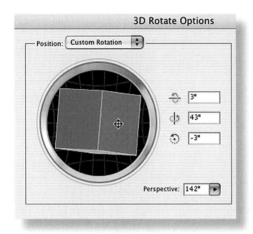

figure | 9–37 |

Adjust simultaneously the x-, y-, and z-axes of the object.

figure | 9–38 |

A profile of a wine glass to be revolved around the y-axis.

1. Draw a profile of an object that, when revolved around an axis, produces a symmetrical shape, such as the profile of a wine glass (see Figure 9–38), a chess piece, a pine tree, or an ornament. Use guides to help you align the top and bottom edges of the profile.

2. Select the profile. Choose Effect > 3D > Revolve.

3. Enter your specifications in the 3D Revolve Options box. See Figure 9–39. Turn on Preview as you make adjustments to see how it looks on your selected path. For the wine glass profile, we chose the following 3D Revolve options:

   • *Position:* Off-Axis Front
   • *Revolve angle:* 360 degrees
   • *Offset:* 0 pt from Right Edge
   • *Surface:* Plastic Shading

   Click OK. See Figure 9–40.

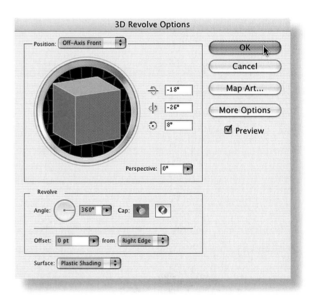

figure | 9–39 |

The 3D Revolve Options box.

4. The color of the completed object is specified by the stroke color of the original profile path. To alter the color, select the object's original path and change the stroke color. The stroke color in our example is set to a bright blue with an opacity setting at 40% (Window > Transparency). See Figure 9–41.

5. To fine-tune, if necessary, the original path, select and move individual anchor points with the Direct Selection tool. The Revolve updates with each new adjustment. The adjusted version of the wine glass is shown in Figure 9–42.

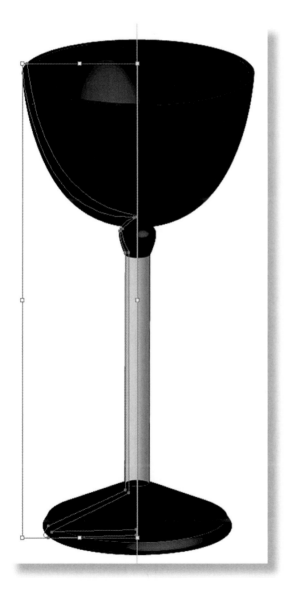

figure |9–40|

The completed Revolve.

figure |9–41|

Set the color and transparency on the original profile path—the revolved object is updated.

figure |9–42|

The final version of the wine glass.

6. As with all Illustrator Effects, go to the Appearance panel of the selected path to adjust or remove the effect. Double-click on the effect in the panel to open its options box and make adjustments. To remove an effect, select it in the panel, and choose Clear Appearance in the panel options. See Figure 9–43. Alternatively, you can drag the effect to the trash icon at the bottom of the panel.

7. Save your file often when using computationally intensive commands, such as the 3D Effect.

Graphic Style 3D Effects and the Free Distort Effect

Before sending you out on your own with these new found tools and commands, we must show you two more things: the 3D Effects Graphic Styles Library and the Free Distort effect.

For quick and easy application of a 3D Effect, go to Window > Graphic Styles. Then, in the Graphic Styles panel options, choose Open Graphic Style Library > 3D Effects. See Figure 9–44. Draw a simple path or geometric shape on the artboard, select it, and then take your pick of any of the predefined dimensional shapes in the 3D Effects Library.

To further modify your 3D effect or any selected path or shape, use the Free Distort Effect: choose Effect > Distort & Transform > Free Distort. Free Distort allows you to bend selected

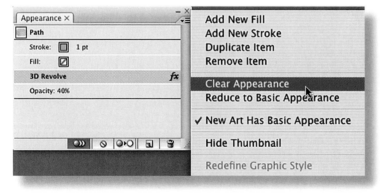

figure |9–43|

Remove the 3D Revolve effect in the Appearance panel.

artwork, within a flexible bounding square. Click and drag on any of the four corners of the square and your artwork acts like a Gumby doll. See Figure 9–45. Figure 9–46 shows the results of combining a 3D Effect graphic style with the Free Distort effect—in essence, applying an effect over an effect.

figure | 9–44 |

Open the 3D Effects Graphic Style Library.

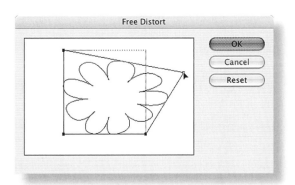

figure | 9–45 |

Bend the shape with the Free Distort effect.

figure | 9–46 |

Four examples of using a Drop Shadow effect (Effect > Stylize > Drop Shadow) and a 3D Effect graphic style with the Free Distort effect—spatial illusion made easy!

SUMMARY

Perhaps this chapter has transported you to another drawing dimension—one that is not flat, but rather filled with spatial possibilities.

in review

1. What are Smart Guides? Why are they so smart?

2. What are the two methods for creating blends?

3. What tool is used to modify individual anchor points of blended, meshed, or warped objects?

4. How do you change the brush size of a Liquify tool?

5. When making an envelope with a different object, where must the object to be used as the envelope be located?

6. How do complex mesh objects affect computer performance?

7. What three options are available when using the 3D Effects feature?

8. How do you change the color of a revolved 3D object?

9. Name four options available in the 3D Effects Options box and what they do.

10. To adjust or modify an effect, where do you go?

exploring on your own

1. Access the Help > Illustrator Help menu option. Under "Contents," read up on Reshaping Objects.

2. Practice your blending and gradient-making skills with the file **shells_blend.ai** in the folder **chap9_lessons/samples**. As reference, see the final version called **shells_final.ai**.

3. Follow Gregory Sinclair's example mentioned in the first part of this chapter. See Figure 9–2. Take a black and white photo of yourself and import it into Illustrator, or import a color photo

and convert it to grayscale (Edit > Edit Colors > Convert to Grayscale). Use the photo as a template to draw a realistic self-portrait. Identify the light and dark areas of the photo and draw each area with light- and dark-colored filled shapes.

4. Create your own perspective boxes (or other dimensional shapes) as shown in Figure 9–1. Use Smart Guides to place the paths and shapes.

5. Create an abstract design, pattern, or collage using the tools discovered in this chapter. See if you can create a sense of dimensionality in the artwork.

Explorer pages

ANN PAIDRICK

Magnolia Blossoms. Compliments of Ann Paidrick.

About Ann Paidrick

Ann Paidrick grew up in a family of artists. She studied sculpture at Kansas City Art Institute for three years. When she left art school, Ann began to work in fabrics and leathers—creating sculptural pieces, clothing, and illustrations.

Ann and business partner Pat Eby formed Eby-Paidrick Designs in 1977. They produced large-scale architectural textiles, banners, and collages for architects, interior designers, and art directors. Their signature fabric solutions animated spaces in buildings, illustrated ad campaigns, and provided unique environments in theme parks, museum exhibits, and theatrical sets.

In 2000, when the physical demands of building, hauling, and installing projects became onerous, Ann and Pat decided to learn computer graphics to continue working in the creative field. Prior to acquiring two Macintosh G-4s in 2000, their experience with computers was limited to catalog searches at the library.

After a year of twice-weekly tutoring sessions with computer artist Peter Richter, Ann fell in love with Adobe Illustrator. She tolerated Adobe Photoshop and Quark as necessary evils, but Illustrator's reliable vectors spoke her love of building things. Her sculptor's soul drove her to find ways to make a two-dimensional object appear three-dimensional.

Today, her realistic drawings not only push the envelope of the Illustrator software, but they also provide clients with images that can be enlarged to the size of an airplane hangar with no loss of detail and no pixilation. The technique mimics photo-realism. The resulting image is rendered flawlessly. Ann's gradient mesh illustrations are especially well suited for food, flowers, glass, metal, and china objects.

To see more of Ann's work, visit *http://www.ebypaidrick.com/*.

About the Work of Ann Paidrick

"I like to start the mesh shapes from a simple rectangle or square," Ann said. "This seems to produce less unruly results. I make my square and place just one set of mesh points in it using Illustrator's Mesh tool. Then I rotate it with an eye toward the final shape. If there's a vein of color down the center of a petal, say, I'll put the center of the square over that. Next, I start "morphing" the outside points toward the edges of the shape. Finally, I start laying in other points to refine the shape and describe the color changes."

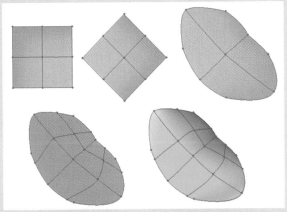

Clockwise from top left, this figure demonstrates the example stages of Ann's process for building a mesh object from a simple to more complex form.

Pepper Triplets is a final example of Ann's detailed, mesh-derived work. Compliments of Ann Paidrick.

Gold Birthday Bow on Red. Compliments of Ann Paidrick.

sbb_logo5.ai   8/21/03   3:09:56 PM

Andrea Linkin-Butler
Principal Broker

STRATTON BUYER BROKERAGE

Exclusive Buyer Representative

(802) 824-4421 – (800) 808-5917
andrea@strattonbroker.com
P.O. Box 2036,
S. Londonderry, VT 05155

www.strattonbroker.com

| print publishing |

charting your course

Chapters 10 and 11 are about what you do when you are ready to present your Illustrator artwork to the world. Where will it go? Will it be printed in a magazine, on a CD cover, on the side of a soup can? Will you be able to view it on a Web page, in a TV commercial, or on a multimedia kiosk? In this chapter, you learn what it takes to prepare your artwork for print. It is not as easy as hitting File > Print and expecting the document to arrive on paper exactly as you see it on screen. There is a host of considerations you should be aware of, such as the types of printing available and the management of color from screen to print. Specific issues unique to the printing process should also be on your output radar—halftoning, color separations, transparency, flattening, and resolution to name a few. There's a lot of information—more than we can cover here without overwhelming you. However, at the least this chapter provides a starting place for asking the right questions about the printing process.

goals

In this chapter you will:

- **Learn about the different methods of printing**

- **Understand halftoning and the color separation process**

- **Know what to do about printing transparencies, gradient meshes, complex paths, and fonts**

- **Get familiar with the Print dialog box**

- **Learn the right questions to ask when consulting a print service bureau**

PRINT PUBLISHING

A FRIENDLY CONVERSION

Have you ever found yourself in a situation where you meet someone who does not speak the same language as you, but you desperately want that person to understand what you are saying?

Donde el baño?

Huh?

Donde el baño?!

It is this type of situation that often occurs when a computer attempts to talk to a printer; they speak different languages, and unless there is an interpreter, the outcome might not be what you intended. Luckily, Illustrator comes equipped with its own translator in the form of a very sophisticated Print dialog box (which we will describe later, with Figure 10–5). However, to understand how to use it, you must have an idea of the printing process and the terminology used to prepare artwork for print.

Ways of Printing

There are several ways to get your artwork onto paper: directly from a desktop printer or digital printing press, from a film negative that is used to create a metal plate for a mechanical press, or in the Portable Document Format (PDF) or a PostScript file. Let us delve into each option.

Desktop Printer

Without a doubt, you will want to print your work on a desktop printer, if not the final version, at least some paper proofs for mock-up and revision purposes. Every desktop printer is different, made by different companies, with different specifications and different levels of printing capabilities. A low-end inkjet printer, for example, deposits ink onto a page much differently than a high-end laser printer. You should read the specifications for your particular desktop printer, so you can accurately gauge whether a printer issue is something you can fix in Illustrator, or is an unavoidable product of your printer.

You should also find out what resolution your printer supports and what will give you the best quality. It can vary greatly, depending on the type of printer and the paper used. Much of it is trial and error—print it and see what it looks like. In general, laser printers have a resolution of about 600 dots per inch (dpi). Inkjet printers have a resolution of between 300 and 1440 dpi. Dpi is usually the resolution measurement for printers. The resolution measurement for computers is pixels per inch (ppi).

> **Note:** For a refresher on resolution, or to find out more about the relationship between resolution and Illustrator, go to Help > Illustrator Help and, under Index, do a search for resolution.

Digital Printing Press

A digital printing press is a beefed-up version of a typical desktop computer (often found in the document processing departments of such places as Kinko's or Staples). As digital printing technologies improve, digital printing services are becoming a more prevalent alternative to traditional offset printing. Because digital printers rasterize PostScript data—printing directly from a computer file, rather than going through the intermediary film and/or metal plate stages (see next section)—they can yield quality output with a quick turnaround. Digital printing is ideal for targeted printing jobs and short-run projects that need to be done quickly but at a much higher quality than a desktop printer. The resolution needed to properly print off a digital printing press should match the resolution of the particular output device. Consult the printing service for the resolution at which your document should be set.

Mechanical Press

The traditional method for getting your virtual work to hard copy is using a mechanical press, the most common being offset printing. A digital file is transferred to a film negative, which is then used to burn a printing plate (or the file is imaged directly to the plate). The plate carries the image the press transfers to paper. If you are printing a photograph or illustration with more than one or two colors in it, things get more complicated and expensive. To simulate a full range of colors (four-color processing), mechanical printers deposit the four ink colors (CMYK) dot by dot, called halftones. See Figure 10–1.

figure |10–1|

Magnifying a section of the flower, you see its color is produced by halftone dots composed of CMYK ink colors.

To create continuous tone color using the halftone method, each color must be inked and pressed separately to the paper—in short, the colors are separated and then layered back together. To do this, each color must have its own metal plate (one plate inked with cyan, one with magenta, one with yellow, and one with black), which is produced from separate film negatives. This is the process of color separation.

The individual colors produced by the mixing of CMYK colors are called process colors. You can also identify spot colors or custom inks. As you learned in Chapter 5, spot colors are special colors composed of premixed inks that require their own printing plate other than the ones used for four-color processing.

For printers using the halftone procedure, Illustrator provides options in the Print dialog box for preparing an image for color separation and the subsequent printing process.

PDF or Postscript file

With Illustrator, you can also print your file in the Portable Document Format (PDF)—a PostScript-based format that can support both vector and bitmapped data. Printing to a PDF is a convenient way to maintain all the attributes of your original Illustrator file in a cross-compatible format. Often print service bureaus will request a PDF version of your file. To set the PDF options, choose a Save command, specify a filename, and choose Adobe PDF as the file format (Mac) or Save as type: (Windows). Click Save and the Adobe PDF Options dialog box appears, where you can indicate general settings and specific presets, such as one specific for [Press Quality]. See Figure 10–2. Check with your print specialist for the settings he or she prefers.

figure |10–2|

The Adobe PDF
Options dialog box.

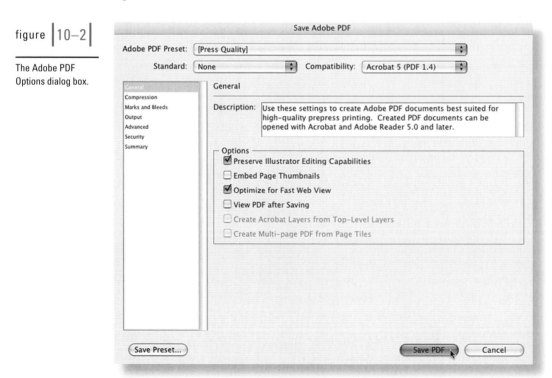

GETTING INTO DETAILS

If professionally printing your artwork, either via a digital or mechanical press, is a definite must, alleviate undue headaches and find yourself a reliable print specialist. A good specialist can identify your printing needs and offer appropriate solutions for getting the best quality print job for your specific situation. That being said, do not underestimate the necessity of *your* knowing something about the printing process and terminology to facilitate print preparation. Properly setting up your Illustrator file before handing it to the printer can save you lots of time and possibly money.

You should also have an idea of what kind of paper the job should be printed on. For instance, do you envision your creation on porous newsprint or slick, heavy card stock? Different types of paper produce varying color effects and require different specifications.

> Note: **Your print specialist can provide paper samples and color swatches to aid you in your decision.**

During the final output stages of your document, consult your printing service bureau to find out how best to prepare your file, such as in what format and resolution (see next section). Also, be aware that the complexity of your artwork determines a lot about how to prepare it for print. Transparencies, overprints, gradients, fonts, and complex paths, for example, might require extra attention to print properly.

Resolution and Screen Ruling

Resolution and screen ruling (or screen frequency) are important for outputting the highest quality artwork possible. For output to printers using halftone dots to render images, you must give consideration to the number of dots to be printed within a given area or screen, or in other words, the "resolution." This consideration is like working with the resolution of bitmap images, which, similarly, are composed of a given number of pixels on a bitmapped grid. Halftone dots are deposited on paper based on a screen ruling—the number of lines or rows within a given screen. Screen rulings for halftones and separations are measured in lines per inch (lpi). The frequency and size of dots are determined by the screen ruling. High lpi creates smaller, tighter dots, like those seen in a glossy magazine or slick brochure. Low lpi creates larger, rougher looking dots that are easier to print, such as in a newspaper. A general rule is that the resolution—ppi or dpi when referring to halftone printing—of a given piece of artwork is about 1.5 times and no more than 2.0 times the screen frequency. Come again? OK, imagine, after consulting a print specialist, you discover that the screen ruling for the glossy flyer you want to print is 150 lpi and needs to be in the TIFF, an uncompressed bitmap format with a lossless LZW compression option. This information gives you some idea of what resolution your TIFF file should be—between 225 and 300 dpi or ppi (hence, 150 lpi x 1.5 = 225). See Figure 10–3. Keep in mind that the resolution of an image and its screen frequency directly relates to what kind of paper it will be printed on and at what quality: the higher the screen frequency, the better the quality.

- Newspapers or similar high porous, coarse papers use screens of 85 to 100 lpi. Therefore, artwork resolution should be between 138 and 150 dpi or ppi.
- News magazines or company publications with medium coarseness use screens of 133 to 150 lpi. Therefore, artwork resolution should be between 200 and 225 dpi or ppi.
- Fine quality brochures and magazines with slick paper surfaces use screens of 150 to 300 lpi. Therefore, artwork resolution should be between 225 and 450 dpi or ppi.

figure | 10–3 |

You can set the resolution of your artwork in the TIFF Options box when you go to export your document (File > Export) or under Effect > Document Raster Effects Settings.

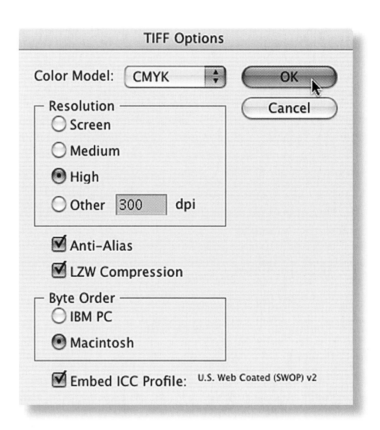

Transparency

If you print or export an Illustrator file that does not recognize Illustrator's transparency effects, Illustrator performs a process called flattening. Flattening identifies colored areas that overlap each other and converts the artwork into components that are more easily recognized by other programs and devices. To specify flattening settings, choose Object > Flatten Transparency or File > Document Setup. To preview how the changes might look when printed, choose Window > Flattener Preview. If you want to make adjustments, do so in the Advanced section of the Print dialog box.

Overprinting

Overprinting relates to transparency as it identifies how overlapping colors are considered in the printing process. By setting certain conditions in the Overprint options of the Attributes panel (Window > Attributes), you can prevent knockout—when a color appears opaque over a different color instead of transparent. See Figure 10–4. To preview how changes to overprint options might occur when printed, choose View > Overprint Preview.

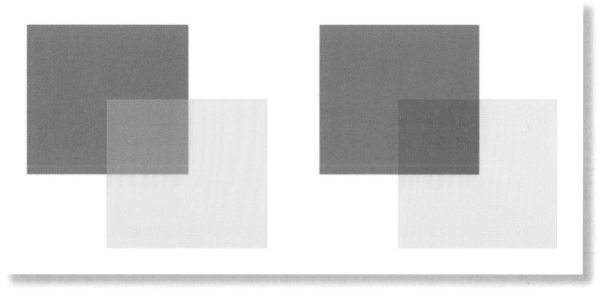

figure |10–4|

The first option shows the overprint preview of how two colors overlap (one with transparency) with the Overprint fill deselected in the Attributes panel. The second option shows the preview with Overprint fill selected.

▶ Don't Go There!

Do not let the preview (i.e., View > Overprint Preview and the Window > Flattener Preview) be the only indicator of how your work might appear in the printed format. Get an actual print proof of your work before going for the full press run.

Gradients

Depending on the type of printer used, gradients, gradient meshes and blends, particularly with transparency, could produce unwanted results. Gradients and blends contain continuous tones of color, which are difficult for some printers to print, causing distinct bands rather than smooth transitions of color. Some general guidelines for successfully printing gradients and blends follow.

- Create blends that change at least 50% between two or more process colors.
- Use short blends—blends that are longer than 7.5 inches can cause banding when printed.
- Use lighter colors if banding occurs between blends.
- Use an appropriate line screen that supports at least 256 levels of gray.
- Adjust the Flatness setting if the curves of the gradient blend or mesh are complex. The Flatness setting (as opposed to the Flatten Transparency setting) is found in the Graphics section of the Print dialog box.
- If the gradient or mesh contains transparency, you can work with its resolution (quality of output) setting in the Object > Flatten Transparency options box.

Fonts

As mentioned in Chapter 7, when exporting and printing fonts, you need the corresponding font files to accurately print the document, or, alternatively, you need to embed the font or font family. Another option is to convert the type into outlines (Type > Create Outlines) to avoid any missing font issues. In either case, it is always a good idea to check the copyright specifications for the fonts used, and if necessary get appropriate permissions for their usage. You can set font downloading specifications in the Graphics section of the Print dialog box.

> Note: Files saved as PDF embed the fonts automatically.

Complex Paths

Artwork containing complex paths, particularly curved paths with many line segments, might receive a "limitcheck" error message when trying to print to PostScript printers with limited memory. You can adjust how the complex paths are rendered with the Flatness setting option in the Graphics section of the Print dialog box. A high setting (toward speed) results in the creation of a path with longer, fewer line segments, making it less accurate visually, but improving print performance.

ABOUT THE PRINT DIALOG BOX

The Print dialog box sets preferences for how you want your artwork to print. If you have different output options—maybe one specific for desktop printing and then another for creating a film negative—you can customize and save your settings in this box. See Figure 10–5.

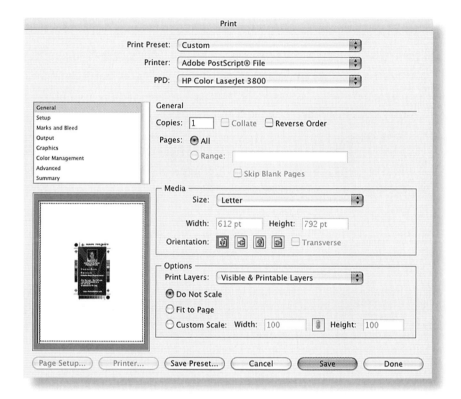

figure |10–5|

The Print dialog box is very useful for specifying and saving print options.

To open the Print dialog box, choose File > Print.

> **Note:** We encourage you to open the Print dialog box in Illustrator and follow along with our description of what is in this box. If you want a document to play with while in the dialog box, choose a pre-made template file. Go to File > New from Template and select a template in the Illustrator's Template folder.

At the top of the Print dialog box, you can choose a Print Preset that you have saved previously, select default, or create a new custom preset. If you are printing the artwork to a desktop printer or creating an Adobe PostScript File (see the next note), select the appropriate option under Printer. If your output device supports PostScript, you can specify a PostScript Printer Description (PPD). Illustrator uses the information in the PPD file to determine which Post-Script information to send to a PostScript printer when printing a document, such as font specifications, optimized screen frequencies, resolution, and color separations and management.

> Note: If your desktop printer does not support PostScript (only a few inkjet printers do), and you want to use some of the specifications PostScript offers, like the ability to make color separations, you might consider purchasing Adobe Acrobat. In Illustrator, you can print the file as an Adobe PostScript file from Acrobat and then send the Acrobat file to the inkjet printer.

Let us briefly go through the print options found on the left-hand side of the dialog box: General, Setup, Marks and Bleeds, Output, Graphics, Color Management, Advanced, and Summary. Keep in mind that the settings in each option area vary depending on the type of printer selected. There is a ton of information in this dialog box, so for more details on each option, choose Help > Illustrator Help > Contents > Printing.

General

In the General section you specify page copies, media size, width, and orientation and options for printing layers.

Setup

Setup is where you define the printable areas of your artwork. You can set the printer to crop artwork to the artboard, artboard bounding box, or to predefined crop marks. To set up crop marks before you print, create a rectangle that defines the edges of where you would like the artwork cropped and then choose Object > Crop Area > Make. The crop marks are then indicated on the document. See Figure 10–6. Another option is to use the Crop Area tool. See Figure 10–7. The Crop Area tool offers a more interactive experience with cropping your artwork. By clicking and dragging out a rectangle, the area inside the crop area shows what will be printed while the dimmed area outside the crop area shows what will be removed. To resize the crop area, click and drag the control points surrounding the perimeter of the crop area rectangle. To exit the crop tool, select any other tool in the toolbox. To make adjustments to the crop area at a later time, select the Crop Area Tool again.

In Setup, you can also adjust the placement of the artwork to best fit on the printed page or film negative. If your artwork is larger than a single page, you can determine how you would like the multiple pages to print by selecting a tiling option.

Marks and Bleeds

In this section, you can set up marks and bleeds specifications. If your document is to go through the color separation process, it is important to include printer marks on each separation page. These marks are needed for the printing device to accurately align the separations at press time (called registration) and verify correct color. See Figure 10–8 for an example of a file with printer marks indicated.

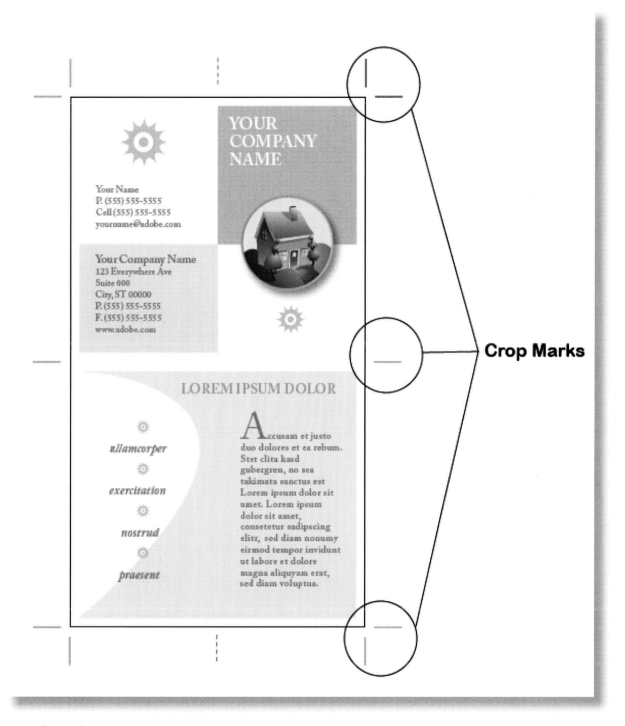

Crop Marks

figure |10–6|

Crop marks are created on this template file provided by Illustrator.

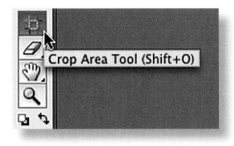

figure |10–7|

The Crop Area tool.

A bleed is defined as any work that spills over or "bleeds" outside the print bounding box. Color, for example, that you want to bleed to the edge of a page requires a bleed setting. Consult your printer for how much of a bleed you should indicate on your document to ensure the ink is still printed to the edge of the paper after it is trimmed (usually around 1/8 to 1/32 of an inch). Figure 10–8 shows a file whose color bleeds beyond the crop marks, ensuring an accurate look after trimming.

figure |10–8|

Artwork with printer marks indicated.

Output

The Output section lets you control how you create color separations. You can choose which CMYK and spot colors to separate and, if necessary, convert spot colors to their closest CMYK equivalent.

Graphics

The Graphics section of the Print dialog box makes clearer some of what was discussed in the section "Getting Into Details," such as setting the flatness of complex paths and adjusting how fonts download.

Color Management

As discussed in Chapter 5, color matching problems can occur when outputting artwork from one kind of device to another, for example, screen to print. One solution to alleviate these discrepancies is to use a color management system (CMS), which can translate color accurately between devices. To find out more about CMS, go to Help > Illustrator Help > Contents > Color Management > Keeping Colors Consistent. If you are using a CMS for your document, you can specify additional color management settings in the Color Management section.

Advanced

Specifications for overprinting and transparencies can be found in the Advanced section, as well as the ability to print artwork as bitmaps (versus vectors) when printing to low-resolution printers.

Summary

The Summary option summarizes all the settings you indicated in the Print dialog box. Conveniently, it also provides warnings about any special things you should consider regarding flattening, resolution of raster effects, color mode, spot and out-of-gamut colors. See Figure 10–9.

Once you have indicated your print options, you choose Print or Save to either print the document to the printer specified or save the document as an Adobe PostScript file, if that was specified. To save the settings you selected so you do not have to repeat the process, click Done.

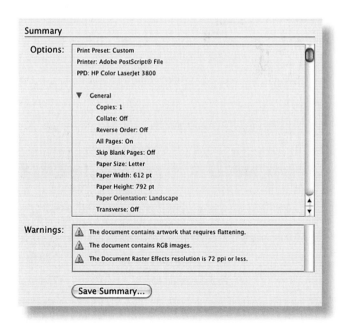

figure |10–9|

The Summary box lets you view your specifications and gives you warnings about special print concerns.

SUMMARY

There is a lot to think about when preparing artwork for print, so you should know the right questions to ask of the professionals in the industry. We also learned the importance of understanding what options are available in Illustrator for streamlining the printing process. Finally, it does not hurt to get a proof or two created of your final, meticulously edited, work before running the full print job.

in review

1. Describe halftone printing.

2. What is a PDF? What is so great about printing to PDF?

3. Screen ruling determines what about the halftone process?

4. The resolution of a piece of artwork is usually how many times greater than its screen ruling?

5. What does Flatten Transparency do?

6. What is overprinting?

7. What does the Flatness setting in the Graphics section of the Print dialog box do?

8. How do you create crop marks for your artwork?

9. What are printer marks for?

10. What is a bleed?

exploring on your own

1. Access the Help > Illustrator Help menu option. Under "Contents," read up on Printing.

2. Find out if your desktop printer supports PostScript and if you have the ability to specify options for color separations in the Print dialog box. If so, try printing separations for a document that has been saved in the CMYK color document mode (File > Document Color Mode).

3. Open the sample file **printlogo.ai** in the folder **chap10_lessons/samples**. Take a look at the printer marks that have been specified around the artwork. Using the Help files, investigate what each printer mark represents. Also, open the Print dialog box (File > Print) and see what print options have been saved for this particular document.

4. Awaken the detective inside you. Call a printing service (or search online) and inquire about what printing services it offers and what file specifications it requires. Be specific with your questions; try out the terminology you learned in this chapter.

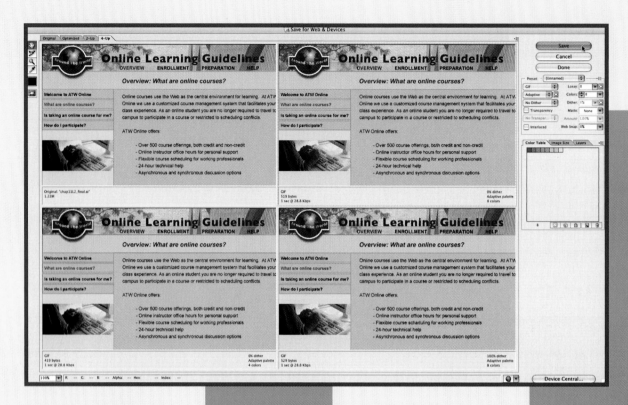

| web publishing |

charting your course

Today, a good percentage of illustrative artwork is used in digital format for Web pages, multimedia presentations, DVDs, TVs, and mobile phones. Designing graphics for the onscreen space is not the same as designing graphics for print (see Chapter 10 for print publishing). Each new version of Illustrator is supplemented with options for saving and preparing artwork and design layouts for the growing digital medium, particularly online. In this chapter, you consider the specifics when working with Web graphics, such as format, size, and color. Also, special attention is given to image slicing, the SVG and SWF vector formats, and reusable graphics called symbols.

goals

In this chapter you will:

- **Become an image optimization master**
- **Get a handle on Web file formats, including SVG and SWF**
- **Learn about Web image color and compression**
- **Discover the reusability of symbols**
- **Slice a Web page**

OPTIMIZATION

When it comes to publishing graphics for the Web, it is all about optimization.

Optimization, when referring to online artwork, is the process of preparing a functionally optimal graphic. It is a balancing act between the visual quality of an image and its quantitative file size. There are three interrelated areas to consider in the Web optimization process: image format, image color, and image size—all of which relate to image compression, reducing an image's file size so it looks good on screen and downloads quickly over an Internet connection.

About Compression

An image's file size can be reduced by compression. If you compress a bitmap image too much—make it smaller in file size—you can lose visual quality. For instance, it might lose its anti-aliased effect, which is the smoothing of pixelated edges through a gradation of color, or it could dither, which is when colors that are lost during the compression are replaced by colors within a reduced palette. See Figure 11–1 and Figure 11–2.

There are two basic types of compression: lossy and lossless (or nonlossy). Lossy compression discards data to make a file smaller. Let us say you are optimizing a line of pixels into the JPEG format, which uses lossy compression. Ten of the pixels are white, followed by a gray pixel, and then five white pixels. With lossy compression, the computer reads the line as 16 white pixels; the gray pixel is converted to white.

figure | 11–1 |

Anti-aliasing close-up creates a stairstep effect of color gradation. When viewed from a distance, the edge of the object looks smoother.

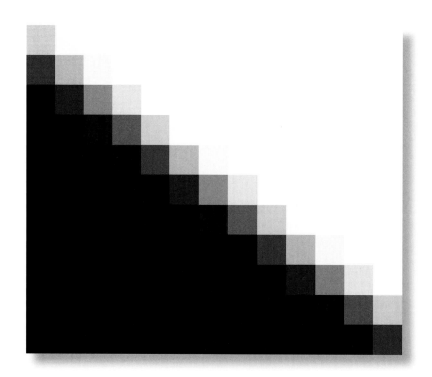

figure |11–2|

Dithering attempts to simulate colors that are lost in the compression process.

Lossless compression, on the other hand, does not eliminate detail or information. Instead it looks for efficient ways to define the image, such as through the use of customized color tables. Ultimately, it varies how compression is applied to images, depending on the image's format, color, and size.

Image Format

Traditionally, most Web images are saved in bitmap formats: Graphic Interchange Format (GIF), Joint Photographic Experts Group (JPEG), or Portable Network Graphic (PNG). Bitmap images are reliant on resolution to determine their file size and quality. In that case, bitmap images are generally larger in file size than vector graphics, and when it comes to "the Web," that means a much bulkier download. Vector-based file formats—including Small Web File (SWF) and Scalable Vector Graphics (SVG)—allow us to save and view graphics as streamlined paths, shapes, text, and effects in the online environment. Such graphics are scalable in size and easier to download—a wonderful combination for experiencing more interactive and animated imagery on the Web and in content for resource-limited handheld devices, like a personal data assistant (PDA) or mobile phone.

The file format you choose for an optimized image depends on the color, tonal, and graphic characteristics of the original image. In general, continuous-tone bitmap images (images with many shades of color), such as photographs, are best compressed in the JPEG or PNG-24 formats. Illustrations or type with flat color or sharp edges and crisp detail are best as GIF or PNG-8 files. Vector-based graphics or animations are either saved in the SVG or SWF formats. The following is a bulleted rundown of the characteristics of each Web-based graphic format—all of which you can export from Illustrator. Further clarification of these characteristics is presented in the sections "Image Color" and "Image Size."

Graphic Interchange Format

The Graphic Interchange Format (GIF):

- Supports an 8-bit color depth. Bit depth determines the amount and range of color an image can contain. A 1-bit image supports two colors, black and white; an 8-bit image can support up to 256 colors. A customized 256-color palette is referred to as indexed color.

- Works best compressing solid areas of color, such as in line art, logos, or illustrations with type, with no gradients or continuous tones.

- Is supported by the most common Web browsers, such as Internet Explorer, Firefox, and Safari.

- Can be animated.

- Traditionally uses a lossless compression method. Lossless compression is when no data is discarded during the file reduction process (see previous section "About Compression"). You can save a GIF file multiple times without discarding data. However, because GIF files are 8-bit color, optimizing an original 24-bit image as an 8-bit GIF will degrade image quality.

> **Note:** You can create a lossy version of a GIF file in Illustrator and Photoshop. The lossy GIF format includes small compression artifacts (similar to those in JPEG files), but yields significantly smaller files.

- Can be interlaced, so images download in multiple passes, or progressively. The downloading process of interlaced images is visible to the user, assuring the user the download is in progress. Keep in mind, however, that interlacing increases file size.

- Includes dithering options: the process of mixing colors to approximate those not present in the image.

- Supports background transparency and background matting: the ability to blend the edges of an image with a Web page background color.

Joint Photographic Experts Group

The Joint Photographic Experts Group (JPEG) format:

- Supports 24-bit color (millions of colors) and preserves the broad range and subtle variations in brightness and hue, such as gradients, found in photographs and other continuous-toned images.

- Is supported by the most common Web browsers.

- Selectively discards data. Because it discards data, JPEG compression is referred to as lossy. The compression is set based on a range between 0% and 100%, or 1 and 10. A higher percentage setting results in less data being discarded. The JPEG compression method tends to degrade sharp detail in an image, particularly in images containing type or vector art. Because of the nature of JPEG compression, you should always save JPEG files from the original image, not from a previously saved JPEG.

- Can be interlaced, so images download in multiple passes.
- Does not support transparency.
- Does not support animation.

Portable Network Graphic-8

The Portable Network Graphic (PNG-8) format:

- Uses 8-bit color. PNG-8 compresses solid areas of color while preserving sharp detail, such as that in line art, logos, or illustrations with type.
- Might not be supported by all browsers (although this is changing). It is advisable to test images saved in the PNG format on browser platforms you and the eventual user might be using to view Web pages.
- Uses a lossless compression method, in which no data is discarded during compression. However, because PNG-8 files are 8-bit color, optimizing an original 24-bit image as a PNG-8 can degrade image quality. PNG-8 files use more advanced compression schemes than GIF, and can be 10% to 30% smaller than GIF files of the same image, depending on the image's color patterns.
- Can be indexed to a specific 256-color palette, such as adaptive or Web.
- Includes dithering options: the process of mixing colors to approximate those not present in the image.
- Supports background transparency and background matting: the ability to blend the edges of an image with a Web page background color.

Portable Network Graphic-24

The Portable Network Graphic (PNG-24) format:

- Supports 24-bit color. PNG-24 preserves the broad range and subtle variations in brightness and hue found in photographs. It also preserves sharp detail, such as that in line art, logos, or illustrations with type.
- Uses the same lossless compression method as the PNG-8 format, in which no data is discarded. For that reason, PNG-24 files are usually larger than JPEG files of the same image.
- Is not necessarily supported by all browsers.
- Supports background transparency and background matting: the ability to blend the edges of an image with a Web page background color.
- Supports multilevel transparency, in which you can preserve up to 256 levels of transparency to blend the edges of an image smoothly with any background color. However, multilevel transparency is not supported by all browsers.

Small Web File

The Small Web File (SWF) format:

- Supports full-screen, scalable, vector graphics, and animated objects.
- Is an Adobe Flash format that must be viewed using Adobe's Shockwave and/or Flash Player. Any Web browser equipped with the Flash Player can view SWF formatted artwork. This player is free and can be downloaded from the Adobe Web site *http://www.adobe.com*.
- Is a cross-compatible file format for importing into Adobe's Flash program.

> **Note:** Artwork on Illustrator layers can be converted to vector-based SWF frames for use in Flash.

- Supports the use of reusable symbol objects (see the section "About Symbols" later in this chapter).
- Uses a sophisticated, lossless compression scheme.

Scalable Vector Graphic

Scalable Vector Graphic (SVG) format:

- Supports full-screen, scalable, vector graphics, and animated objects.
- Is entirely XML-based, which is quite advantageous for Web developers and designers. Extensible Markup Language (XML) is a flexible text standard that has become widely used as a means to exchange data on the Web and elsewhere.
- Supports the use of JavaScript to create interactive events directly on graphics, such as button rollover actions. This can be done in Illustrator using the SVG Interactivity panel (Window > SVG Interactivity).
- Requires the SVG plug-in, which is normally installed with Illustrator. To download the plug-in, if necessary, go to *http://www.adobe.com/svg*.
- Supports the use of reusable symbol objects (see the section "About Symbols").

The Wireless Bitmat format

The Wireless Bitmap (WBMP) format:

- Supports 1-bit color, which means images are reduced to contain only black and white pixels.
- Is the standard format for optimizing images for older mobile devices, such as cell phones and PDAs that do not support viewing complex images in color.

Image Color

Photographs and artwork to be viewed onscreen, such as on a Web page, must be saved in the RGB color mode. Why? For an answer to that question, review Chapter 5. To convert your artwork to the RGB color mode, choose File > Document Color Mode > RGB Color.

Color Reduction Algorithms

Color reduction algorithms is what Adobe calls the methods used to generate a specific color table for an optimized image. You will get a better idea of how color tables work in "Lesson 1: Preparing Artwork for the Web." Color reduction algorithms apply only to the GIF and PNG-8 formats. Because these two formats support the 8-bit format, an image with 256 colors or less, the color tables determine how the computer calculates which of the 256 colors of the image to keep.

> Note: If the original image has less than 256 colors, you can adjust the maximum number of colors that are calculated, further reducing the image's size.

Each color reduction palette produces slightly different results, so you need to understand how each type works. The descriptions for the following first five color tables we extracted from the Illustrator Help files. In addition, there are more color tables you can choose from the Save for Web & Devices settings for the GIF and PNG-8 formats.

Perceptual: Creates a custom color table by giving priority to colors for which the human eye has greater sensitivity.

Selective: Creates a color table similar to the perceptual color table, but it favors broad areas of color and the preservation of Web colors. This color table usually produces images with the greatest color integrity. Selective is the default option.

Adaptive: Creates a custom color table by sampling colors from the spectrum appearing most commonly in the image. For example, an image with only the colors green and blue produces a color table made primarily of greens and blues. Most images concentrate colors in particular areas of the spectrum.

Restrictive (Web): Uses the standard 216-color color table common to the Windows and Mac OS 8-bit (256-color) palettes. This option ensures no browser dither is applied to colors when the image is displayed using 8-bit color. Using the Web palette can create larger files, and is recommended only when avoiding browser dither is a high priority.

Custom: Preserves the current perceptual, selective, or adaptive color table as a fixed palette that does not update with changes to the image.

Black and White: Builds a color table of only two colors: black and white.

Grayscale: Creates a custom table of grays, black, and white.

Mac OS and Windows: Builds an 8-bit palette, capable of displaying 256 colors, using the color table of the system you select.

Image Size

Size does matter. But wait . . . before we get into that, we need to discuss resolution. Remember resolution, the somewhat elusive concept of measuring bitmap images in pixels per inch (ppi)?

If you recall from Chapter 10, the resolution of artwork going to print varies depending on where it is being printed and on what kind of paper stock. For online display, an image's resolution is much easier to grasp; it needs to match only a standard monitor's resolution, which is 72 ppi for Mac and 96 ppi for Windows.

Of course, the concept of resolution does not apply to vector-based graphics, such as those saved in the SWF or SVG formats. These types of images are unique in their application to the Web: They are inherently scalable and compact in size. So keep in mind that much of what we are talking about in regard to file size and compression applies to bitmap (or rasterized) images. Until more Web designers use the latest online vector graphic formats, many of the graphics on the Web will be in a bitmap format.

A bitmap image's size is related to its resolution. Image size can be referred to in two ways, and both impact optimization: 1) actual dimensions (i.e., 5-by-5 inches or 400-by-600 pixels); and 2) file size—the image's actual weight, per se, in digital bits. This is measured in bytes, kilobytes (KB), megabytes (MB), or gigabytes (GB). A byte is 8 bits, a kilobyte is 1,024 bytes, a megabyte is 1,024 kilobytes, and a gigabyte is 1,024 megabytes. How big is too big for a Web image? That depends on how many images you have on a single Web page, whether they are bitmap or vector based, dimensionally large or small.

We prefer to keep our Web images, especially bulky bitmap ones, to no more than 10 to 20 KB each in file size. In fact, when building Web pages, it is not uncommon to keep the total file size of everything on a Web page under 30 KB for those viewers with slow Internet connections. The ultimate, of course, is to actually post your optimized images to the Web and test how long it takes to download them on different Internet connections.

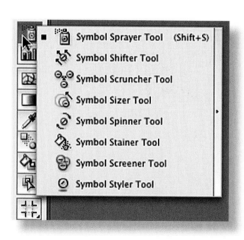

About Symbols

A symbol is a reusable object. You can reuse a symbol in an illustration and, unlike the traditional way of duplicating an object, it produces copies of a much smaller file size. This is great when developing graphics for the bandwidth-dependent, online environment. Imagine you need to create an illustration of a school of swimming minnows. It will eventually go to the Web, so you want to keep the artwork's file size down. First, you draw a minnow. Then you save it as a symbol in Illustrator's Symbol panel or Library (Window > Symbols). After you save the symbol, drag virtual copies (or instances) of it to the artboard. Each instance is linked to the original symbol in the Library, resulting in an overall smaller file size.

When you redefine an original symbol or change its attributes, the instances of it in the artwork will also be redefined. You can modify instances of a symbol with the Symbolism tools in the toolbox. Modifications might include scaling, rotating, moving, coloring, or duplicating instances. See Figure 11–3 and Figure 11–4. To view the options for the Symbolism tools, double-click on them in the toolbox. See Figure 11–5. To use a premade symbol, choose Window > Symbol Libraries.

figure |11–4|

Examples of modified instances of a fish symbol.

figure |11–5|

Options for the
Symbolism tools.

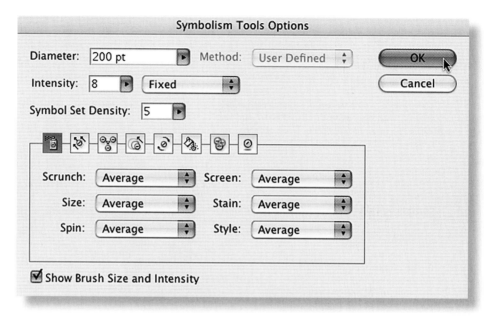

Using symbols is highly compatible with the SWF and SVG vector-based file formats. A plus is that you can save an SWF file of Illustrator symbols and then import it into the Adobe Flash program. The symbols will appear in Flash's symbol library and can be placed on a single frame or multiple frames, ready to be animated. See Figure 11–6 and Figure 11–7.

figure |11–6|

Symbols located on
individual sublayers in
Illustrator.

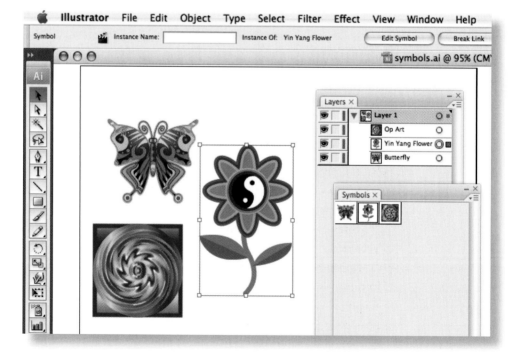

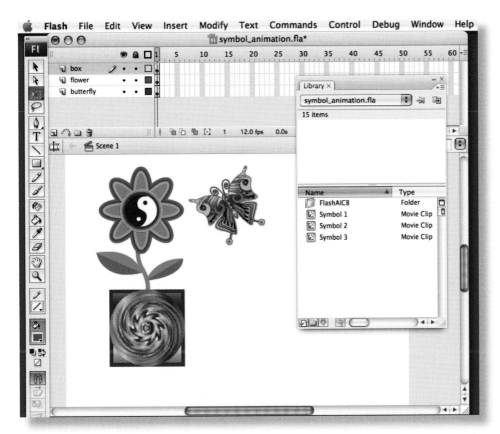

figure |11–7|

Symbols imported from Illustrator to the Adobe Flash program. The symbols appear in Flash's symbol library and their instances as individual frames on the Timeline.

SAVE FOR WEB & DEVICES

Think of the Save for Web & Devices feature as a fitness program for artwork. Depending on your image's body type (format), you can try various fitness regimes (compression schemes) to produce the best looking, leanest image possible. A two- or four-window view lets you compare and contrast an image's optimization settings to the original file. See Figure 11–8.

There are general guidelines for what kind of artwork to save as what kind of format—photos as JPEGs, line art as GIFs. However, the finesse to finding the right size and quality comes from subtly adjusting the options in the Save for Web & Devices dialog box. A simple adjustment to the bit depth of a GIF image, for example, can reduce the file size of the image immensely, resulting in a much more efficient Internet download. There are many options to choose from in the Save for Web & Devices dialog box, but do not let that overwhelm you. When you are ready to review said options, go to the Illustrator Help files. For now, we are going to concentrate on some of the basics and help make you comfortable trusting your visual instincts when comparing and contrasting settings in the Save for Web & Devices dialog box.

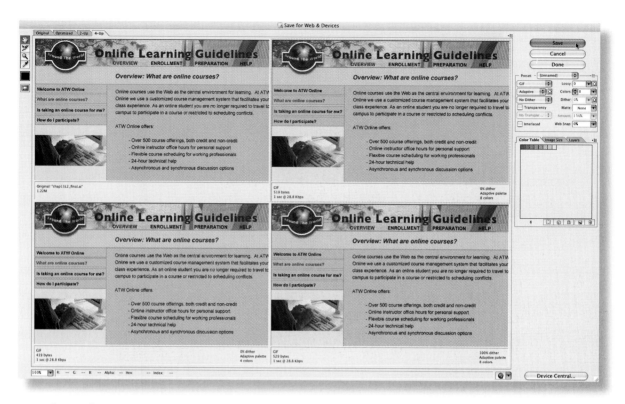

figure | 11–8 |

The Save for Web & Devices window is filled with options for optimizing artwork, including four-window viewing for comparing different optimization settings.

Lesson 1: Preparing Artwork for the Web

In this lesson, you optimally save for the Web a basic black and white logo, originally in the Encapsulated PostScript (EPS) format, using the settings in Illustrator's Save for Web & Devices dialog box.

Setting Up the File

1. In Illustrator, choose File > New. Name the file **optimization1**; new document profile: **Basic RGB**; size: **640 x 480**. Click OK.

2. Choose File > Place. In the folder **chap11_lessons/assets**, select the **sbblogo.eps**. Uncheck Link and choose Place.

3. Choose Select > Deselect.

4. Choose View > Pixel Preview to view the graphic as it might appear when rasterized into the GIF, JPEG, or PNG formats. Note the difference visually when Pixel Preview is turned off and on. See Figure 11–9 and Figure 11–10. You should turn on Pixel Preview when you want to control the precise placement, anti-aliasing, and size in the final rasterized object.

figure | 11–9 |

Example of artwork
with Pixel Preview
turned off. Notice the
uneven edges of
the shapes.

figure | 11–10 |

Example of artwork
with Pixel Preview
turned on. Anti-
aliasing smoothes the
edges.

Setting the Save for Web & Devices Options

1. Select the logo.

2. Choose File > Save for Web & Devices.

3. In the Save for Web & Devices window, select the 4-Up window tab in the upper-left corner of the window. A four-window view of the logo becomes available. See Figure 11–11.

figure | 11–11 |

The 4-Up window of the Save for Web & Devices window.

4. Click on the upper-left window to highlight it—a highlighted frame appears around the image. Note the first window shows the original image at a file size of about 1.17M. Also, in the information area to the right of the dialog box, notice the setting is set to Original.

5. Click on the upper-right window—a highlighted frame appears around the image, and the settings for the image become available. Notice the viewing annotations at the bottom of the selected window. These provide valuable information about the optimizations settings for that particular window, including format type, file size, estimated download time, and color panel (table) specifics.

6. The download time is determined by a specified Internet speed. By default, this is set to the lowest possible modem speed, 28.8 Kbps (kilobytes per second). Adjust this setting to a more standard 56 Kbps modem speed. Click on the arrow with three horizontal lines above and to the right of the selected window. From the preview menu, choose Size/Download Time (56.6 Kbps Modem/ISDN). See Figure 11–12.

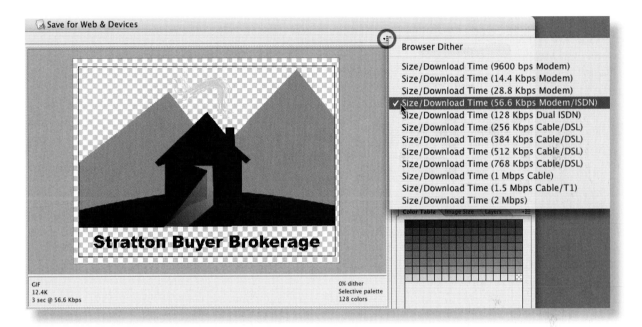

figure | 11–12 |

The preview menu.

7. Under Settings, leave it [Unnamed]. Then select the following options (see Figure 11–13):

- *Optimized file format:* **GIF**
- *Color reduction algorithm:* **Grayscale**
- *Dither algorithm:* **No Dither**
- *Transparency:* **Uncheck**
- *Interlaced:* **Uncheck**
- *Lossy:* **0**
- *Colors:* **Auto**
- *Matte:* **None**
- *Web Snap:* **0%**

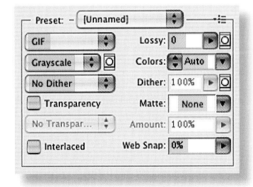

figure | 11–13 |

Settings for the second window.

figure | 11–14 |

A color table shows the colors used in an optimized image.

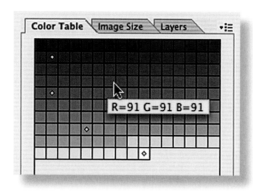

8. The Color Table for the selected window shows the colors used in the image; this is determined by the color reduction algorithm setting (Grayscale) and the maximum number of colors in the algorithm setting (Auto). The swatches with a diamond in the middle indicate Web-safe colors (for more on the restrictive, Web-safe color table, see the section "Color Reduction Algorithms"). The other swatches are in the general RGB color space. Place—do not click—your cursor over a swatch to reveal the color's attributes. See Figure 11–14.

9. Select the lower-left window and adjust its settings as follows:

   - *Optimized file format:* **GIF**
   - *Color reduction algorithm:* **Restrictive (Web)**
   - *Dither algorithm:* **Pattern**
   - *Transparency:* **Uncheck**
   - *Interlaced:* **Uncheck**
   - *Lossy:* **0**
   - *Colors:* **Auto**
   - *Matte:* **None**
   - *Web Snap:* **0%**

10. In the Color Table for the selected window, notice each swatch has a diamond icon in the middle. The icons indicate that all of the colors are within the Web-safe color palette. Place—do not click—your cursor over one of the swatches, and the hexadecimal color number is revealed.

11. Select the lower-right window and adjust its settings as follows:

   - *Optimized file format:* **JPEG**
   - *Compression Quality:* **Very High**
   - *Quality:* **80**
   - *Progressive:* **Check**
   - *Blur:* **0**

Comparing and Contrasting Settings

1. OK. Take a close look at what each optimization setting has done to the artwork. Magnify each window with the Zoom tool (located on the left side of the Save for Web & Devices window), and examine the artifacts of each compression scheme. Use the Hand tool to move the magnified artwork around in a window.

2. Double-click on the Zoom tool icon to set the view of each window back to the original artwork size. Which version looks best to you?

3. Compare and contrast the viewing annotations at the bottom of each window. What are the size differences? Is the one you visually like the best a reasonable size for Web display (under 10K for example)?

Getting Picky

1. Fine-tune and try to reduce the file size of the artwork without sacrificing quality. Select the upper-right window.

2. Change the color reduction algorithm to **Selective**, and reduce the colors to **128**. The file size is reduced, but it does not look any better. The gradient in the logo (the beam of light coming from the doorway) is banding and not looking too good. This is because gradient blends are composed of many shades of color.

3. Look at the lower-right window—the JPEG. The gradient in this version looks good, but the file size is too big.

4. Select the lower-left window and change the JPEG compression quality to **Medium**. The file size is lower, but the artwork is not looking as good. Where is the happy medium?

5. Type in a quality setting of **50** and press Tab. That looks pretty good and the file size is more respectable.

6. Select Save to save this version of the file. Name it **weblogo.jpg**. For format, choose Images Only. Save the file in the folder **chap11_lessons**.

> **Note:** If you do not want to save the file right away, choose Done rather than Save. This will close the Save for Web & Devices window, but maintain your optimization settings.

IMAGE SLICING

Image slicing is dividing up areas of an image or a complete Web page layout into smaller, independent files. If you are familiar with constructing Web pages and working in HTML, you probably have an understanding of the benefits of slicing. If you are new to Web page design and development, this might seem like a crazy thing to do to your artwork, but slicing is useful for the following uses:

- Accurate HTML table placement
- Creating independent files, each containing its own optimization settings
- Creating several smaller files for faster download
- Creating interactive effects, such as button rollovers

Lesson 2: Slicing a Home Page

In this lesson, you revisit the Web page layout created in Chapter 8. Using the Illustrator Slice tool, you will slice and optimize areas of the layout for optimal Web performance.

Setting Up the File

1. Open **chap11L2.ai** in the folder **chap11_lessons**.

2. Choose View > Actual Size and View > Pixel Preview.

3. Choose Window > Workspace > [Basic].

4. Press Shift-Tab to hide unneeded docks/panels.

5. Choose Window > Layers.

6. Hide all the layers, except the layer called **web_template**.

7. Unhide the layer called **guides**. You will use the template and guides to accurately place the slices you create in the next section. See Figure 11–15.

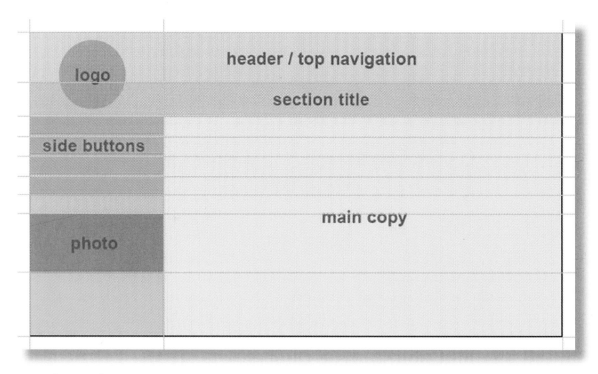

figure |11–15|

The Web template and guides are used for accurate placement of slices.

Making Slices

1. Choose Object > Slice > Clip to Artboard to keep your slices defined to the artboard area.

2. Create a new layer in the Layers panel and name it **slices**. The slice areas you define will be saved in this layer.

> **Note:** When you make slices, you do not actually "cut up" your artwork, but rather create an overlay of divided areas that determine how the individual files will be created when you save the document.

3. Select the Slice tool in the toolbox (hidden under the Crop Area tool). See Figure 11–16.

4. Place the point end of the Slice tool in the upper-left corner of the template and click and drag, defining a box around the green **header/top navigation** area. See Figure 11–17. Notice a number for the slice is indicated in the upper-left corner of the defined box. To show or hide the slice number, choose View > Show/Hide Slices. To change its color, choose Illustrator > Preferences > Smart Guides & Slices (Mac) or Edit > Preferences > Smart Guides & Slices (Windows).

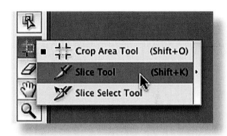

figure |11–16|

The Slice tool.

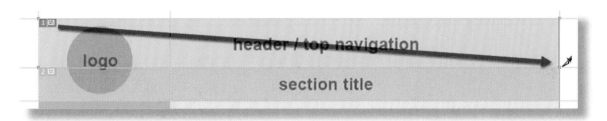

figure |11–17|

Click and drag down to define a slice area.

5. Create another divided area with the Slice tool, covering the pink **section title** area.

6. Slice the **main copy** area—the light orange area. Do not add the side buttons to this slice!

7. Define a slice for each side button, the **photo** area, and the orange spaces above and below that area. Use the guides to align the slices. See Figure 11–18.

> **Note:** If you make a mistake, choose Edit > Undo and try again. Each individual slice can also be deleted in the Layers panel.

figure |11–18|

Divide each section
(content zone) with
the Slice tool.

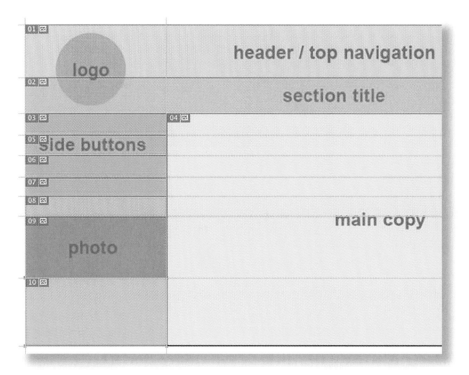

figure |11–19|

Place the Slice tool in the upper-left corner of the
header where the textured navigation bar begins.

8. Choose View > Actual Size.

9. Save the file **chap11L2_yourname.ai**, and place it in your lessons
folder.

10. Unhide all the layers to see how the slices overlay the actual Web
page layout.

11. The top navigation bar needs to be further divided. The title
areas—overview, enrollment, preparation, and help—will eventually become linkable rollover buttons. You will not create the
rollover actions or links in this lesson; however, you will prepare
the slices for that next step in the process.

12. Select the Slice tool in the toolbox. Place the tool in the upper-left
corner of the header where the textured navigation bar begins.
See Figure 11–19.

13. Click and drag, creating a box along the textured area until you
hit the vertical guide right before the word *OVERVIEW*. See
Figure 11–20.

figure |11–20|

Create a new slice in the top
navigation area.

14. Continue creating divided areas around each button title, similar to Figure 11–21. Keep the slices aligned.

> **Note:** Slicing always occurs in a grid-like pattern. Even if you do not define a slice in a particular area, Illustrator automatically creates one to maintain the table structure necessary for importing into an HTML page.

figure |11–21|

Create six new slices, defined around each button title and the side margins of the navigation bar.

15. Save your file.

> **Note:** If you need to select and modify individual slices, use the Slice Select tool, hidden under the Slice tool in the toolbox. See Figure 11–22. To see the options for individually selected slices, choose Object > Slice > Slice Options. Here you can create a name for the sliced area or add a link (URL), a message for the browser's status bar, or an Alt tag to it. See Figure 11–23.

Optimizing and Saving the Slices

1. Choose File > Save for Web & Devices. Select the 2-Up Window option. On the left side is the original artwork, on the right will be the one you modify. Make sure the right side is selected (with a highlighted frame around the window).

2. Select the Slice Select tool (located on the left side of the Save for Web & Devices window). See Figure 11–24.

figure |11–22|

The Slice Select tool.

figure |11–23|

The Slice Options.

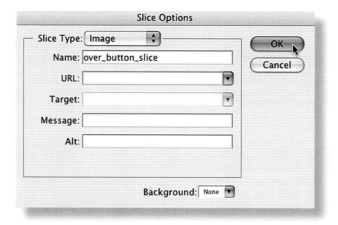

figure |11–24|

Select the
Slice Select tool.

figure |11–25|

Optimization settings
for one of the side
buttons.

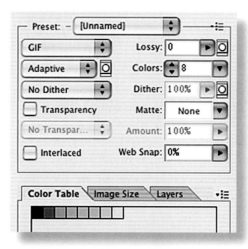

figure |11–26|

Option to turn off slice
visibility.

3. Select slice number 1 in the second window to highlight it. Adjust the optimization settings of this sliced area. We chose JPEG, Medium, quality 50 because of the many gradations of color in the header and logo graphics.

4. Select the first side button and adjust the optimization settings. We chose GIF, Adaptive, No Dither, and reduced Colors to 8, producing a very efficient graphic. See Figure 11–25.

5. Select each slice and optimize it to your liking. Balance the image file size with visual appeal.

6. Turn off the slice view (located in the tools area to the left of the window) to view the final, optimized artwork. See Figure 11–26.

7. Choose Save in the Save for Web & Devices window.

8. In the Save Optimized As box, enter the following (see Figure 11–27):

   • *Save As:* **mywebpage.jpg**

   • *Where: Your lesson folder*

   • *Format:* **Images Only**

   • *Settings:* **Custom**

   • *Slices:* **All Slices**

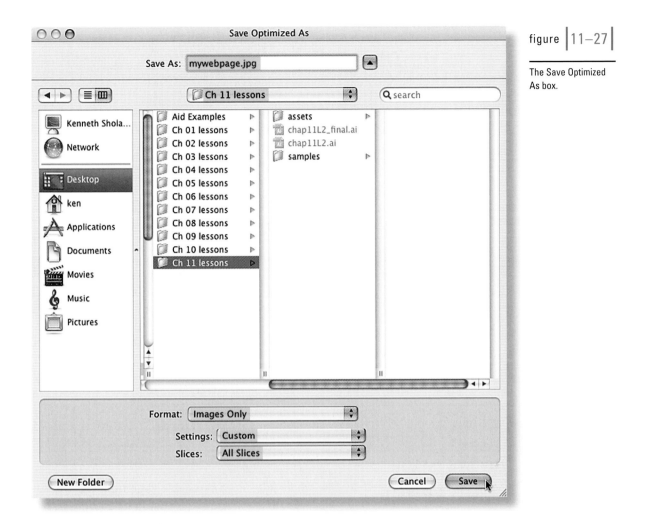

figure | 11–27 |

The Save Optimized
As box.

Wait! Before you hit Save, we want to show you something. Under Settings, choose Other. In the Output Settings, choose Saving Files. See Figure 11–28. In the Saving Files options, make sure Put Images in Folder is checked and **images** is indicated for the folder name. See Figure 11–29. We know there is a lot of stuff in this dialog box to distract you, but that is for later, when you really get into Web design work using Illustrator. For now, just click OK.

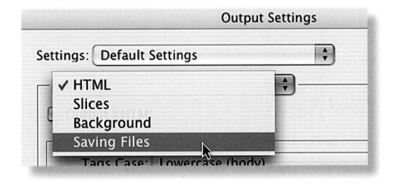

figure | 11–28 |

The Saving Files option in the
Output Settings.

figure 11–29

Check the Put Images
in Folder option.

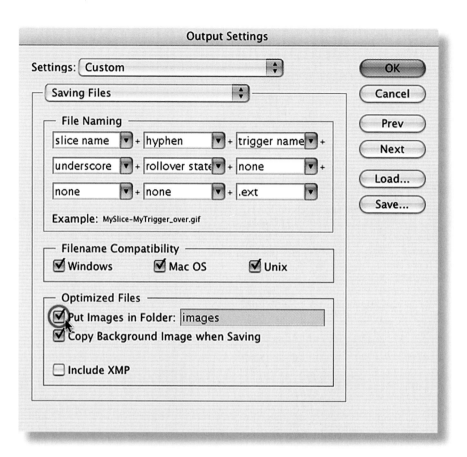

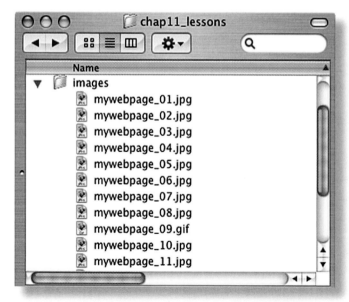

figure 11–30

Find your saved images.

9. Click Save to save the individually divided files to the **images** folder you just selected. This folder will be located in your lessons folder. Minimize the Illustrator program and find this folder. Open it and, amazingly, all your sliced images are there! See Figure 11–30.

SUMMARY

Illustrator is a resource for exploring the elements of drawing and design, and producing a finished product suitable for print and the World Wide Web.

in review

1. Describe image optimization.

2. Photographs are best saved in what format? What about graphics with gradient blends and meshes?

3. To view SVG and SWF formatted graphics, you must have what? And where do you get it?

4. What image formats use color reduction algorithms and why?

5. How many bytes are in a kilobyte? Why is that important to know?

6. What is *dithering*?

7. How are symbols useful for Web graphics?

8. Name three useful things about slicing images.

9. Where do sliced images go after you save them?

10. Name the five elements of visual design.

exploring on your own

1. For more information about Web graphics with Illustrator, choose Help > Illustrator Help > Contents > Web Graphics. Information not covered in this chapter you might want to read is found under Slices and image maps > Create image maps.

2. For more information on using SVG with Illustrator, choose Help > Illustrator Help > Contents > Web Graphics > SVG, or visit the World Wide Web Consortium (W3C) site at *http://www.w3.org/Graphics/SVG*. For more information on the SWF format, visit the Adobe site at *http://www.adobe.com*.

3. Using what you have learned about the Save for Web & Devices window, decide which optimization settings are best for the example artwork, **weblogo2.ai**, located in the folder **chap11_lessons/samples**.

index

A

B

INDEX

M

X

Z

IMPORTANT! READ CAREFULLY: This End User License Agreement ("Agreement") sets forth the conditions by which Delmar Cengage Learning will make electronic access to the Delmar Cengage Learning-owned licensed content and associated media, software, documentation, printed materials, and electronic documentation contained in this package and/or made available to you via this product (the "Licensed Content"), available to you (the "End User"). BY CLICKING THE "I ACCEPT" BUTTON AND/OR OPENING THIS PACKAGE, YOU ACKNOWLEDGE THAT YOU HAVE READ ALL OF THE TERMS AND CONDITIONS, AND THAT YOU AGREE TO BE BOUND BY ITS TERMS, CONDITIONS, AND ALL APPLICABLE LAWS AND REGULATIONS GOVERNING THE USE OF THE LICENSED CONTENT.

1.0 SCOPE OF LICENSE

1.1 Licensed Content. The Licensed Content may contain portions of modifiable content ("Modifiable Content") and content which may not be modified or otherwise altered by the End User ("Non-Modifiable Content"). For purposes of this Agreement, Modifiable Content and Non-Modifiable Content may be collectively referred to herein as the "Licensed Content." All Licensed Content shall be considered Non-Modifiable Content, unless such Licensed Content is presented to the End User in a modifiable format and it is clearly indicated that modification of the Licensed Content is permitted.

1.2 Subject to the End User's compliance with the terms and conditions of this Agreement, Delmar Cengage Learning hereby grants the End User, a nontransferable, nonexclusive, limited right to access and view a single copy of the Licensed Content on a single personal computer system for noncommercial, internal, personal use only. The End User shall not (i) reproduce, copy, modify (except in the case of Modifiable Content), distribute, display, transfer, sublicense, prepare derivative work(s) based on, sell, exchange, barter or transfer, rent, lease, loan, resell, or in any other manner exploit the Licensed Content; (ii) remove, obscure, or alter any notice of Delmar Cengage Learning's intellectual property rights present on or in the Licensed Content, including, but not limited to, copyright, trademark, and/or patent notices; or (iii) disassemble, decompile, translate, reverse engineer, or otherwise reduce the Licensed Content.

2.0 TERMINATION

2.1 Delmar Cengage Learning may at any time (without prejudice to its other rights or remedies) immediately terminate this Agreement and/or suspend access to some or all of the Licensed Content, in the event that the End User does not comply with any of the terms and conditions of this Agreement. In the event of such termination by Delmar Cengage Learning, the End User shall immediately return any and all copies of the Licensed Content to Delmar Cengage Learning.

3.0 PROPRIETARY RIGHTS

3.1 The End User acknowledges that Delmar Cengage Learning owns all rights, title and interest, including, but not limited to all copyright rights therein, in and to the Licensed Content, and that the End User shall not take any action inconsistent with such ownership. The Licensed Content is protected by U.S., Canadian and other applicable copyright laws and by international treaties, including the Berne Convention and the Universal Copyright Convention. Nothing contained in this Agreement shall be construed as granting the End User any ownership rights in or to the Licensed Content.

3.2 Delmar Cengage Learning reserves the right at any time to withdraw from the Licensed Content any item or part of an item for which it no longer retains the right to publish, or which it has reasonable grounds to believe infringes copyright or is defamatory, unlawful, or otherwise objectionable.

4.0 PROTECTION AND SECURITY

4.1 The End User shall use its best efforts and take all reasonable steps to safeguard its copy of the Licensed Content to ensure that no unauthorized reproduction, publication, disclosure, modification, or distribution of the Licensed Content, in whole or in part, is made. To the extent that the End User becomes aware of any such unauthorized use of the Licensed Content, the End User shall immediately notify Delmar Cengage Learning. Notification of such violations may be made by sending an e-mail to delmarhelp@cengage.com.

5.0 MISUSE OF THE LICENSED PRODUCT

5.1 In the event that the End User uses the Licensed Content in violation of this Agreement, Delmar Cengage Learning shall have the option of electing liquidated damages, which shall include all profits generated by the End User's use of the Licensed Content plus interest computed at the maximum rate permitted by law and all legal fees and other expenses incurred by Delmar Cengage Learning in enforcing its rights, plus penalties.

6.0 FEDERAL GOVERNMENT CLIENTS

6.1 Except as expressly authorized by Delmar Cengage Learning, Federal Government clients obtain only the rights specified in this Agreement and no other rights. The Government acknowledges that (i) all software and related documentation incorporated in the Licensed Content is existing commercial computer software within the meaning of FAR 27.405(b)(2); and (2) all other data delivered in whatever form, is limited rights data within the meaning of FAR 27.401. The restrictions in this section are acceptable as consistent with the Government's need for software and other data under this Agreement.

7.0 DISCLAIMER OF WARRANTIES AND LIABILITIES

7.1 Although Delmar Cengage Learning believes the Licensed Content to be reliable, Delmar Cengage Learning does not guarantee or warrant (i) any information or materials contained in or produced by the Licensed Content, (ii) the accuracy, completeness or reliability of the Licensed Content, or (iii) that the Licensed Content is free from errors or other material defects. THE LICENSED PRODUCT IS PROVIDED "AS IS," WITHOUT ANY WARRANTY OF ANY KIND AND DELMAR CENGAGE LEARNING DISCLAIMS ANY AND ALL WARRANTIES, EXPRESSED OR IMPLIED, INCLUDING, WITHOUT LIMITATION, WARRANTIES OF MERCHANTABILITY OR FITNESS FOR A PARTICULAR PURPOSE. IN NO EVENT SHALL DELMAR CENGAGE LEARNING BE LIABLE FOR: INDIRECT, SPECIAL, PUNITIVE OR CONSEQUENTIAL DAMAGES INCLUDING FOR LOST PROFITS, LOST DATA, OR OTHERWISE. IN NO EVENT SHALL DELMAR CENGAGE LEARNING'S AGGREGATE LIABILITY HEREUNDER, WHETHER ARISING IN CONTRACT, TORT, STRICT LIABILITY OR OTHERWISE, EXCEED THE AMOUNT OF FEES PAID BY THE END USER HEREUNDER FOR THE LICENSE OF THE LICENSED CONTENT.

8.0 GENERAL

8.1 Entire Agreement. This Agreement shall constitute the entire Agreement between the Parties and supercedes all prior Agreements and understandings oral or written relating to the subject matter hereof.

8.2 Enhancements/Modifications of Licensed Content. From time to time, and in Delmar Cengage Learning's sole discretion, Delmar Cengage Learning may advise the End User of updates, upgrades, enhancements and/or improvements to the Licensed Content, and may permit the End User to access and use, subject to the terms and conditions of this Agreement, such modifications, upon payment of prices as may be established by Delmar Cengage Learning.

8.3 No Export. The End User shall use the Licensed Content solely in the United States and shall not transfer or export, directly or indirectly, the Licensed Content outside the United States.

8.4 Severability. If any provision of this Agreement is invalid, illegal, or unenforceable under any applicable statute or rule of law, the provision shall be deemed omitted to the extent that it is invalid, illegal, or unenforceable. In such a case, the remainder of the Agreement shall be construed in a manner as to give greatest effect to the original intention of the parties hereto.

8.5 Waiver. The waiver of any right or failure of either party to exercise in any respect any right provided in this Agreement in any instance shall not be deemed to be a waiver of such right in the future or a waiver of any other right under this Agreement.

8.6 Choice of Law/Venue. This Agreement shall be interpreted, construed, and governed by and in accordance with the laws of the State of New York, applicable to contracts executed and to be wholly preformed therein, without regard to its principles governing conflicts of law. Each party agrees that any proceeding arising out of or relating to this Agreement or the breach or threatened breach of this Agreement may be commenced and prosecuted in a court in the State and County of New York. Each party consents and submits to the nonexclusive personal jurisdiction of any court in the State and County of New York in respect of any such proceeding.

8.7 Acknowledgment. By opening this package and/or by accessing the Licensed Content on this Web site, THE END USER ACKNOWLEDGES THAT IT HAS READ THIS AGREEMENT, UNDERSTANDS IT, AND AGREES TO BE BOUND BY ITS TERMS AND CONDITIONS. IF YOU DO NOT ACCEPT THESE TERMS AND CONDITIONS, YOU MUST NOT ACCESS THE LICENSED CONTENT AND RETURN THE LICENSED PRODUCT TO DELMAR CENGAGE LEARNING (WITHIN 30 CALENDAR DAYS OF THE END USER'S PURCHASE) WITH PROOF OF PAYMENT ACCEPTABLE TO DELMAR CENGAGE LEARNING, FOR A CREDIT OR A REFUND. Should the End User have any questions/comments regarding this Agreement, please contact Delmar Cengage Learning at delmarhelp@cemgage.com.